I Love being your student.

Merry Christmas.

Love Rachel

12-12-94

Rose's Christmas Cookies

Rose's Christmas Cookies

Rose Levy Beranbaum

Photographs by Louis Wallach

Art direction and design by
Richard Oriolo

William Morrow and Company, Inc.
New York

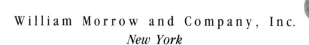

Recognizing the importance of preserving what has been written, it is the policy of William
Morrow and Company, Inc., and its imprints and affiliates to have the books it publishes
printed on acid-free paper, and we exert our best efforts to that end.

Library of Congress Cataloging-in-Publication Data
Beranbaum, Rose Levy.
    Rose's Christmas cookies / Rose Levy Beranbaum; photographs by Louis Wallach.
        p.   cm.
    Includes index.
    ISBN 0-688-10136-4
    1. Cookies.   2. Christmas cookery.   I. Title.
TX772.B47   1991
641.8′654—dc20   90-6505
                                                                          CIP

Printed in the United States of America

First Edition

2 3 4 5 6 7 8 9 10

BOOK DESIGN BY RICHARD ORIOLO

To Aunt Ruth,
who taught me how to make my
first Christmas cookies

To two dear friends,
Dr. Maurice F. Goodbody and Jeanne Bauer,
who live the Christmas spirit
every day of the year

To Maria D. Guarnaschelli
and Al Marchioni,
who gave this book so much
love and care

and

To my nephew, Alexander,
who loves cookies and is the
cutest cookie of all

It was a very special team of professionals who have given their unique talents to create the uniqueness of this book. Working together on this joyful project has not only resulted in a book we all adore, it has also established strong bonds of respect and friendship (and lots of extra pounds!).

A big kiss and salute to each of you:

Maria D. Guarnaschelli: my incomparable editor, whose passion and devotion is more than equal to my own;

Deborah Weiss Geline: my ever-enthusiastic, patient, and discerning copy editor, whose critical eye ensures the success of these recipes;

Richard Oriolo: art director and book designer, who has sweetly involved himself, with a whole heart, in every possible aspect of the appearance of this book;

Rick Rodgers: esteemed colleague, and also the best recipe tester I have ever known: generously creative, untiring, and thorough;

Louis Wallach: photographer with the rare ability to portray precisely and accurately what is, while giving us something to dream about that is a work of art;

Andrea Swenson: food stylist, gifted with hands of gold, good judgment, *and* an unfailingly cheerful disposition, even after having been run over by a van (she's fine now);

Judy Singer: prop stylist, who knows so well how to enhance and entice the eye without ever overshadowing the subject;

Helen Raffels and Slobodan Saramandic: craftswoman and architect team, who built the gingerbread cathedral. Both are artists totally devoted to their crafts. Helen was there to watch the sun rise with me after we had spent the whole night writing the painstakingly detailed instructions for making the edifice. (I have not shared the dawn with many people!)

Laura Hartman Maestro: illustrator of my dreams. Not only are Laura's drawings beautiful to behold, they are breathtakingly clear and show exactly what needs to be seen. Together with all her other gifts, she also has the most precious one of all: imagination;

Shirley Corriher: scientific consultant, beloved and generous friend who has, once again, contributed her invaluable knowledge as a research biochemist and cook to how cookies work;

Lillian Wager Levy: proofreader, my devoted mother, retired dentist, and former Latin gold-medal winner, whose judgment is unswervingly reliable;

Elliott R. Beranbaum: my husband, whose contributions are everywhere in this book—beyond the telling.

Special thanks to Lisa Queen, Pat Adrian, and Bill Adler for their encouragement and support.

Grateful acknowledgment is made to the following people who so generously shared their recipes with me: to Jeanne Bauer for "Mother Bauer's Buttered Rum Cookies" and "Jeanne Bauer's Maple Macadamia Bars"; to Lillian Levy for "Mom's Coconut Kisses"; to Margaret Morris for "Aunt Margaret's Star-Spangled Meringues"; to Marion Bush for "Marion Bush's Cranberry-Chocolate Chippers"; to Helen King for "Mrs. King's Irresistibles"; to Barbara Vanderbilt for "Bone à Fidos"; to David Shamah for "David's Dreambars" and "David Shamah's Jumbles"; and to Lora Brody for "Lora Brody's Rugelach" (from *Cooking with Memories* by Lora Brody) and "Lora Brody's Chocolate Phantoms" (from *Growing Up on the Chocolate Diet* by Lora Brody).

Contents

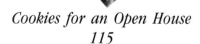

I grew up dreaming of white Christmases on a farm, horse-drawn sleighs, ice-skating on frozen ponds—all from storybooks. But my child-hood Christmases were actually spent in New York City. They were magical, too, but in a different way. There was ice-skating on the rink at Rockefeller Center, amid silvery skyscrapers and the world's most enormous Christmas tree. There was the comforting smell of roasting chestnuts warming the frosty air, and the sound of many Santas clanging large brass bells. I grew up with the feeling that in New York Christmas was a joyous cultural celebration belonging to everyone and not restricted only to those who observed it as a religious holiday.

Every Christmas my great-aunt Bertha would take my cousins Joanie and the twins and me to McCreery's Department Store to see Santa Claus and then for a stroll past the store windows that displayed festively ani-mated figures of families at home for the holidays, moving to the special Christmas music piped onto Fifth Avenue. Aunt Bertha would always treat us to a self-service lunch at Horn & Hardart, which featured entire walls of little glass windows that contained food. We were given money with which to choose our own lunch and out our selections would pop. (It was a sad day when we thought we were too grown up for Horn & Hardart.)

Christmas eve I would go down two flights to my best friend Susie Bernstein's apartment and help decorate her tree with tinsel. While we did this, we would share our secret hopes (we both wanted sisters—we each got brothers who arc to this day each other's best friend). I remem-ber very little pine showing on Susie's tree because we always overdid the tinsel; it was such great silvery stuff. I felt privileged that she would let me share in the enjoyment of such a fun activity.

Perhaps my most vivid Christmas memory is when I played the part of a toy soldier in the second annual Christmas production of George Bal-lanchine's ballet of *The Nutcracker*. Amazingly to me (I was ten at the time), we all got paid for our performances. Every once in a while, when we soldiers started moving out of our wooden box onto the stage, there would be a burst of mad applause. We learned afterward that it was one of the children's parents in the audience that night. But it sure was a great morale booster, not to mention the sheer thrill of being in a real production on the stage of New York's City Center.

Another cherished Christmas memory of more recent vintage is of Martha Stewart's quintessential Christmas party at Turkey Hill Farm in Westport, Connecticut. There was snow on the ground and pine trees everywhere. Candles softly glowing in paper bag lanterns lined the long walkway between the main house and the barn, where carolers sang from the rafters and we helped ourselves to an enormous buffet. Then, we wandered back to the warmly lit main house for a delectable array of desserts—all manner of cookies, cakes, and tartlets. It was the fantasy of entering into one of Martha's enchanting dream books come true.

Warm Christmases in recent years have been spent with my husband, Elliott, as part of Bert Greene and Phillip Schulz's extended family. We were invited the first time because two of the usual family members had to be away, leaving room in the full-to-bursting party for two more. Without discussion of any sort, we immediately considered ourselves and were considered (fortunately) part of all future Greene/Schulz Christmases.

Gifts were exchanged beneath Phillip's tree, the most beautiful, exquisitely trimmed Christmas tree in my memory. (Knowing that his father is a minister made it somehow more authentic.) Elliott and I especially looked forward to the jars of jams and chutneys put up every summer by Bert and Phillip from their East Hampton garden. But more than anything, it was the warmth and love that brought us back.

Sometimes we forget, but when all is said and done, it is love that we all want most. It is the best, most exalting emotion we know. No matter what else we experience or must suffer, love, again and again, in its many forms, is what makes life worth living. It redeems us and transports us. It is reflected in the resilience of the human spirit.

The Christmas season itself is, without a doubt, the most enchanting time of year. But the reason that the spirit of Christmas is most magical is because it is about loving and giving. I've often heard children wish it could be Christmas every day. But we know in our hearts that if it were Christmas all year round it would be too easy for most of us to lose the impact of its true meaning. So every year, we get to experience the joy and excitement all over again.

There is a reason that the word *cookie* follows *Christmas* with such inevitability. After all, what would Christmas be without Christmas cookies? Nothing represents the spirit of loving, nurturing, and giving more than a homemade cookie. It is made and given from the heart. It is small and pretty, sweet and comforting. It is something friends and family can make together. A cookie is a treat that doesn't need to be eaten right away but will last, in many instances for months, to be savored when one desires (only, of course, if it is well hidden).

One of the most touching examples of how much Christmas cookies are associated with love is what my special friend Paula Perlis said when I asked her for her favorite cookie recipe. "Oh yes, I have a wonderful recipe I used to make with my mother. Well . . . maybe it isn't all that wonderful; maybe it's just that it makes me remember my mother."

Another dear friend, Jeanne Bauer, moved me by reminiscing about how even when she had grown up and left home, her mother would purposely not finish making all the Christmas cookies so that a few would remain for them to make together when she visited for the holidays. She remembered how "a lot of things were solved over those cookies—things you wouldn't feel comfortable saying if your hands were not busy." It seems that making cookies with a loved one is one of life's bonding experiences.

I have always loved the idea of Christmas cookies; in fact, I've always loved cookies any time of year, but what finally made me decide to write a book about them was a country weekend with *my* mother. Every time she had coffee and my father had tea, which seemed to be every few hours, she requested a cookie to go with it. It started off simply: "Do you have a little something sweet to go with it?" And ended up by the fourth request as: "Are you sure you don't have even *one* little cookie?" It made me aware of just how important and wonderful cookies are (my mother is good at doing that with many things), even to my mother, who hardly eats any sweets. I realized then that I had better have them available for her next visit. I also knew that if I were going to have cookies, they certainly weren't going to be packaged ones. They would be the best I could create. I am, after all, a baker.

As I started falling in love with cookies all over again, remembering a vast range of favorites I had been collecting and creating over the years for numerous articles in food magazines, it naturally evolved into a book. And it seemed that if there was to be a cookie book, it would have to be Christmas cookies, a collection of my very favorites, because the best is always saved for Christmas.

A Note on Making Cookies

Cookie is a word that derives from the Dutch *koekje,* the diminutive of the Dutch word for cake, *koek.* Most cookies, however, are actually more like sweetened pastry than like cake. Unlike both cake and pastry, however, most cookies are very easy to make because they are much more forgiving of overmixing and overhandling. Scraps of dough can be reshaped many times without changing a cookie's texture.

There are three basic methods of mixing cookie dough:

1. Food processor (my favorite because it's the fastest)
   This method is given for each recipe, where applicable.
2. Electric mixer (stand mixer or hand-held)
   This method is also given for each recipe, where applicable.
3. Hand (a large bowl and spoon)
   This method is described on page 247.

All three methods produce essentially the same results. The only minimal difference is with cookies that contain liquids, such as sour cream, or a large amount of eggs. The electric mixer will make them slightly more puffy. However, no matter which method you use, you are guaranteed to make terrific cookies.

Smart Cookie

Highlights for Success

- Measure or weigh carefully.
- Use unsalted butter and unsalted nuts.
- Make cookies in the same batch the same size, shape, and thickness so they bake evenly.
- Arrange cookies at even intervals on the baking sheet so that they bake evenly. (Don't leave large, unevenly empty spaces.)
- Preheat the oven for at least 15 minutes before baking the cookies.
- Don't overbake the cookies; they continue baking after they are removed from the oven.
- Rearrange and rotate the cookie sheets in the oven for even baking.
- Cool cookie sheets between batches so that the cookies don't start melting and thinning at the edges before they can be set by the heat of the oven.
- Use flat cookie sheets with very low edges so that the air can circulate over the cookies and make them crisp.
- Use shiny heavy-gauge aluminum cookie sheets, not darkened ones, so the cookies will brown evenly and not excessively.
- Remove the cookies from the cookie sheets as soon as they are rigid enough to transfer and cool on racks so that they remain crisp and do not continue cooking from the heat of the sheets.
- Cool the cookies completely before storing them airtight to maintain the best possible texture.
- Store soft cookies together, not with crisp cookies, or they will soften the crisp ones. To preserve each cookie's special flavor, it is best to store each variety of cookie in its own container.

Storing Cookies

- Most cookie doughs can be refrigerated for at least 3 days or frozen for several weeks and thawed overnight in the refrigerator. It is easiest to shape cookie dough, however, if it has not been refrigerated for more than 3 hours. If the dough cracks on rolling or shaping, the dough is too cold. Divide the chilled dough into quarters and allow the dough to sit at room temperature for about 15 minutes or until it is malleable and soft enough to roll but is still chilled.
- Most baked cookies are superb for weeks after baking if they are stored carefully. If they are stored in a cool room, they will keep for months. There is, however, something extra special about certain cookies that are freshly baked, especially those containing pieces of chocolate. Within 4 to 6 hours after baking, the chocolate is still slightly soft and adds an extra dimension to both texture and taste. (This explains the enormous success of cookie bakeries throughout America.)
- Freezing cookies keeps them almost as fresh as the day they were baked. I usually don't find it necessary to freeze cookies, however: Freezer space is limited, and things in the freezer are often forgotten, whereas cookies stored in cookie jars or airtight containers at room temperature always get eaten long before there is any noticeable decrease in quality!

- If you do want to freeze cookies, use heavy-duty freezer bags, expelling as much air as possible, or airtight containers, filling any air space at the top with crumpled plastic wrap or wax paper. Fragile cookies can be flash-frozen in single layers on cookie sheets and, when frozen solid, packed in airtight containers. Bar cookies can be frozen whole, before cutting, wrapped in plastic wrap and then heavy-duty aluminum foil.
- Individual cookies will defrost at room temperature in about 20 minutes if they are taken out of their containers.
- *When storing cookies, always be sure to cool them completely first and to store crisp cookies separately from soft ones.* It is also best to store each variety of cookie separately to prevent transfer of flavors.
- Separate layers of cookies with wax paper to keep the cookies crisp and to separate those that are sticky.
- For cookies that are stored in the refrigerator, such as mini-cheesecakes and lemon butter bars, be sure to store them airtight so that they don't pick up conflicting aromas from other foods (such as garlic or spices). For the best flavor and texture, allow them to warm to room temperature before serving them.
- To recrisp cookies, place them on cookie sheets in a 300°F oven for about 5 minutes. Cool them on wire racks.

Packaging Cookies To Ship

Shipping my glass mercury thermometers over the years has provided me with the experience and basic rules for shipping fragile, breakable things so they arrive shipshape:

- Cookies with long keeping qualities are more suitable than others for shipping. Less delicate cookies are easier to pack and ship, but even the most delicate can be shipped successfully if care is taken.
- Pack individual containers so that the cookies can't rattle around in them. Crumpled wax paper works well for this and also helps to maintain the texture of the cookies, especially crunchy ones. Colored tinsel makes a beautiful protective bed for holiday cookies.
- The shipping box should be constructed of heavy corrugated cardboard (with rigid sides) and should be considerably larger than the packing containers, leaving lots of room for packing material as a buffer between the outside of the box and the containers.
- Air is the greatest of all buffers. Packing material should be lightweight and as airy as possible. Several inches of packing material should come between all four sides of the box and the cookie containers.
- Ideal packing materials:

Styrofoam "peanuts": Little bits of Styrofoam can be saved in large, clean, plastic garbage bags whenever you receive a package containing them.

Popcorn: Popped popcorn makes a delightful packing material. If you line the box with aluminum foil, or place the popcorn and cookie containers in a large plastic bag before placing them in the shipping box, the popcorn becomes an edible packing material.

Newspaper: Big poufs of crumpled-up newspaper are not as attractive as Styrofoam or popcorn, but newspaper is readily available and works perfectly to absorb the shocks of shipping.

Tissue paper: Colored tissue paper, crumpled into poufs, makes an attractive and festive protective material. To make it more decorative still, after crumpling the paper, paste little gold and silver stars on it. The self-stick variety is available on rolls in stationery stores.

To Hand Deliver as Gifts

There is something heartfelt about giving your favorite cookies at Christmastime. And it is a gift that is always appreciated and always appropriate.

Friends of mine have created a tradition of offering Christmas cookies in antique decorative tins that they collect all year around. They tell me that when the cookies are finished, their friends return the tins to ensure that they will receive another batch the following year!

There are many festive and exciting ways to present your cookies as gifts:

- in beautiful tins, on beds of colored tinsel
- in antique cookie jars
- in tissue-lined shoe boxes, perhaps wrapped with decorative paper
- in small hatboxes lined with crumpled tissue paper or tinsel
- wrapped in special decorative candy papers and foil cups (available from cake-decorating and candy-making supply houses)
- in a cookie tin, boxed, wrapped, and tied with ribbons, perhaps with a favorite cookie cutter attached to the ribbon
- cookies made with holes in them tied together in bunches with gold cord or beautiful slim ribbons.

Tree and Mantelpiece Cookies

Stained Glass

Makes about 4 dozen
3-inch cookies

This is a cookie and a candy all in one. The cookie itself is a crisp sugar-butter cookie, and the candy panes add a sweet fruity flavor and crunch. It was these cookies, hanging on a Christmas tree, with light shining through their transparent candy panes, that inspired me to create a gingerbread cathedral with a stained-glass rose window (page 188). For greater ease of preparation, the cookies can be made with one larger cutout in the center, but with their many cutouts (admittedly painstaking) they are so breathtaking to behold that they are worth the effort.

EQUIPMENT: *cookie sheets lined with aluminum foil, then sprayed with nonstick vegetable cooking spray or greased; rolling pin; 3-inch round cookie cutters and small canapé cutters.*

Food Processor Method

In a small bowl, whisk together the flour, baking powder, and salt.

In a food processor with the metal blade, process the sugar until it is very fine. Cut the butter into a few pieces and add it with the motor running. Process until smooth and creamy. Add the egg and extracts and process until incorporated, scraping the sides of the bowl. Add the flour mixture and pulse in, just until the dough begins to clump together.

INGREDIENTS	MEASURE volume	WEIGHT ounces	grams
bleached all-purpose flour	2¾ cups (dip and sweep method)	13.75 ounces	390 grams
baking powder	½ teaspoon	•	•
salt	½ teaspoon	•	•
sugar	⅔ cup	4.75 ounces	132 grams
unsalted butter	1 cup	8 ounces	227 grams
about half a large egg, lightly beaten	2 teaspoons	•	•
pure vanilla extract	1½ teaspoons	•	6 grams
lemon extract	⅛ teaspoon	•	•
sour balls	1 package (1 cup)	6.5 ounces	184 grams

Electric Mixer Method

Soften the butter. In a mixing bowl, cream together the sugar and butter until fluffy. Add the egg and extracts and beat until blended. In a small bowl, whisk together the remaining dry ingredients. On low speed, gradually add them to the butter mixture and mix just until the dough can be gathered into a ball.

For Both Methods

Scrape the dough onto a sheet of plastic wrap and use the wrap, not your fingers, to press the dough together to form a thick flat disc. Wrap it well and refrigerate for at least 30 minutes, preferably no longer than 3 hours.

Place 2 oven racks in the upper and lower thirds of the oven.
Preheat oven to 350°F.
Separate the sour balls into individual colors and pulverize them separately in a blender or food processor. Place each color in a small container and set aside.

Using about a quarter of the dough at a time, roll out the dough to ⅛-inch thickness between 2 sheets of plastic wrap or on a lightly floured counter. Cut out cookies with a 3-inch cookie cutter, spraying or greasing the cutter as needed to prevent sticking. With a small, angled metal spatula or pancake turner, transfer the cookies to the prepared cookie sheets. If you are planning to hang the cookies, make small holes with the blunt end of a wooden skewer.

Cut out shapes for the stained glass in each cookie with small cutters or with a small sharp knife. Use the tip of a small sharp knife to fill the holes with candy pieces, filling just to the top of the dough.

Bake for 10 to 12 minutes or until the cookies are lightly browned and the candy has melted completely. For even baking, rotate the cookie sheets from top to bottom and front to back halfway through the baking period. Watch carefully toward the end of baking to see that the candy does not start to caramelize and turn brown.

Allow the cookies to cool completely on the sheets. Carefully peel off the aluminum foil.

Store: In an airtight container, between sheets of wax paper, at room temperature.

Keeps: Several weeks.

 Smart Cookie

- Saran Wrap is the ideal plastic wrap for rolling the dough because it lies very flat. Wax paper is the second choice.
- For precise cutouts, chill the dough after the impressions are made and remove the cutout with the tip of a sharp knife after the dough has firmed enough for each cutout to come out in a clean piece.
- If you are using a blender to pulverize the sour balls, drop the balls with the motor running in order to keep them from getting stuck under the blades.
- Allow the cookie sheet(s) to cool completely before using for the next batch.
- Distribute the cookies evenly around the cookie sheet. Avoid crowding the cookies into one section of the cookie sheet, leaving a large area bare.

Traditional Rolled Christmas Sugar Cookies

Makes about 4 dozen
3-inch cookies

These sugar cookies can be as simple or as decorative as your fancy dictates. The dough is ideal for rolling and cutting into special shapes. Now is the time to get out your favorite Christmas cookie cutters. For an extra-special touch, add to your loved ones' cookie cutter collections by tying one or two cutters with gold ribbons to the cookie tins when you give the cookies as gifts.

INGREDIENTS	MEASURE volume	WEIGHT ounces	grams
bleached all-purpose flour	2¼ cups (dip and sweep method)	11.25 ounces	320 grams
salt	¼ teaspoon	•	•
sugar	¾ cup	5.25 ounces	150 grams
unsalted butter	12 tablespoons	6 ounces	170 grams
1 large egg	3 tablespoons + ½ teaspoon	1.75 ounces (weighed without the shell)	50 grams
lemon zest	1 tablespoon (finely grated)	•	6 grams
pure vanilla extract	1 teaspoon	•	4 grams
Edible Tempera Color (recipe follows)			
Royal Icing (recipe follows)			

EQUIPMENT: *nonstick or buttered or greased cookie sheets; rolling pin; cookie cutters.*

Food Processor Method

In a small bowl, whisk together the flour and salt.

In a food processor with the metal blade, process the sugar until very fine. Cut the butter into a few pieces and add it with the motor running. Process until smooth and creamy. Add the egg, lemon zest, and vanilla extract and process until incorporated, scraping the sides of the bowl. Add the flour mixture and pulse in just until incorporated. If the mixture seems dry, add a few droplets of water and pulse in just until the dough begins to clump together.

Electric Mixer Method

Soften the butter. In a mixing bowl, cream together the sugar and butter until fluffy. Add the egg, lemon zest, and vanilla extract and beat until blended. In a small bowl, whisk together the remaining dry ingredients. On low speed, gradually add them to the butter mixture and mix until incorporated. Add water, a few drops at a time, only until the dough starts to come away from the sides of the bowl.

For Both Methods

Scrape the dough onto a sheet of plastic wrap and use the wrap, not your fingers, to press the dough together to form a thick flat disc. Wrap it well and refrigerate for at least two hours, preferably no longer than 3.

Place 2 oven racks in the upper and lower thirds of the oven.
Preheat oven to 350°F.

On a lightly floured surface, roll out the dough to a ⅛-inch thickness. Cut shapes using your favorite Christmas cookie cutters or homemade cardboard patterns or even freehand. With a small, angled metal spatula or pancake turner, transfer the cookies to the prepared cookie sheets. If desired, paint the cookies with Edible Tempera Color. If you are planning to hang the cookies, make small holes with the blunt end of a wooden skewer.

Reroll the scraps, chilling them first, if necessary.

Bake for 8 to 12 minutes or until the cookies begin to brown

Royal Icing

INGREDIENTS Do not make on a humid day	MEASURE volume	WEIGHT pounds/ ounces	grams
3 large egg whites	3 fluid ounces	3 ounces	90 grams
powdered sugar	4 cups (lightly spooned into the cup)	1 pound	460 grams

around the edges. For even baking, rotate the cookie sheets from top to bottom and front to back halfway through the baking period.

Use a small, angled metal spatula or pancake turner to transfer the cookies to wire racks to cool before decorating with Royal Icing, dragées, sprinkles, and glittering holiday edibles.

Store: In an airtight container at room temperature.

Keeps: For several months.

Edible Tempera Color

Lightly beat 2 large egg yolks and spoon equal amounts of them into 5 small bowls or cups. Use liquid food coloring to color each mixture. For yellow, use 1/2 teaspoon

of yellow; for red, use 1/2 teaspoon of red; for green, use 1/4 teaspoon of green; for blue, use 1/4 teaspoon of blue; for black, use 1 1/2 teaspoons of green, 1 1/2 teaspoons of red, and 5 drops of blue.

Use a small clean paintbrush to paint the designs on the cookies before baking.

Royal Icing

This recipe has an excellent consistency for piping. For painting, thin the icing with water.

In a large mixing bowl, place the egg whites and powdered sugar and beat, preferably with the whisk beater, at low speed, until the sugar is moistened. Beat at high speed until very glossy and stiff peaks form when the beater is lifted (5 to 7 minutes). The tips of the peaks should curve slightly. If

necessary, more powdered sugar may be added. Keeps 3 days in an airtight container at room temperature. Rebeat lightly.

Royal Icing with Meringue Powder: * Replace the egg whites with 3 tablespoons of meringue powder and 3 fluid ounces (6 tablespoons) of warm water (this is approximately the amount of water contained in the eggs). Proceed as for basic Royal Icing. Keeps 2 weeks in an airtight container at room temperature. Rebeat lightly.

Smart Cookie

- Cookies can be rolled to a 1/4-inch thickness and underbaked slightly for a softer, chewier cookie.
- If the dough cracks while rolling it, cut it in quarters and allow it to soften until it is more malleable before continuing.
- Allow the cookie sheet(s) to cool completely before using for the next batch.
- Distribute the cookies evenly around the cookie sheet. Avoid crowding the cookies into one section of the cookie sheet, leaving a large area bare.

*Meringue powder is available through cake-decorating supply houses such as Maid of Scandinavia and the Chocolate Gallery (page 229).

Snowflakes

Makes 2 dozen 4-inch snowflakes

These brittle, sugary snow-flakes are almost too pretty to eat. Secret sugar eaters, however, will enjoy nibbling on them. They take hours to make, but the results are pure magic and provide the most exquisite Christmas tree and wreath decorations. The snowflakes can also be made as permanent ornaments with an inedible substance that holds up indefinitely, providing they don't get broken (page 11).

When I was ten, I was one of the toy soldiers in George Ballanchine's ballet of Tchaikovsky's *The Nutcracker,* performed at New York's City Center. The dance of the toy soldiers was followed by the dance of the snowflakes. I still remember the music of our cue. The memory of the final few flakes of the glittering artificial snow that were still falling onto the stage at curtain call inspired this cookie.

EQUIPMENT: *templates (see diagram); parchment; reclosable gallon-size freezer bag or pastry bag, fitted with a coupler and number 8 (³/8-inch diameter) decorating tube; small, clean paintbrush.*
At least 24 hours ahead, pipe the snowflakes.
In a large mixing bowl, place the egg whites and sugar and beat, preferably with the whisk beater,

INGREDIENTS *Do not make on a humid day*	MEASURE *volume*	WEIGHT	
		pounds/ ounces	*grams*
Royal Icing			
3 large egg whites	¹/4 liquid cup	3 ounces	90 grams
powdered sugar	4 cups (lightly spooned into the cup)	1 pound	460 grams
Topping			
2 large egg whites, lightly beaten	¹/4 liquid cup	2 ounces	60 grams
coarse crystal sugar*	¹/2 cup	3.5 ounces	100 grams

*Available through Maid of Scandinavia (page 229).

at low speed, until the sugar is moistened. Beat at high speed until very glossy and stiff peaks form when the beater is lifted (5 to 7 minutes). The tips of the peaks should curve slightly. If necessary, more powdered sugar may be added. Keeps 3 days in an airtight container at room temperature. Rebeat lightly.

Royal Icing with Meringue Powder:*
Replace the egg whites with 3 tablespoons of meringue powder and 3 fluid ounces (6 tablespoons) of warm water (this is approximately the amount of water contained in the eggs). Proceed as for basic Royal Icing. Keeps 2 weeks in an airtight container at room temperature. Rebeat lightly.

Scrape the icing immediately into the prepared decorating bag

*Meringue powder is available through cake-decorating supply houses such as Maid of Scandinavia and the Chocolate Gallery (page 229).

and close tightly so that the icing does not dry. When not piping, keep the tip covered at all times with a damp towel.

Place the templates (see diagram) on a counter and place round pieces of parchment (about 6 inches in diameter) on top of them. Tape them to the counter in a few places so that they do not slip while you are piping the snowflakes.

Follow the outline of each template. First pipe the 6 long "legs" of the flake, starting at the outside perimeter and stopping in the center. Use the paintbrush, dipped in water, to smooth any irregularities in the icing. Remove the tape and slip out the template to use for other snowflakes.

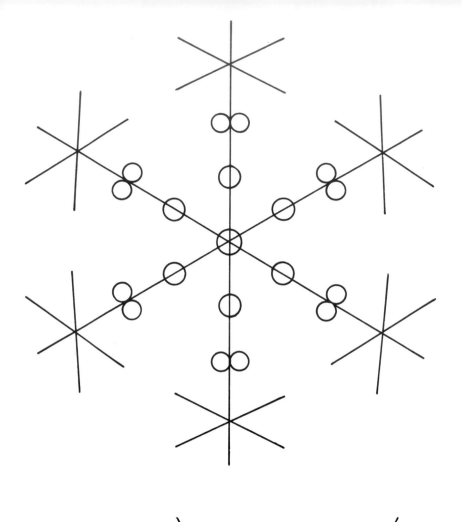

When all the snowflakes are piped, brush one at a time with the beaten egg whites and sprinkle each immediately with about 1 teaspoon of the crystal sugar. Allow the snowflakes to dry for at least 24 hours before removing them from the parchment.

To remove the snowflakes from the parchment, hold the snowflakes on a flat counter, allowing small sections to extend over the edge. Support the snowflake with a broad spatula while you pull the parchment down and away from the extended section. A *very thin* spatula or pancake turner also works if carefully slipped under the snowflake.

Use loops of thin nylon thread or fishing line, ribbon, or fine gold cord to suspend the snowflakes from the Christmas tree or wreath. If parts should break, use them anyway. They create a naturally beautiful look, and after all, no two snowflakes in nature are the same!

Store: In an airtight container, between sheets of wax paper, at room temperature at low humidity.

Keeps: Indefinitely at low humidity.

Smart Cookie

- The freezer bag works wonderfully for Royal Icing because it closes securely and keeps the icing from drying. A coupler, available from cake-decorating supply houses such as Maid of Scandinavia (page 249), is necessary, however, to keep the tube from slipping back into the bag.
- For the best texture, use old egg whites (page 219).
- Make sure that the bowl, beater, and egg whites are free of grease, including even a speck of egg yolk, or the whites will not beat well.
- Royal Icing can be stored in an airtight container up to 3 days. If it is made with meringue powder, it keeps up to 2 weeks. Rewhisk stored Royal Icing before using.
- Silica gel, available from florist or crafts shops, will improve the keeping quality of Royal Icing snowflakes if they are exposed to humidity.
- Perma Ice, available from Parrish (page 229), is an excellent piping material that resembles Royal Icing but is a lot more durable, unaffected by humidity, and is for decorative purposes only (it is not edible). It works well to pipe it on wax paper.

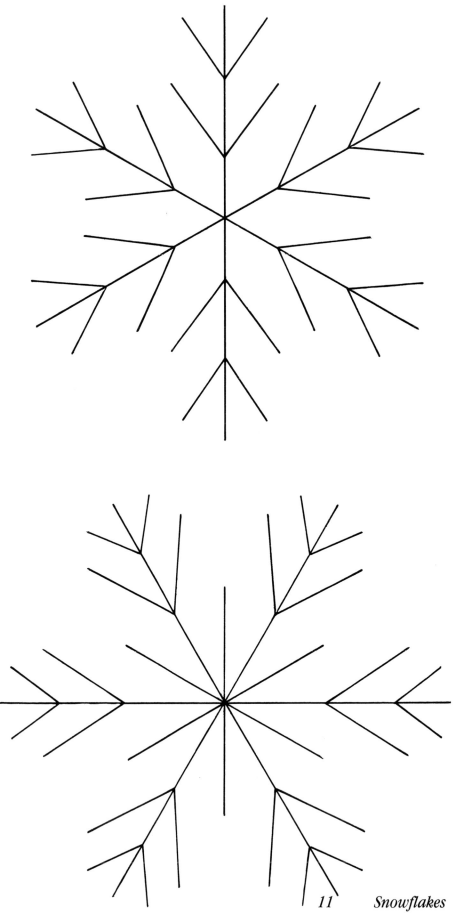

Gingerbread People

Makes 19 dozen 2-inch by ¼-inch small cookies or 40 5-inch by 3-inch by ¼-inch large cookies

I made my first gingerbread man from scraps of pie dough left over from what was the only pie I can ever remember my grandmother making. I had great fun shaping the "cookie man," and giving him raisin buttons and eyes. I remember that Grandma even baked him for me along with the pie, but she wouldn't let me eat my cookie because it had turned gray from overhandling. I didn't know until many years later that gingerbread men were supposed to be made from gingerbread dough and are called *gingerbread* because they are fragrant with ginger. Nobody ever talked about gingerbread women in those days either.

This gingerbread is delicious to eat and not too spicy, even for children. The cookies are perfect to string with bright fresh cranberries as garlands on the tree. Teddy bears and other favorite shapes are also fun to make.

EQUIPMENT: *nonstick or greased or buttered cookie sheets; floured pastry cloth and floured rolling pin sleeve; rolling pin; gingerbread men and women cookie cutters and/or hearts or other shapes.*

INGREDIENTS	MEASURE	WEIGHT	
	volume	ounces	grams
bleached all-purpose flour	3 cups (dip and sweep method)	15 ounces	425 grams
salt	¼ teaspoon	•	
baking soda	1 teaspoon	•	5 grams
ground ginger	2 teaspoons	•	•
ground cinnamon	1 teaspoon	•	•
grated nutmeg	½ teaspoon	•	•
ground cloves	¼ teaspoon	•	•
dark brown sugar	¾ cup (firmly packed)	6.25 ounces	179 grams
unsalted butter	12 tablespoons	6 ounces	170 grams
unsulfured molasses (preferably Grandma's)	½ cup (use a greased liquid measuring cup)	5.5 ounces	161 grams
1 large egg	3 tablespoons + ½ teaspoon	1.75 ounces (weighed without the shell)	50 grams

Optional: raisins, currants, decorative candies, and Royal Icing (recipe follows)

Food Processor Method

In a medium bowl, sift together the flour, salt, baking soda, and spices, then whisk together to mix evenly.

In a food processor with the metal blade, process the brown sugar until fine. Cut the butter into a few pieces and add it with the motor running. Process until smooth and creamy. Add the molasses and egg and process until incorporated, scraping the sides of the bowl. Add the flour mixture and pulse in just until the dough begins to clump together.

Electric Mixer Method

Soften the butter. In a small bowl, sift together the flour, salt, baking soda, and spices, then whisk together to mix evenly. In a mixing

bowl, cream together the brown sugar and butter until fluffy. Add the molasses and egg and beat until blended. On low speed, gradually beat in the flour mixture until incorporated.

For Both Methods

Scrape the dough onto a sheet of plastic wrap and use the wrap, not your fingers, to press the dough together to form a thick flat disc. Wrap it well and refrigerate it for at least 2 hours.

Place 2 oven racks in the upper and lower thirds of the oven.
Preheat oven to 350°F.

On a floured pastry cloth, roll out the dough to about ¹/₈-inch thickness. Use gingerbread cutters to cut out the dough. With a small, angled metal spatula or pancake turner, lift the cut dough onto the cookie sheets, placing the cutouts about 1 inch apart. If desired, make holes for hanging, either at the tops or hands, using the blunt edge of a wooden skewer.

Bake for about 8 to 10 minutes for the small cookies, up to about 10 to 12 minutes for the larger ones, or until firm to the touch and just beginning to color around the edges. For even baking, rotate the cookie sheets from top to bottom and front to back halfway through the baking period.

Royal Icing

INGREDIENTS	MEASURE	WEIGHT	
	volume	*pounds/ ounces*	*grams*
3 large egg whites	3 fluid ounces	3 ounces	90 grams
powdered sugar	4 cups (lightly spooned into the cup)	1 pound	460 grams

Cool the cookies on the sheets for about 1 minute. When they are firm enough to lift, use a small, angled metal spatula or pancake turner to transfer the cookies to wire racks to cool completely.

While the cookies are still hot and slightly soft, if desired, press raisins, currants, cinnamon red-hots, or other candy into the dough (for eyes and buttons). They can also be attached, using dots of Royal Icing as glue, after the cookies have cooled. Royal Icing, either white or tinted with food coloring, can be used to pipe details or frilly borders. The icing can be thinned slightly with a few drops of water and used to paint decorative motifs on the baked cookies. For a very special, dramatic effect, cut out rectangular or other shape plaques from the dough and personalize them for use as place cards or even as menus or greeting cards. The writing can be done with piped Royal Icing. To create stands, cut and bake triangles of gingerbread and attach them with Royal Icing to the back of the gingerbread plaques. Allow the icing to dry at least 24 hours before standing the plaques upright.

Note: Gingerbread for a cathedral or house can be made even more sturdy by reducing the amounts of sugar and butter. Use ¹/₂ cup firmly packed (4.25 ounces/120 grams) dark brown sugar and ¹/₂ cup (4 ounces/113 grams) unsalted butter. For further stability plus a delicious flavor, spread melted bittersweet or semisweet chocolate onto the back of the baked, cooled gingerbread.

Store: In an airtight container at room temperature.

Keeps: For several months.

Royal Icing

This recipe has an excellent consistency for piping. For painting, thin the icing with water.

In a large mixing bowl, place the egg whites and sugar and beat, preferably with the whisk beater, at low speed, until the sugar is moistened. Beat at high speed until very glossy and stiff peaks form when the beater is lifted (5 to 7 minutes). The tips of the peaks should curve slightly. If necessary, more powdered sugar may be added. Keeps 3 days in an airtight container at room temperature. Rebeat lightly.

Royal Icing with Meringue Powder: *
Replace the egg whites with 3 tablespoons of meringue powder and 3 fluid ounces (6 tablespoons) of warm water (this is approximately the amount of water contained in the eggs). Proceed as for basic Royal Icing. Keeps 2 weeks in an airtight container at room temperature. Rebeat lightly.

Smart Cookie

- If you like your gingerbread people soft, chewy, and pudgy, roll the dough to 1/4-inch thickness and underbake it slightly so that upon cooling the cookies remain soft.
- Well-chilled dough rolls easily on a floured surface without plastic wrap or a pastry cloth.
- Dough can also be rolled between plastic wrap layers but needs to be refrigerated after cutting as the dough becomes too soft to hold its shape well.
- Saran Wrap is the ideal plastic wrap for rolling the dough because it lies very flat. Wax paper is the second choice.
- Allow the cookie sheet(s) to cool completely before using for the next batch.
- Distribute the cookies evenly around the cookie sheet. Avoid crowding the cookies into one section of the cookie sheet, leaving a large area bare.
- Gingerbread is delicious and crunchy eaten plain. It becomes softer and equally delicious dunked in coffee, tea, or Cognac.

*Meringue powder is available through cake-decorating supply houses such as Maid of Scandinavia and the Chocolate Gallery (page 229).

Spritz Butter Cookies

Makes about 3½ dozen 2-inch cookies

When I hear the words *Christmas cookies,* I immediately think of spritz cookies because they are the first traditional Christmas cookies I ever made. My father's sister, Ruth, was the only person in the family who baked on a regular basis. She came from a tradition of fine handwork and crafts so she adored creating the most decorative cookies imaginable. When she made spritz cookies, she would set out little glass custard cups filled with appealingly colorful dragées, candied fruit, nuts, colored sugar, and sprinkles, and beautifully decorated cookie tins in which to pack the cookies. Every Christmas Aunt Ruth baked spritz cookies to take to her bosses at the glove company where she worked as a bookkeeper. They were as Jewish as she, but in New York, it seems, Christmas belongs to everyone, and Aunt Ruth, a born giver, got right into the holiday spirit.

This recipe produces spritz cookies with a lovely almond flavor and very tender texture. They are delicious to eat and, because they are so pretty and do not become stale quickly, they are perfect for setting on the mantel for company.

INGREDIENTS	MEASURE volume	WEIGHT ounces	grams
blanched sliced almonds	½ cup	1.5 ounces	43 grams
sugar	¾ cup	5.25 ounces	150 grams
unsalted butter	1 cup	8 ounces	227 grams
1 large egg	3 tablespoons + ½ teaspoon	1.75 ounces (weighed without the shell)	50 grams
pure vanilla extract	1 teaspoon	•	4 grams
pure almond extract	1 teaspoon	•	4 grams
bleached all-purpose flour	2 cups (dip and sweep method)	10 ounces	285 grams
salt	pinch	•	•

Optional: glacé cherries, sugar sprinkles, or dragées

EQUIPMENT: *ungreased cookie sheets; large pastry bag, fitted with a number 6 (½-inch diameter) large star pastry tube, or a cookie press.*

Place 2 oven racks in the upper and lower thirds of the oven.

Preheat oven to 375°F.

Place the almonds on a cookie sheet and bake them, stirring occasionally, for about 10 minutes, or until lightly browned. Cool completely.

Food Processor Method

In a food processor with the metal blade, process the almonds and sugar until they are ground powder fine. Cut the butter into a few pieces and add it with the motor running. Process until smooth and creamy. Add the egg and extracts and process until incorporated, scraping the sides of the bowl. Add the flour and salt and pulse in just until blended.

Electric Mixer Method

Soften the butter. Grate the almonds powder fine. In a mixing bowl, cream together the sugar and butter until fluffy. Add the egg and extracts and beat until blended. On low speed, gradually add the flour and salt and mix until incorporated.

For Both Methods

Scoop the dough into the pastry bag and pipe rosettes or stars about 1³/₄ inches in diameter onto the cookie sheets, 2 inches apart. To get the best possible shape, hold the bag so that the tube is straight up with the toothed edge just barely touching the cookie sheet. Squeeze the bag firmly without moving it until the shape is as wide as you desire. Stop squeezing and push the tube down slightly. Lift the tube straight up and away.

Decorate with optional glacé cherries, sugar sprinkles, or dragées.

Bake for 10 to 12 minutes, depending on the size, or until pale golden. For even baking, rotate the cookie sheets from top to bottom and front to back halfway through the baking period.

Use a small, angled metal spatula or pancake turner to transfer the cookies to wire racks to cool completely.

Store: In an airtight container at room temperature, or in the refrigerator or freezer.

Keeps: 1 month at room temperature, several months frozen.

Smart Cookie

- This recipe is less sweet than most spritz cookies. The almonds create a more tender cookie so the sugar can be reduced. This also results in a more attractive shape.
- Using a bag to "spritz" the cookies is easier than using a cookie press because the exact consistency of the dough is far less important. A reclosable freezer bag does not work well for this dough because the dough is very heavy and tends to squeeze out around the tube.
- Use the dough immediately after preparing it; chilling will make it too firm to pipe.
- If using a press and the impressions of the dough do not come out distinctly, chill the dough briefly to make it slightly more firm.
- Allow the cookie sheet(s) to cool completely before using for the next batch.
- Distribute the cookies evenly around the cookie sheet. Avoid crowding the cookies into one section of the cookie sheet, leaving a large area bare.

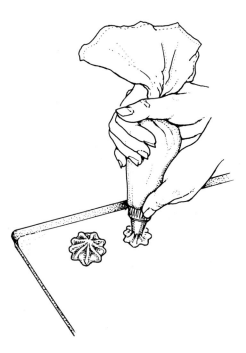

Spritz Butter Cookies 18

Mrs. King's Irresistibles

**Makes about 3 dozen
3-inch cookies**

The very first cookie I ever made on my own was from the back of an oatmeal box. I remember following the recipe with great care and my disappointment when I opened the oven and found that the carefully spooned cookies had all joined together to form one enormous and inedible cookie! Needless to say, the experience discouraged me from trying again for quite some time.

Mrs. King's cookies fall at the other end of the spectrum. Mrs. King is innkeeper of the charming Babbling Brook Inn in Santa Cruz, California. My brother and I stayed there only two days before the 1989 earthquake. Aside from the quake itself, these cookies, put out on the mantelpiece to welcome guests, were the most memorable part of my visit to California. Everyone is wild about them. My husband, Elliott, proclaims them the best oatmeal cookies he's ever tasted because they stay soft and chewy for many days, not

INGREDIENTS	MEASURE volume	WEIGHT ounces	grams
walnut halves	1 1/2 cups	5.25 ounces	150 grams
raisins	1 1/2 cups	7.5 ounces	215 grams
unsweetened granola mix*	1 1/2 cups	6.75 ounces	190 grams
old-fashioned rolled oats	1 cup	2.5 ounces	74 grams
semisweet chocolate chips	1 cup	6 ounces	170 grams
bleached all-purpose flour	1 2/3 cups (dip and sweep method)	8 ounces	227 grams
baking soda	1 teaspoon	•	5 grams
baking powder	1 teaspoon	•	5 grams
salt	1/2 teaspoon	•	•
dark brown sugar	1 cup (firmly packed)	8.5 ounces	240 grams
granulated sugar	3/4 cup	5.25 ounces	150 grams
unsalted butter	1 cup	8 ounces	227 grams
2 large eggs	3 fluid ounces	3.5 ounces (weighed without the shells)	100 grams
pure vanilla extract	1 teaspoon	•	4 grams

*I use "pecan splendor," a mix that contains cinnamon and was created by my local health food store; Mrs. King uses orange-almond. Use your favorite *unsweetened* granola. Sweetened granola will be much too sweet.

to mention that they contain loads of chocolate chips and granola. Without a doubt, you will want to make them all year round.

EQUIPMENT: *ungreased cookie sheets.*

Place 2 oven racks in the upper and lower thirds of the oven.
Preheat oven to 375°F.
Place the walnuts on a cookie sheet and bake them, stirring them occasionally, for about 10 minutes, or until lightly browned. Cool completely.

Food Processor Method

In a large bowl, toss together the raisins, granola, rolled oats, and chocolate chips.

Into a small bowl, sift together the flour, baking soda, baking powder, and salt. Whisk to combine well. Add the walnuts and set aside.

In a food processor with the metal blade, process the sugars until blended. Cut the butter into a few pieces and add it with the motor running. Process until smooth and creamy. Add the eggs and vanilla extract and process until incorporated, scraping the sides of the bowl. Add the flour mixture and pulse in just until incorporated. (The nuts will be coarsely chopped.)

Scrape the mixture into the bowl containing the chocolate chip mixture and stir together.

Electric Mixer Method

Soften the butter. Chop the walnuts coarsely. In a large bowl, toss together the raisins, granola, rolled oats, and chocolate chips. Into a small bowl, sift together the flour, baking soda, baking powder, and salt. Whisk to combine well. Add the walnuts and set aside. In a mixing bowl, beat the sugars until blended. Add the butter and beat until smooth and creamy. Scrape the sides of the bowl. Beat in the eggs and vanilla until incorporated, scraping the sides of the bowl. At low speed, add the flour mixture and beat it in just until incorporated. Scrape

the mixture into the bowl containing the chocolate chip mixture and stir together.

For Both Methods

Use your hands, or a 2-inch (number 30) scoop, to shape the dough into 1³/₄-inch diameter golf balls (2 level tablespoons) and place them 2 inches apart on the cookie sheets (12 cookies will fit on a 10-inch by 15-inch cookie sheet).

Bake for 12 to 15 minutes or just until the tops are turning light brown. The cookies should still be very soft when lightly pressed in the centers, although the edges will be set. (It's better to underbake than overbake.) For even baking, rotate the cookie sheets from top to bottom and front to back halfway through the baking period.

Cool for a few minutes on the sheets until firm enough to lift. Use a small, angled metal spatula or pancake turner to transfer the cookies to wire racks to cool completely.

Store: In an airtight container at room temperature or in the freezer.

Keeps: Several weeks at room temperature, several months frozen.

Smart Cookie

- Mrs. King's original recipe uses 1 cup of granulated sugar. A recent addition is 1 cup of white chocolate chips. If you have a real "sweet tooth," you may want to try these variations.
- These cookies may seem underdone when hot, but on cooling they continue to crisp. If not overbaked, they will stay soft and chewy for days.
- The unbaked dough keeps at least 5 days covered tightly and refrigerated.
- Allow the cookie sheet(s) to cool completely before using for the next batch.
- Distribute the cookies evenly around the cookie sheet. Avoid crowding the cookies into one section of the cookie sheet, leaving a large area bare.

Golden Biscotti

Mandelbröt

Makes 3 dozen 3-inch by 1¹/₂-inch cookies

I never really liked this cookie when I was growing up. I found it too plain and too brittle. But I once worked in the test kitchen of *Ladies' Home Journal,* and the food editor, Sue Huffman, gave me good advice about food prejudices: "If you don't like a recipe or an ingredient, make it so even *you* will like it." So I took the challenge to heart and made this version.

The mother of my accountant, Arnie Civins, contributed the base for a dough that is higher than usual in oil and nuts, making it less brittle. My husband, Elliott, gave me his mother's secret about putting in unblanched whole almonds for texture and appearance. And I added the large quantity of orange zest, giving it a lovely golden color and a little extra zip. It's great for snacking and dunking, and everyone loves it (including me)!

INGREDIENTS	MEASURE	WEIGHT	
	volume	ounces	grams
unbleached all-purpose flour	2 cups (dip and sweep method)	10 ounces	290 grams
baking soda	¹/₄ teaspoon	•	•
baking powder	1 teaspoon	•	5 grams
salt	¹/₄ teaspoon	•	•
sugar	²/₃ cup	4.75 ounces	132 grams
zest from 1 large orange, removed in lengthwise strips with a vegetable peeler	2 scant tablespoons (finely chopped)	•	10 grams
2 large eggs	3 fluid ounces	3.5 ounces (weighed without the shells)	100 grams
flavorless vegetable oil	¹/₂ liquid cup	3.75 ounces	108 grams
pure vanilla extract	1¹/₂ teaspoons	•	6 grams
pure almond extract	¹/₂ teaspoon	•	2 grams
unblanched sliced almonds	1²/₃ cups	5 ounces	142 grams
unblanched whole almonds	¹/₃ cup	2.25 ounces	64 grams
Topping			
sugar	2 tablespoons	1 ounce	25 grams
ground cinnamon	¹/₈ teaspoon	•	•
1 large egg white	2 tablespoons	1 ounce	30 grams

EQUIPMENT: *nonstick or greased cookie sheets.*

Place 2 oven racks in the upper and lower thirds of the oven.
Preheat oven to 350°F.

Food Processor Method

In a medium bowl, sift together all but ¹/₄ cup of the flour with the baking powder, baking soda, and salt, and whisk to mix it well.

In a food processor with the metal blade, process the sugar and orange zest until the zest is finely minced. Add the eggs and process for about 30 seconds or until thoroughly blended. Scrape the sides of the bowl.

With the motor running, add the oil and extracts and process until blended. Add the sliced al-

monds and process until finely chopped. Add the flour mixture and process for about 7 seconds or until the flour is almost incorporated. (There will be some flour clinging to the sides of the work bowl. Do not overprocess as the dough will be too stiff to incorporate the flour completely in the processor.)

Electric Mixer Method

Finely grate the orange zest. Finely chop the sliced almonds. Place them both in a medium bowl. Sift together all but 1/4 cup of the flour with the baking powder, baking soda, and salt, and add to the nuts and zest. Whisk together to mix them well. In a large mixing bowl, beat the sugar and eggs for several minutes, until very thick and pale in color. With the mixer at medium speed, beat in the oil and extracts. At low speed, gradually beat in the flour mixture.

For Both Methods

Scrape the dough (including any flour from the work bowl) onto a lightly floured counter and knead the dough, adding the remaining 1/4 cup of flour to form a soft, nonsticky dough.

Shape the dough into two 2-inch-wide cylinders. Each will be about 7 1/2 inches long. Line up the whole almonds lengthwise in rows along the dough and press them well into the dough. With the palms of your hands, roll the cylinders on the counter, enclosing the almonds and maintaining the 2-inch diameters of the cylinders. Place the cylinders 2 inches apart on a cookie sheet. In a small bowl, stir together the sugar and cinnamon for the topping. Beat the egg white. Brush the cylinders lightly with the beaten egg white and sprinkle them with the cinnamon topping.

Bake on the upper rack of the oven for 30 minutes or until lightly browned and very firm.

Cool the cylinders on the cookie sheet for 15 minutes or until just warm. Slip them off the sheet and onto a counter. With a serrated knife, cut diagonal 1/2-inch slices. Place the slices closely together on lightly buttered cookie sheets.

Toast the slices for about 8 minutes. Using a small metal spatula, turn them and bake for another 8 minutes or until golden brown. For even baking, rotate the cookie sheets from top to bottom and front to back halfway through the baking period. Use a small, angled metal spatula or pancake turner to transfer the cookies to wire racks to cool completely.

Store: In an airtight container at room temperature.

Keeps: Several months.

Smart Cookie

- Use only the orange portion of the zest, not the bitter white pith beneath.
- Unbleached flour has more gluten-forming proteins, which help to hold the almonds in the dough and make the dough less fragile.
- When the almonds are placed lengthwise, they do not fall out of the baked dough as readily and are more attractive when sliced.
- *Biscotti* can be tricky to cut into neat slices. If the cylinders are too hot or completely cold, the slices tend to break. When cutting the *biscotti,* hold the cylinder near the end being sliced and press it gently on top. If it is still crumbly, try popping it in the oven for another 5 minutes. Using coarsely chopped almonds instead of whole almonds is another solution, but they are less dramatic in appearance.
- Distribute the cookies evenly around the cookie sheet. Avoid crowding the cookies into one section of the cookie sheet, leaving a large area bare.
- For a pleasant variation, try replacing the almonds with hazelnuts (skins removed and finely chopped for the initial dough and coarsely chopped for kneading). If you still want to call the cookie by its German name, you will have to rename it Hasselnüssbröt, as *mandel* means "almond" in German.

Golden Biscotti   24

Springerle

Makes about 6 dozen 2-inch by
1½-inch cookies

Springerle are German in
origin and have been adopted
by many other countries. They
are hard, dry, anise-flavored
cookies, ideal for dunking in
tea or coffee but perhaps most
loved for their visual quality.
To my mind, springerle are
the most elegant of all Christmas cookies. The subtle raised
relief of pale ivory on ivory is
beautiful and traditional. In
Switzerland, the relief is sometimes painted with food-coloring–tinted egg yolk, and the
cookies returned to the oven
for a few minutes just to set
the color. For special designs
like the rose and angel in the
photograph, I love to paint the
relief with edible gold petal
dust, for the most dazzling effect of all.

Every trip I've taken to
Switzerland has added to my
wooden springerle mold collection. Some are antiques,
carved from mellow but durable pear wood. (One even has
a pear motif that serves as our
family crest since *Beranbaum*
means "pear tree.") Others of
my molds are reproductions of
antiques in a resin that resembles wood. All are treasures

INGREDIENTS	MEASURE	WEIGHT	
	volume	*pounds/ ounces*	*grams*
bleached all-purpose flour	4¼ cups (dip and sweep method)	1 pound 5 ounces	602 grams
baking soda	1 teaspoon	•	5 grams
4 large eggs (room temperature)	6 full fluid ounces	7 ounces (weighed without the shells)	200 grams
sugar	2 cups	14 ounces	400 grams
anise extract	1½ teaspoons	•	6 grams
Optional: gold petal dust*			

*Available in cake-decorating supply houses such as Maid of Scandinavia and the Chocolate Gallery (page 229).

that grace my kitchen walls
until I take them down at
Christmas baking time.

PREPARE AT LEAST 2 WEEKS
BEFORE SERVING

EQUIPMENT: *nonstick or greased
cookie sheets; rolling pin; springerle molds.*

Electric Mixer Method

In a medium bowl, sift together
the flour and baking soda, then
whisk together to mix evenly.

In a mixing bowl, preferably
with the whisk beater, beat the
eggs on high speed until light and
fluffy. Add the sugar and continue
beating on high speed until very
thick (about 5 minutes using a
KitchenAid, 15 minutes· using
a hand-held electric mixer).

If using a whisk beater, change
to the flat spade beater. On low
speed, beat in the anise extract.
Gradually beat in the flour mixture until well mixed. The dough
will be crumbly.

Scrape the dough onto a sheet
of plastic wrap and use the wrap,
not your fingers, to press the
dough together into a thick flat
disc. Wrap the dough well and refrigerate for about 1 hour. (Longer chilling may make the dough
difficult to roll.)

On a well-floured surface, roll
the dough into a ³/₈-inch-thick
rectangle. Press a springerle mold
into the dough, applying as much
pressure as possible to obtain a
good impression. If you are using
a multiple-pattern mold, use a
large, sharp knife to cut the dough
apart into individual rectangles at
the pattern edges.

Place the cookies on the prepared cookie sheets. Reroll the
scraps and repeat the procedure.
Allow the cookies to stand uncovered overnight at room temperature.

*Place 2 oven racks in the upper
and lower thirds of the oven.*

Preheat oven to 350°F.

Place the cookies in the preheated oven and lower the tem-

perature to 300°F. Bake for 25 to 30 minutes or until the cookies turn white on the unpainted portion of the tops and slightly golden on the bottoms. For even baking, rotate the cookie sheets from top to bottom and front to back halfway through the baking period.

Use a small, angled metal spatula or pancake turner to transfer the cookies to wire racks to cool completely.

To Apply Gold Petal Dust

Sprinkle a little petal dust into a small cup and add a few droplets of vodka or other clear high-proof drinking alcohol to dilute the "dust" and produce a thick "paint." Use a small clean paintbrush to apply the liquid gold to the raised portion of the design.

Store: In an airtight container at room temperature. Allow the cookies to ripen for at least 2 weeks before serving.

Keeps: For many months.

 Smart Cookie

- Allowing the molded dough to dry overnight before baking keeps these shapes from distorting. If using the gold petal dust, the high-proof alcohol dilutes it and then quickly evaporates, leaving behind only the golden color on the surface of the cookie.
- Springerle rolling pins do not work as well as the molds because you have to exert more pressure to get the best impressions.
- If you do not have enough cookie sheets for the whole batch, lay pieces of aluminum foil, the size of your cookie sheet, on the counter and place the springerle on the foil. When the first batch is baked, remove them from the cookie sheet and simply slip the cookie sheet under the foil of the next batch.
- Distribute the cookies evenly around the cookie sheet or aluminum foil. Avoid crowding the cookies into one section of the cookie sheet, leaving a large area bare.
- If baking larger pieces, increase the baking time. If the cookies are still moist in the center, the white surface will become golden again from the moisture and will need further baking.
- If you plan to hang the cookies, before baking, make holes using the blunt end of a wooden skewer.

Christmas Wreaths

Makes 1½ dozen 2-inch wreaths

I first encountered this old-time recipe fifteen years ago, when I worked in the test kitchen of *Ladies' Home Journal.* I was a bit of a food snob in those days and questioned how anything with marshmallows and cornflakes, not to mention green food coloring and cinnamon red-hots, could be considered edible. To my surprise, the crunchy, wheaty, sticky sweetness of these wreaths was quite pleasing when freshly made, and the air-dried wreaths were shiny, adorable, and perfect for adorning the mantelpiece as well as hanging from window frames and on the Christmas tree.

EQUIPMENT: *flat counter or cookie sheet, lined with wax paper, sprayed with nonstick vegetable cooking spray or lightly greased or buttered; 2 small spoons sprayed with nonstick vegetable cooking spray or lightly greased or buttered.*

Spray a medium saucepan with nonstick vegetable shortening or lightly grease it.

INGREDIENTS	MEASURE	WEIGHT	
	volume	*ounces*	*grams*
unsalted butter	½ cup	4 ounces	113 grams
30 large marshmallows	3 cups	7.25 ounces	208 grams
green liquid food coloring	1½ teaspoons	•	•
pure vanilla extract	1 teaspoon	•	4 grams
cornflakes	4 cups	5 ounces	140 grams
cinnamon red-hots (candies)	2 tablespoons	1 ounce	30 grams

Melt the butter over low heat. Add the marshmallows and melt them over low heat, stirring constantly, until smooth (about 6 minutes). Remove the pan from the heat and whisk in the food coloring and vanilla extract until well blended. Stir in the cornflakes to coat them well. Keep the mixture warm by placing the saucepan in a large pot or skillet filled with 1 inch of very hot tap water. Replace the water as it cools.

Working quickly so the mixture does not harden, use the 2 spoons, or lightly greased fingers, to drop small (1 heaping tablespoon) mounds of the cornflake mixture onto the wax paper. With lightly greased fingers, quickly form cornflake mounds into wreaths with holes in the centers. Immediately, while the wreaths are still sticky, decorate the wreaths with red-hots. (The red-hots may also be attached in a more leisurely fashion by using small dabs of Royal Icing, page 14.)

When wreaths dry, they may be strung with nylon string or gold ribbons as tree ornaments.

Store: In an airtight container.

Keeps: For eating, about 1 month; as ornaments, indefinitely.

 Smart Cookie

- Do not use the microwave to melt the marshmallows unless you have an enormous microwave-proof bowl; marshmallows swell considerably on heating.
- For easy cleanup, place your spoons and whisk in the saucepan; fill it with water and bring it to a boil.

Heirlooms

Salt Dough

Makes 3 cups (1 kilogram
48 grams/2 pounds 5 ounces)
of modeling dough
(enough for about
3 sets of Magi)

INGREDIENTS	MEASURE	WEIGHT	
	volume	*ounces*	*grams*
bleached all-purpose flour	3 cups (dip and sweep method)	15.25 ounces	436 grams
ordinary table salt	1½ cups	15.25 ounces	436 grams
water	1 liquid cup	8.25 ounces	236 grams

This dough is so smooth and malleable it can even be used to sculpt figures. My ingenious friend and colleague Rick Rodgers uses a garlic press to squeeze bits of the dough to form hair. This dough is not edible, but it is ideal for Christmas ornaments to treasure year after year or to give as gifts, such as the exquisitely graceful Three Magi designed and crafted by Helen Raffels and pictured here.

EQUIPMENT: *tracing paper; aluminum foil; rolling pin; ungreased cookie sheets; acrylic cutting board or other cutting surface; X-Acto knife with number 11 blades;* 2-ply bristol or heavy paper* for Magi templates; scissors; sharp paring knife; acrylic craft paints (white, violet, blue, red, rose, green);* gold and bronze paint;* assorted small paintbrushes for applying paints;* acrylic craft spray for final glaze;* hot glue gun and glue sticks (for making support stands).**

Food Processor Method

In a food processor with the metal blade, process the flour and salt for several minutes, until the salt

*Available in hobby, crafts, or art-supply stores.

is very fine. Add the water and pulse in to combine it and form a soft dough.

Electric Mixer Method

If using a mixer, it is best to buy popcorn salt, which is finer than ordinary table salt. Place the flour and salt in a large mixing bowl and beat for 30 seconds on medium speed to blend them together. With the mixer on low speed, add the water. Beat until the dough comes together.

For Both Methods

Empty the mixture onto a counter and knead it until it is smooth and malleable. If the dough is sticky, sprinkle on a little more flour; if too crumbly, sprinkle it with droplets of water.

Wrap the dough well in plastic wrap and store it overnight at room temperature before using it.

Trace the template patterns and transfer them to the heavy paper. Use the scissors to cut out the templates.

Cut 9 pieces of aluminum foil, 10 inches by 5 inches, for rolling the dough. Tape each piece to the counter as you need it. Roll out the dough to an even ³/₁₆-inch thickness. Sprinkle a little flour on the surface of the dough and

smooth it with your fingers. This will keep the knife from sticking to the dough when you're cutting it.

With a sharp knife trim the dough to measure 4 inches by 8 inches. Leave the dough on the foil and set aside. Continue with the remaining dough, keeping the trimmed scraps covered to prevent drying, and reroll them.

Preheat oven to 350°F. for 15 minutes and turn it off. Allow it to cool for 10 minutes. Place the dough pieces, still on the aluminum foil, on the cookie sheets. Place them in the oven and heat until a light crust forms on the top of the dough (about 6 to 8 minutes). Forming a thin crust on the surface of the dough facilitates even cutting. Overheating, however, will cause puffing and curling.

Remove the dough rectangles from the oven and allow them to cool completely on the sheets on wire racks.

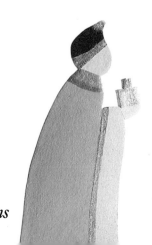

To Cut and Dry the Dough

With your fingers, lift each cookie from the foil and place it, one at a time, on the cutting board. Lightly sprinkle the surface of the cookie with flour and lay the template on top of it. With the X-Acto knife, cut around the edges of the template. For the cleanest cut and to prevent stretching of the dough, hold the knife vertically and use an up-and-down motion. Use a pancake turner to lift the shapes onto cookie sheets.

The dough must be thoroughly dry before painting. To air-dry, set the cookie sheets in a warm dry spot such as on a warm radiator, in a warm room, or in an oven with a pilot light for at least 3 days or until the pieces become very white and dry. If the edges start to curl slightly, turn the pieces upside down and weight them down under heavy books for about 1 hour, as often as required.

To Paint the Magi

Paint one side of the dough with a primer coat of white. Allow it to dry for about 20 minutes. Turn the piece over, paint the other side, and allow it to dry.

Paint one color at a time, allowing colors to dry 20 minutes. You will need at least 2 coats of each color. For the most even color use a short dabbing motion to apply the paint. If desired, make triangles of dough to use as stands and paint them the same color as the Magi.

To preserve the cookies for many years, spray them and the stands with several light coats of clear acrylic spray. Allow about 10 minutes of drying time between each coat and be sure to work in a well-ventilated area.

When the stands are dry, attach them to the backs of the Magi with hot glue.

Store: In boxes at room temperature wrapped in tissue paper.

Keeps: Fresh dough: 5 days. Dried dough: indefinitely, sprayed on both sides with acrylic.

Smart Cookie

- Other designs can be made using decorative cutters, a sharp knife to create free-form designs, or by pressing pieces of dough into oiled and floured molds. Cutouts of dough can be attached to one another using water and a small paintbrush.
- If you are planning to hang the salt dough cookies, be sure to make a small hole in the undried piece using the blunt end of a wooden skewer.

Enlarge template 175 percent

Cookies to Make for and/or with Kids

Peanut Butter and Jelly Jewels

Makes about 5 dozen
1³/₄-inch cookies

If you love peanut butter, these cookies will be It. I created what I believe to be quintessential peanut butter cookies to honor the one hundredth anniversary of peanut butter. They are *very* peanut buttery yet exceptionally light, with a lovely "sandy" bite. At my husband's urging, I doubled up on the peanut butter and decreased the flour, making the chocolate cookie centers seem like biting into a Reese's peanut butter cup.

Chocolate centers blend wonderfully with the peanut flavor, but the bright, tart, sticky cherry centers are my first choice.

EQUIPMENT: *ungreased cookie sheets, 1¹/₄-inch cookie scoop or a measuring teaspoon.*

Place 2 oven racks in the upper and lower thirds of the oven.
Preheat oven to 375°F.

Food Processor Method

Into a small bowl, sift together the flour, baking soda, and salt, then whisk to mix evenly. In a food processor with the metal blade, process the sugars for several minutes until very fine. Cut the butter into a few pieces and add it with the motor running. Add the pea-

INGREDIENTS	MEASURE volume	WEIGHT	
		ounces	*grams*
bleached all-purpose flour	1 cup (dip and sweet method)	5 ounces	142 grams
baking soda	1 teaspoon	•	5 grams
salt	¹/₈ teaspoon	•	•
light brown sugar	¹/₂ cup (firmly packed)	3.75 ounces	108 grams
granulated sugar	¹/₄ cup	1.75 ounces	50 grams
unsalted butter	¹/₂ cup	4 ounces	113 grams
smooth peanut butter	1 cup	9.25 ounces	266 grams
1 large egg	3 tablespoons + ¹/₂ teaspoon	1.75 ounces 50 grams (weighed without the shell)	
pure vanilla extract	¹/₂ teaspoon	•	2 grams

nut butter and process until smooth and creamy. Add the egg and vanilla extract and process until incorporated, scraping the sides of the bowl. Add the flour mixture and pulse in just until incorporated.

Electric Mixer Method

Soften the butter. Into a small bowl, sift together the flour, baking soda, and salt. Whisk to combine well. Set aside. In a mixing bowl, beat the sugars until well mixed. Add the butter and peanut butter and beat for several minutes, until very smooth and creamy. Add the egg and vanilla extract and beat until incorporated, scraping the sides of the bowl. At low speed, gradually beat in the flour mixture just until incorporated.

For Both Methods

Scrape the dough into a bowl and refrigerate for at least 1 hour or overnight. (This keeps the dough from cracking when shaped.)

Measure the dough into a 1¹/₄-inch cookie scoop or 2 level teaspoons and roll it between the palms of your hands to shape 1-inch balls. Place the balls 1¹/₂ inches apart on the cookie sheets. As soon as you roll each ball, use your index finger or the handle of a wooden spoon to make a depression going down almost to the cookie sheet in the center of each ball.

Bake for 10 to 12 minutes or until lightly browned and set. For even baking, rotate the cookie sheets from top to bottom and front to back halfway through the baking period.

Cool the cookies on the sheets for a few minutes or until firm enough to lift. Use a small, angled metal spatula or pancake turner to transfer the cookies to wire racks to cool completely. If necessary, while the cookies are still hot, use the greased handle of a wooden spoon to deepen the depressions.

Fill the centers with the cherry preserves or milk chocolate toppings.

Cherry Preserves Topping

In a microwave oven or a saucepan, heat the preserves until boiling. Strain the jelly into a small heavy saucepan. Place the cherries remaining in the strainer in the centers of the cookies. If some are crushed, piece them together.

On medium heat, boil the jelly for about 5 minutes, stirring constantly until, when it is dropped from the stirring spoon, the last drops gather to form one large sticky drop that hangs from the spoon. The jelly will be reduced to about $3/4$ cup. Allow the jelly to cool about 1 minute or until the bubbling stops. Spoon heaping $1/4$ to $1/2$ teaspoons over each cherry.

Milk Chocolate Topping

Break the chocolate into squares and place them in the top of a double boiler. Set it over hot but not simmering water. The water must not touch the bottom of the double-boiler insert. Stir until the chocolate begins to melt. Return the pan to low heat if the water cools, but be careful that the water does not get too hot. Stir the

Cherry Preserves Topping

INGREDIENTS	MEASURE	WEIGHT	
	volume	pounds/ ounces	grams
cherry preserves	1½ (12-ounce) jars	1 pound 2 ounces	510 grams

Milk Chocolate Topping

INGREDIENTS	MEASURE	WEIGHT	
	volume	ounces	grams
milk chocolate	2 (3-ounce) bars	6 ounces	170 grams
bittersweet chocolate	2 (3-ounce) bars	6 ounces	170 grams
unsalted butter (room temperature)	6 tablespoons	3 ounces	85 grams

chocolate until smooth, and cool it until it is no longer warm to the touch. (The chocolate may be melted in a microwave oven *if stirred every 15 seconds*. Remove it before it is fully melted and stir, using residual heat to complete melting). Whisk in the softened butter. The mixture will immediately thicken. Do not overwhisk. Use a reclosable quart-size freezer bag with one corner cut off to pipe the chocolate into the centers of the cookies or use a small metal spatula to spread on a dollop. You can also use a coupler with a number 22 star decorating tube to pipe the chocolate decoratively into the centers. Allow the chocolate to set until firm.

Store: Cookies filled with chocolate can be stacked in an airtight container at room temperature. Cookies with cherry centers need to be placed in single layers in airtight containers at room temperature. Do not cover the surface of

the cookie with plastic wrap as the cherry center remains slightly sticky.

Keeps: 1 month if filled, several months unfilled.

Smart Cookie

- For the best texture and flavor, be sure to use commercially prepared peanut butter such as Skippy and not homemade or health food varieties, which are less smooth.
- The dry ingredients are sifted together because baking soda has a tendency to lump.
- Using superfine sugar will result in fewer cracks in the cookie's surface. It can be prepared easily in a food processor by processing granulated sugar for a few minutes or until it is as fine as sand.

- These cookies are much lighter than the usual peanut butter cookie, despite the high amount of peanut butter, because there is less flour, which offsets the bulk of the peanuts.
- For a more delicate flavor and a finer, less "sandy" texture that does not crack, try a batch using half the amount of peanut butter. The cookies will also be flatter and crisper.
- Cherry preserves, straight from the jar, can be placed in the center of the unbaked cookie and baked in it, but the cookie is far less attractive.

- Allow the cookie sheet(s) to cool completely before using for the next batch.
- Distribute the cookies evenly around the cookie sheet. Avoid crowding the cookies into one section of the cookie sheet, leaving a large area bare.
- For a delicious variation that will enable you to pack the cherry variety without their sticking together, top the cherry centers with melted chocolate. Use 3 ounces of bittersweet or semisweet chocolate and 2 ounces of *finely* chopped milk chocolate. Melt the bittersweet choc-

olate as indicated for the Milk Chocolate Topping. Scrape it into a small container, immediately add the finely chopped milk chocolate, and stir until the chocolate is completely melted. Use a small spoon to cover the cherry center with the chocolate or pipe it from a reclosable quart-size freezer bag with a small piece cut from one of the corners of the bag. Place the cookies in a cool place or the refrigerator for about 5 minutes or until the chocolate is set and no longer shiny.

Turtles

Makes 28 2-inch turtles

We are all kids when it comes to turtles—beloved first pet and endearing shape—especially when they come in this deliciously edible form containing pecans, chocolate, and caramel—one of life's unbeatable flavor and texture combinations.

EQUIPMENT: *heavy, medium-size saucepan; accurate candy thermometer; greased or buttered 2-cup heatproof measure; small pan, such as an 8-inch by 8-inch by 2-inch baking pan, lined with aluminum foil, greased or buttered (if making the caramel ahead and storing); 9-inch by 13-inch baking pan, lightly greased or buttered; 7 parchment triangles or a greased teaspoon.*

INGREDIENTS	MEASURE	WEIGHT	
	volume	*pounds/ ounces*	*grams*
Caramel			
light brown sugar	2/3 cup (firmly packed)	5 ounces	143 grams
granulated sugar	1/3 cup	2.25 ounces	66 grams
corn syrup	3/4 liquid cup	8.75 ounces	246 grams
heavy cream	3/4 liquid cup	6 ounces	174 grams
unsalted butter	3 tablespoons	1.5 ounces	43 grams
pure vanilla extract	3/4 teaspoon	•	3 grams
Turtles			
pecan halves	4 2/3 cups	1 pound	454 grams
bittersweet or semisweet chocolate	1 (3-ounce) bar	3 ounces	85 grams

To Make the Caramel

In a heavy, medium-size saucepan, preferably with a nonstick lining, combine all ingredients for the caramel except for the vanilla extract and cook over medium-low heat, stirring often, until a candy thermometer reads 248°F. (the firm ball stage: The syrup, dropped into ice water, can be formed into a firm ball that does not lose its shape when removed from the water). Immediately pour the mixture into the heatproof measure. Allow the mixture to cool to about 145°F. Stir in the vanilla extract and use the caramel at once or pour it into a baking pan lined with aluminum foil, allow it to harden, and wrap it in foil. Keeps at least 1 month in an airtight container at room temperature. Makes 1 1/2 cups (about 1 pound/500 grams).

To Make the Turtles

Spread the pecans, rounded sides up, evenly in the prepared pan and press to level them. (To make picture-perfect turtles, place sheets of aluminum foil on the counter and arrange symmetrical clusters of 5 pecan halves—1 for the head, 2 for the arms, and 2 for the legs.)

If the caramel has been made ahead, heat enough water to surround the top container in the bottom of a double boiler until boiling. Turn off the heat. Place the caramel in the top of the double boiler and stir occasionally until melted (about 15 minutes). Reheat the water in the bottom after 10 minutes. The temperature of the caramel will be about 140°F., and the caramel will be fluid enough to spoon into the parchment bags. (The caramel can also be heated in the microwave oven on medium power for 1 or 2 minutes, stirring about four times. Stir well before transferring it to the parchment bag.)

Make bags from the parchment triangles (page 242), and put one inside the other to make 3 double bags and 1 single one for the melted chocolate. (This will protect your hand from the heat of the caramel.) Fill 1 parchment bag no more than two-thirds full with caramel. Fold over the top several

times to seal in the caramel. Cut off a small piece from the tip of the bag.

Using a pistol grip (thumb on top and index and middle fingers on either side, palm facing up), or both hands, squeeze quarter-size pools of caramel onto the pecans using a circular motion. The caramel will sink down between the pecans, so a few layers of caramel will be necessary. The circles of caramel will become somewhat irregular, but the freeform shape of these "turtles" is part of their charm. Leave about 1½ inches between the caramel circles. Allow the caramel to cool for about 2 minutes or until the circles are firm enough to pick up.

Lift out the caramel circles with attached pecans and transfer them to a wax paper–lined work surface. Push the pecans so that no spaces form between them. Reheat the remaining caramel, fill the second bag, and proceed as before. Repeat the procedure with the third bag and with the remaining caramel. Allow the turtles to cool completely.

Break the chocolate into squares and place in the top of a double boiler set over very hot water (but no hotter than 160°F.). The water must not simmer or touch the bottom of the double-boiler insert. Stir until the chocolate begins to melt. Return the pan to low heat if the water cools, but be careful that it does not get too hot. (The chocolate may be melted in a microwave oven *if stirred every 15 seconds.*) Remove the chocolate from the heat source before it is fully melted and stir, using residual heat to complete the melting. Allow the chocolate to cool, stirring it often, until it is slightly thickened.

Dry any moisture that formed on the bottom of the chocolate container and pour the melted chocolate into a reclosable quart-size freezer bag. Close it securely and cut off a small piece from one of the corners of the bag. Squeeze a coating of chocolate on top of the caramel, allowing a small amount of caramel to show around the edges. Allow the chocolate to set.

For a whimsical touch, as shown in the photograph, decorate the chocolate-topped turtles with small dots of piped melted white chocolate. (You will need about 1 ounce of white chocolate. Use the same technique to melt it as for the dark chocolate. Make an extra parchment bag or use a reclosable freezer bag with a tiny piece cut from one corner to pipe the dots.)

Store: In an airtight container at cool room temperature.

Keeps: At least 1 month. (If refrigerated, turtles will keep for about 6 months, but the chocolate will lose its attractive appearance. It is the pecans that shorten their shelf life because the nut oil eventually becomes rancid.)

 ## Smart Cookie

- A greased spoon can be used for caramel instead of parchment bags. The bags, of course, are quicker and neater to use.
- If you welcome shortcuts, premade caramel (available from Maid of Scandinavia, page 229) or unwrapped squares of caramel candies can be melted and used. Needless to say, when time allows, nothing beats homemade caramel.

Lion's Paws

Makes 22 2-inch cookies

I designed these butter cookies many years ago for a Safari Supper for *Co-ed,* a magazine for teenagers. Lion's Paws are actually seamless sandwiches made up of two pieces of dough that encase six chocolate chips. The chips create the knucklelike effect and slivered almonds, to simulate claws, are pressed into the dough between them to further the illusion of paws. The winsome shapes are time-consuming, but the result will so delight children of all ages that it makes the effort worthwhile.

EQUIPMENT: *nonstick, greased, or buttered, cookie sheets.*

Place 2 oven racks in the upper and lower thirds of the oven.

Preheat oven to 300°F.

Place the almonds on a cookie sheet and bake them, stirring occasionally, for about 10 minutes or until they are lightly browned. Cool completely. Turn off the oven.

INGREDIENTS	MEASURE volume	WEIGHT ounces	grams
blanched slivered almonds	1/2 cup	2 ounces	60 grams
bleached all-purpose flour	1 1/2 cups (dip and sweep method)	7.5 ounces	215 grams
baking powder	1/2 teaspoon	•	•
salt	1/2 teaspoon	•	•
sugar	1/4 cup	1.75 ounces	50 grams
unsalted butter	6 tablespoons	3 ounces	85 grams
1 large egg	3 tablespoons + 1/2 teaspoon	1.75 ounces (weighed without the shell)	50 grams
pure vanilla extract	1 teaspoon	•	4 grams
semisweet chocolate chips	1/2 cup	3 ounces	80 grams
Topping			
sugar	1/4 cup	1.75 ounces	50 grams
cinnamon	1/8 teaspoon	•	•
1 large egg white, lightly beaten	2 tablespoons	1 ounce	30 grams

Food Processor Method

In a small bowl, whisk together the flour, baking powder, and salt.

In a food processor with the metal blade, process the sugar until fine. Cut the butter into a few pieces and add it with the motor running. Process until smooth and creamy. Add the egg and vanilla extract and process until incorporated, scraping the sides of the bowl. Add the flour mixture and pulse in just until incorporated.

Electric Mixer Method

Soften the butter. In a small bowl, whisk together the flour, baking powder, and salt. In a mixing bowl, cream the sugar and butter until light and fluffy. Beat in the egg and vanilla extract until well blended. On low speed, beat in the flour mixture until incorporated.

For Both Methods

Scrape the dough onto a piece of plastic wrap, press it into a thick disc, wrap it tightly, and refrigerate it at least 1 hour.

Measure 22 level teaspoons of dough for the bottoms. As you shape each piece of dough, knead it by flattening it between your palms and then rolling it into a ball. (This keeps it from cracking around the edges when pressed down.)

Place each ball on the cookie sheet, pressing it to flatten to about a 1/8-inch thickness. Using your fingers, shape the dough into

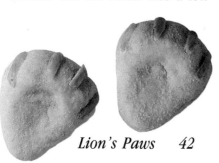

Lion's Paws 42

a triangular form with rounded corners, 2 inches long by 1 1/2 inches at its widest point. Leave about 1 inch between the cookies.

Place 3 chocolate chips in a row, points down, toward the wide end of the triangle. To create a knuckle effect, place 3 more chips points up, directly on top of the first 3. The chips will be sandwiched in by the top cookie dough.

For the tops of the cookies, measure 22 slightly rounded teaspoons of dough. Shape the dough as for the bottoms, but shape them a little larger and thicker at the widest part so they will drape over the chips. Starting at the pointed end of the triangle, place the cookie tops over the bottoms, matching the shapes and covering the entire bottom. Press lightly around the edges to seal them. Using your thumb, press down the dough in the longer area between the chocolate chips and the

pointed end to flatten and shape them to resemble paws. Don't worry if a little chocolate shows through. Firmly press in 4 almond slivers between and on either side of the chocolate chips to form the claws.

In a small bowl, stir together the sugar and cinnamon.

Brush the surface of the dough lightly with the beaten egg white, and dust the cookies with the cinnamon sugar. You will need only about 1 tablespoon, so reserve the remainder for other cookies.

At least 15 minutes before you are ready to bake the cookies, *preheat oven to 350°F.*

Bake for 20 to 30 minutes or until golden. For even baking, rotate the cookie sheets from top to bottom and front to back halfway through the baking period.

Cool for a few minutes on the sheets. When the cookies are firm enough to lift, use a small, angled metal spatula or small pancake turner to transfer them to wire racks to cool completely.

Store: In an airtight container at room temperature or in the freezer.

Keeps: Several months.

 ## Smart Cookie

- This cookie has a low sugar content, because more sugar makes the dough spread and the resulting cookies are less attractive.
- Allow the cookie sheet(s) to cool completely before using for the next batch.
- Distribute the cookies evenly around the cookie sheet. Avoid crowding the cookies into one section of the cookie sheet, leaving a large area bare.

Mom's Coconut Kisses

Makes 2 dozen
1³/₄-inch kisses

INGREDIENTS	MEASURE	WEIGHT	
	volume	*ounces*	*grams*
coconut, freshly shredded (see below)	3¹/₂ cups	9.75 ounces	276 grams
sweetened condensed milk	7 fluid ounces	9.75 ounces	276 grams
cornstarch	2 tablespoons	0.5 ounce	15 grams
lemon juice	1 teaspoon	•	5 grams
pure vanilla extract	1 teaspoon	•	4 grams
salt	pinch	•	•

My mother didn't bake cookies when I was growing up. The only smell of spice I associated with her was from the oil of cloves she used in her dental practice. However, she has fond memories from her own childhood of a special cookie that her aunt Edith's cook, Katie, used to make for all the children. This cookie is so easy to make, in fact, that it's ideal to make *with* the kids. No doubt they will think that these kisses look like toasted snowballs! And they'll love the milky/creamy tropical blend of fresh coconut and sweetened condensed milk. The flavor is strongly reminiscent of coconut macaroons traditionally eaten for Hanukkah.

EQUIPMENT: *food processor with a fine shredding or hand shredder; cookie sheets lined with parchment or aluminum foil; 1¹/₄-inch cookie scoop or tablespoon.*

Place 2 oven racks in the upper and lower thirds of the oven.
Preheat oven to 400°F.

With an ice pick or nail and hammer, pierce the 3 holes at one end of the coconut. Drain the liquid and reserve it, if desired, for another use. Bake the coconut until the shell cracks (about 20 minutes). *Reduce oven temperature to 350°F.*

Wrap the coconut with a towel to keep the shell from flying about, and use a hammer to crack open the shell. Separate the coconut meat from the shell and, using a small paring knife, peel the dark outer skin from the white coconut meat. (Discard this outer skin.) With the fine shredding disk of a food processor or hand shredder, shred the coconut meat. Do not grate the coconut as the shape of the finished cookie will be flatter.

In a medium bowl, using a wooden spoon, mix all the ingredients together until well blended, but do not add all of the milk until you check the consistency. The mixture should be moist and hold together. If necessary, add up to 2 extra tablespoons of the condensed milk.

Use a rounded cookie scoop, or a scant tablespoon and your fingers, to form 1-inch mounds of the mixture about 1¹/₂ inches high. Place about 1¹/₂ inches apart on the prepared baking sheet.

Bake for 15 to 20 minutes or until most of each cookie's surface is light golden. There will still be white spots. For even baking, rotate the cookie sheets from top to bottom and front to back halfway through the baking period.

Use a small, angled metal spatula or pancake turner to transfer the cookies to wire racks to cool completely.

Store: In an airtight container in the refrigerator or freezer.

Keeps: 2 months refrigerated, several months frozen.

Smart Cookie

- Fresh coconut is a lot less sweet and a lot more delicious than canned or packaged coconut. Don't even think about substituting here!
- Allow the cookie sheet(s) to cool completely before using for the next batch.
- Distribute the cookies evenly around the cookie sheet. Avoid crowding the cookies into one section of the cookie sheet, leaving a large area bare.

Cocoa Brownies

Makes 16 2-inch by
2-inch by 1½-inch
squares

There are many wonderful recipes for this American classic, and the truth is, chocolate doesn't ever get better than in the form of a brownie. Everyone has a favorite brownie recipe; in fact, I have several. But this one really is tops. It is chewy yet slightly spongy and cakey—a miracle of textures. My friend Brigitte Weil, who created and ran Dean & DeLuca's bakery department for years, commented that what makes these brownies particularly unusual is that they don't even *need* milk to wash them down.

I make these brownies with cocoa for its deeper, duskier flavor. Since cocoa contains a lot less cocoa butter than does chocolate, butter is added to this recipe to replace it. At room temperature butter is soft, while cocoa butter is very hard. This means that the texture of the cocoa brownies is less chewy than that of chocolate brownies. If you like your brownies intensely chocolatey *and* very chewy, there's a simple solution: Store these cocoa brownies in the refrigerator and eat them cold. That's something like having your brownie and eating it too!

INGREDIENTS	MEASURE	WEIGHT	
	volume	*ounces*	*grams*
pecan pieces *or* coarsely chopped pecans	1½ cups	6 ounces	213 grams
unsalted butter	14 tablespoons	7 ounces	200 grams
unsweetened cocoa (preferably Dutch-processed)	½ cup + 2 teaspoons (lightly spooned into the cup)	1.75 ounces	50 grams
sugar	1 cup + 3 tablespoons	8.25 ounces	238 grams
3 large eggs	4.5 fluid ounces	5.25 ounces (weighed without the shells)	150 grams
pure vanilla extract	2 teaspoons	•	8 grams
bleached all-purpose flour	½ cup	2.5 ounces	71 grams
salt	pinch	•	•

EQUIPMENT: *8-inch by 8-inch by 2-inch baking pan, preferably metal (if using a glass pan, lower the oven temperature 25°F.), bottom lined with parchment or wax paper, sprayed with nonstick vegetable spray or buttered (if buttering, butter the bottom of the pan too so the liner won't slip).*

Place 1 oven rack in the middle of the oven.

Preheat oven to 325°F.

Place the pecans on a cookie sheet and toast them, stirring occasionally, for about 10 minutes or until lightly browned. Cool completely.

In a medium saucepan or microwave-proof bowl, melt the butter. Remove from the heat source and whisk in the cocoa. Whisk in the sugar, then the eggs and vanilla extract. Add the flour, salt, and nuts and stir into the mixture using a large rubber spatula or wooden spoon.

Scrape the batter into the prepared pan and spread it evenly.

Bake for 30 to 40 minutes. A wooden pick inserted in the center should come out with moist crumbs still clinging to it. Do not overbake.

Place the pan on a wire rack and cool completely. Use a small metal spatula to loosen the brownie from the sides of the pan and invert onto the back of a cookie sheet. Peel off the liner and reinvert the brownie onto a cutting

surface. Use a serrated knife to cut 2-inch squares. (First cut the brownie into fourths in one direction, then into fourths the other direction, at right angles to the first.)

Store: Wrap each brownie in plastic wrap and store in an airtight container at room temperature, or in the refrigerator or freezer.

Keeps: 1 week at room temperature, 1 month refrigerated, or several months frozen.

Smart Cookie

- A nonalkalized cocoa (not Dutch-processed) can be used, but Dutch-processed gives a darker, richer color and a smoother cocoa taste.
- It's fine to replace the pecans with walnuts. I prefer the softer texture and flavor of the pecans.
- Combining the cocoa with the hot butter brings out more cocoa flavor.
- A serrated knife works best to cut the brownies because it cuts well through the nuts.
- If you are a fanatic for perfection, you may want to do as they do at Walt Disney World: Cut the drier edges from the outside of the brownie before cutting it into squares, and serve only the perfect moist inner section. Their pastry chef, George Geary, tells me that they grind up the drier edges and use them as a delicious crumb coating for the buttercream on the sides of their cakes. Actually, these brownies are so high in butter content that even the edges go down easily.
- Brownies stay the moistest and freshest when wrapped airtight. Saran Wrap is the least "breathable" of current plastic wraps and therefore the best choice.

Cocoa Brownies   48

Cookies for Giving

Mexican Wedding Cakes

Makes about 4½ dozen
1½-inch cookies

This is a recipe with many names and claims of origin. Some people call it Portuguese Wedding Cakes and Wedding Bells, but this version containing pecans is said to have come from Mexico.

These innocent-looking mounds, pristinely dusted with powdered sugar, are so ethereal they seem to explode in your mouth. A real favorite with most everyone, they are lovely to serve for afternoon tea and, placed in an attractive container, make a charming and welcome holiday gift.

EQUIPMENT: *ungreased cookie sheets.*

Place 2 oven racks in the upper and lower thirds of the oven.
Preheat oven to 350°F.

Place the pecans on a cookie sheet and bake them, stirring occasionally, for 10 minutes or until lightly browned. Cool completely.

Food Processor Method

In a food processor with the metal blade, process the sugar with the pecans and salt until the pecans are powder fine. Cut the butter into a few pieces and add it with the motor running. Process until

INGREDIENTS	MEASURE	WEIGHT	
	volume	*ounces*	*grams*
pecan halves	½ cup	1.75 ounces	50 grams
powdered sugar	1 cup (lightly spooned into the cup)	4 ounces	115 grams
salt	pinch	•	•
unsalted butter	1 cup	8 ounces	227 grams
pure vanilla extract	½ teaspoon	•	2 grams
bleached all-purpose flour	1¾ cups (dip and sweep method)	8.75 ounces	250 grams
Topping			
powdered sugar	1½ cups (lightly spooned into the cup)	6 ounces	172 grams

smooth and creamy. Scrape the sides of the bowl. Add the vanilla extract and pulse in. Add the flour and pulse in until it starts to clump together.

Electric Mixer Method

Soften the butter. Grate the nuts so that they are powder fine. In a medium bowl, whisk together the flour, salt, and grated nuts. In a mixing bowl, at low speed, cream the sugar and butter until light and fluffy. Beat in the vanilla extract and scrape the sides of the bowl. Still on low speed, gradually beat in the flour mixture just until incorporated.

For Both Methods

Scrape the dough into a bowl, cover it tightly, and refrigerate for at least 1 hour and preferably no longer than 3 hours.

Measure the dough into a 1¼-inch scoop, gently rounded, or 1 scant tablespoon and roll it between the palms of your hands to form 1-inch balls. Lightly flour your hands if necessary.

Place the balls 1½ inches apart on the cookie sheets. Bake for 15 to 20 minutes or until the cookies barely begin to brown. (The undersides will be lightly browned.) For even baking, rotate the cookie sheets from top to bottom and front to back halfway through the baking period.

Cool the cookies on the sheets for 2 to 3 minutes. Use a small, angled metal spatula or pancake turner to lift them from the sheets.

Roll them in the powdered sugar while still hot. Several rollings create a lovely powdery coating. Transfer the cookies to wire racks to cool completely. Roll again in the powdered sugar.

Store: In an airtight container at room temperature.

Keeps: About 1 month.

Smart Cookie

- If you have a scale, pecan pieces can be used. The halves are given for consistency of weight.
- Allow the cookie sheet(s) to cool completely before using for the next batch.

- Distribute the cookies evenly around the cookie sheet. Avoid crowding the cookies into one section of the cookie sheet, leaving a large area bare.
- These cookies look lovely well powdered with sugar. If you are storing the cookies, it's fine to reroll them in powdered sugar up to several hours before serving.

Scottish Shortbread Cathedral Cookies and Traditional Wedges

Makes 4 dozen
1¹/₂-inch cookies or
16 3¹/₂-inch long wedges

INGREDIENTS	MEASURE	WEIGHT	
	volume	*ounces*	*grams*
unsalted butter (cold)	1¹/₄ cups	10 ounces	284 grams
powdered sugar	¹/₄ cup (lightly spooned into the cup)	1 ounce	28 grams
granulated sugar	¹/₄ cup	1.75 ounces	50 grams
bleached all-purpose flour	2¹/₂ cups (dip and sweep method)	12.5 ounces	362 grams

If there could be but one cookie in all the world, this would be it for me, perhaps because there really is perfection in simplicity. Its buttery flavor and tender texture with just the right amount of bite are perfection. In order to avoid temptation, I like to store these cookies in the freezer and take out just one to put in the oven with the pilot light while brewing my afternoon coffee. By the time the cup is brewed, the cookie is no longer cold—just right.

Traditionally, shortbread was baked in round discs with notches radiating around the edges to represent the sun. But shortbread can be as creative as the person who makes it. My favorite shortbread press comes from my good friend, the brilliant cook and food columnist Bonnie Stern of the Bonnie Stern School of Cooking in Toronto. My editor, Maria Guarnaschelli, took one look at the cookies produced with this press and dubbed them "cathedral cookies."

EQUIPMENT: *ungreased cookie sheets.*

Food Processor Method

Cut the butter into 1-inch cubes, wrap it, and refrigerate.

In a food processor with the metal blade, process the sugars for 1 minute or so, until the sugar is very fine. Add the butter and pulse until the sugar disappears. Add the flour and pulse until there are a lot of moist, crumbly little pieces and no dry flour particles remain.

Dump the mixture into a plastic bag and press it together. Remove the dough from the plastic bag and knead it lightly until it holds together.

Electric Mixer or by Hand

In Scotland it is said that the best shortbread is mixed with the fin-gers and that each woman's fingers lend something distinctive and special to the finished cookie. I find that the texture is more delicate when the dough is mixed with the fingers rather than in a machine. For either method, use superfine sugar for the best texture and be sure to soften the butter.

In a medium bowl, whisk together the sugars. In a large bowl, cream the butter with the sugars until light and fluffy. With your fingers or with the electric mixer, mix in the flour until the mixture holds together. If using the mixer, add the flour in 2 parts.

For Both Methods

Place 2 oven racks in the upper and lower thirds of the oven.
Preheat oven to 275°F.
Measure 2 level teaspoons or 1 scant tablespoon of the dough and knead each piece by flattening it between your palms and then rolling it into a 1-inch ball. (This keeps it from cracking around the edges when pressed flat.)

Place each ball on the cookie sheet, flattening it with a cookie press, fork, or the bottom of a

tumbler, lightly moistened with water. Leave about 1 inch between flattened cookies.

Bake for 45 minutes to 1 hour or until pale golden (do not brown). For even baking, rotate the cookie sheets from top to bottom and front to back halfway through the baking period.

Use a small, angled metal spatula or pancake turner to transfer the cookies to wire racks to cool completely.

Wedge-Shaped Shortbread

Decrease the butter to 1 cup (8 ounces/227 grams). Divide the dough into 2 equal parts. Pat each half into an ungreased 8-inch round cake pan. Use the tines of a fork to press 3/4-inch lines radiating like rays of sun all around the perimeter of the dough. Prick the rest of the dough all over with the tines of the fork. This keeps the shortbread even and creates the traditional design.

Bake for 60 to 70 minutes or until pale golden (do not brown). For even baking, rotate the pans from top to bottom and front to back halfway through the baking period.

Cool in the pans, on a wire rack, for 10 minutes. Invert the shortbread onto a flat cookie sheet and slide it onto a cutting board. While still warm, use a long sharp knife to cut each 8-inch round of shortbread into 8 pie-shaped wedges. Transfer the wedges to wire racks to cool completely.

Store: In an airtight container at room temperature or in the freezer.

Keeps: Several months.

 Smart Cookie

- In Scotland, part rice flour (1/6 the total volume of flour) is used in making the shortbread. It results in a crisper texture. I prefer shortbread made with all-purpose flour. If you use rice flour, be sure it is fresh, and store the leftover flour in the refrigerator as it can become rancid.
- Cookies require slightly more butter than the discs so that they don't crack around the edges when rolled into balls and pressed flat.
- In Canada, the sugar in the shortbread is sometimes replaced with an equal weight or 6 tablespoons of firmly packed light brown sugar for a "richer" cookie.
- Shortbread dough can be pressed into lightly oiled and floured decorative wooden molds and then inverted onto cookie sheets to bake; however, I find that large discs of shortbread have the best texture when shaped and baked in aluminum cake pans. Perhaps it's because the sides of the pan keep the dough from spreading and the resulting shortbread is somewhat more compact.
- Allow the cookie sheet(s) to cool completely before using for the next batch.
- Distribute the cookies evenly around the cookie sheet. Avoid crowding the cookies into one section of the cookie sheet, leaving a large area bare.

Rose's Crescents

Makes 5 dozen 2-inch
by 1-inch crescents

This is the first cookie I successfully made and has always been one of my very favorites. The original recipe was given to me years ago, when I was a young bride, and contained half Crisco for ease in handling. As my confidence grew, I eventually changed to all butter. This is a fragile, flavorful, buttery cookie with a fine dusting of cinnamon sugar. Over the years, it has served as the perfect gift that "money can't buy" to offer to the person who has everything. The last person to receive a "thank you" batch was too busy consuming the cookies even to look up to say good-bye.

EQUIPMENT: *ungreased cookie sheets.*

Food Processor Method

In a food processor with the metal blade, process the almonds and sugar until the almonds are ground very finely. Cut the butter into a few pieces and add it with the motor running. Process until smooth and creamy. Scrape the sides of the bowl. Add the flour and sprinkle the salt on top. Pulse in just until the flour is incorporated.

INGREDIENTS	MEASURE	WEIGHT	
	volume	*ounces*	*grams*
blanched sliced almonds	2/3 cup	2 ounces	56 grams
sugar	1/3 cup	2.25 ounces	66 grams
unsalted butter	1 cup	8 ounces	227 grams
bleached all-purpose flour	1 2/3 cups (dip and sweep method)	8.25 ounces	235 grams
salt	1/4 teaspoon	•	•
Topping			
superfine sugar	1/2 cup	3.5 ounces	100 grams
cinnamon	1/2 teaspoon	•	•

Electric Mixer Method

Soften the butter. Grind the almonds very finely. In a large mixing bowl, combine the almonds, butter, and sugar and beat until light and fluffy. Stir together the flour and salt and beat them into the mixture, on low speed, until incorporated.

For Both Methods

Scrape the dough onto a piece of plastic wrap, press it into a thick disc, wrap it tightly, and refrigerate about 2 hours or until the dough is firm.

For the topping, stir together the sugar and cinnamon until uniform in color.

Place 2 oven racks in the upper and lower thirds of the oven.
Preheat oven to 325°F.
Divide the dough into 8 portions. Work with 1 section at a time, keeping the remainder of the dough refrigerated. Knead the dough between floured hands until malleable. Pinch off a portion of the dough and roll it into a 3/4-inch round ball. On a lightly floured counter, roll each ball into a cylinder with tapered ends, about 3 inches long by 1/2 inch thick. Form each cylinder into a crescent shape and place on the cookie sheet 1 inch apart.

Bake for 14 to 16 minutes or until set but not brown. For even baking, rotate the cookie sheets from top to bottom and front to back halfway through the baking period.

Cool the cookies on the sheets for 10 minutes. While they are still warm, use a small, angled metal spatula or pancake turner to lift them from the sheets and dip them, 1 at a time, in the cinnamon

sugar, turning gently to coat all over. Finish cooling the cookies on wire racks.

Store: In an airtight container at room temperature, or in the refrigerator or freezer.

Keeps: 1 month at room temperature, 1 month refrigerated, or several months frozen.

Smart Cookie

- Superfine sugar can be prepared easily in a food processor by processing granulated sugar for a few minutes or until it is as fine as sand. This produces a finer, more pleasant topping for the cookies.

- Allow the cookie sheet(s) to cool completely before using for the next batch.
- Distribute the cookies evenly around the cookie sheet. Avoid crowding the cookies into one section of the cookie sheet, leaving a large area bare.

Bernachons' Biarritz

Makes about 6 dozen
2¹/₂-inch cookies

When I went to France to work with Maurice and Jean-Jacques Bernachon in Lyon on the adaptation of their book *A Passion for Chocolate*, this became my favorite of all their cookies. Crisp yet slightly chewy and deliciously fragrant with hazelnuts, these cookies are as elegant as is the famous beach resort on the Atlantic coast after which they are named.

EQUIPMENT: *nonstick, lightly buttered, or greased cookie sheets; teaspoon or pastry bag, or reclosable quart-size freezer bag with a coupler, fitted with a number 12 (⁵/₁₆-inch diameter) round decorating tube.*

Place 2 oven racks in the upper and lower thirds of the oven.

Preheat oven to 350°F.

In a medium saucepan, bring the water to a boil. Add the hazelnuts and baking soda, and boil for 3 minutes. (The water will turn black from the color in the skins.) Test a nut by running it under cold water. If the skin is not easy to remove with slight pressure from the fingers, boil the nuts another minute or so more. Drain, rinse, and peel them.

Place the hazelnuts on a cookie sheet and bake them, stirring occasionally, for 10 to 15 minutes or until golden brown. Cool completely.

In a food processor with the metal blade, process the sugar for a few minutes or until it is as fine as sand. Remove the sugar to a small bowl and set aside.

In the container of a food processor, place the hazelnuts with the flour, ¹/₂ cup of the sugar, and the salt. Process until the nuts are finely ground. Add the milk and vanilla extract and process to combine them. Add the butter and pulse in to combine. Transfer the mixture to a large bowl.

Electric Mixer Method

In a mixing bowl, beat the egg whites until foamy, add the cream of tartar, and beat until soft peaks form when the beater is raised slowly. Gradually beat in the remaining 2 tablespoons of sugar until stiff peaks form when the beater is raised slowly. Using a

INGREDIENTS	MEASURE	WEIGHT	
	volume	ounces	grams
water	1¹/₂ cups	12.5 ounces	355 grams
whole hazelnuts	1 scant cup	4.5 ounces	125 grams
baking soda	2 tablespoons	1 ounce	30 grams
sugar	¹/₂ cup + 2 tablespoons	4.5 ounces	125 grams
bleached all-purpose flour, sifted	³/₄ cup + 2 tablespoons (sift into the cup and level off)	3.5 ounces	100 grams
salt	pinch	•	•
milk	¹/₂ liquid cup	4.25 ounces	121 grams
pure vanilla extract	¹/₂ teaspoon	•	2 grams
unsalted butter (softened)	5 tablespoons	2.5 ounces	70 grams
2¹/₂ large egg whites (room temperature) *or* 2 jumbo egg whites	2.5 fluid ounces	2.75 ounces	75 grams
cream of tartar	¹/₄ teaspoon	•	•
bittersweet or semisweet chocolate	4 (3-ounce) bars	12 ounces	340 grams

large rubber spatula, fold the whites into the batter.

Using a teaspoon or a pastry bag or reclosable quart-size freezer bag with a coupler, fitted with a number 12 round decorating tube, form 1-inch rounds (about ¾ inch high) about 1½ inches apart on the prepared baking sheets. Tap the baking sheets against the counter to spread and flatten out the batter to 2-inch discs (about 15 will fit on a 10-inch by 15-inch cookie sheet).

Bake for 8 to 10 minutes or until the cookies begin to brown around the edges. For even baking, rotate the cookie sheets from top to bottom and front to back halfway through the baking period.

Allow the cookies to cool for a few minutes on the sheets. When they are firm enough to lift, use a small, angled metal spatula or pancake turner to transfer the cookies to wire racks to cool completely.

Break the chocolate into squares and place them in the top of a double boiler set over very hot water (but not hotter than 160°F.). The water must not simmer or touch the bottom of the double-boiler insert. Stir until the chocolate begins to melt. Return the pan to low heat if the water cools, but be careful that it does not get too hot. (The chocolate may be melted in a microwave oven *if stirred every 15 seconds.*) Remove the chocolate from the heat source before it is fully melted and stir, using residual heat to complete the melting. Allow the chocolate to cool for about 5 minutes, stirring occasionally, or until slightly thickened.

Using a small metal spatula, spread a thick layer of melted chocolate on the underside of each cookie. (Have several paper towels handy as this is a messy task.) If desired, use a cake-decorating triangular comb or a fork to make wavy lines on the chocolate when the chocolate is "tacky" and before it fully sets. Stir the chocolate often to prevent streaking.

Store: In an airtight container, between layers of wax paper, at room temperature or in the freezer. If you are planning to freeze the cookies, apply the choc-olate after removing from the freezer for the best appearance.

Keeps: Several days at room temperature, several months frozen.

Smart Cookie

- There is no need to sift the flour if you have a scale and can weigh it. Sifting is for accurate measure only in this recipe.
- For the best texture, use old egg whites (page 219).
- Make sure that the bowl, beater, and egg whites are free of grease, including even a speck of egg yolk, or the whites will not beat well.
- Allow the cookie sheet(s) to cool completely before using for the next batch.
- Distribute the cookies evenly around the cookie sheet. Avoid crowding the cookies into one section of the cookie sheet, leaving a large area bare.
- For a faster decoration, drizzle the melted chocolate over the tops of the cookies.

Hazelnut Meringue Puffs

Makes about 3 dozen
1¼-inch cookies

These unusual little puffs are a delightful combination of crispy, light meringue filled with crunchy, nutty dacquoise—and both the puffs and filling are made from the same simple meringue batter. Although these cookies have an impeccably sophisticated and complex appearance, they are actually quite easy to make.

INGREDIENTS Do not make on a humid day	MEASURE volume	WEIGHT ounces	grams
water	1½ cups	12.5 ounces	355 grams
baking soda	2 tablespoons	1 ounce	30 grams
whole hazelnuts	½ cup	2.5 ounces	70 grams
powdered sugar	¾ cup (lightly spooned into the cup)	3 ounces	85 grams
lemon zest	½ teaspoon (finely grated)	•	•
3 large egg whites (room temperature)	3 fluid ounces	3 ounces	90 grams
cream of tartar	⅜ teaspoon	•	•
superfine sugar	2 tablespoons + ¼ cup	1.5 ounces	75 grams

EQUIPMENT: *cookie sheets, non-stick or lined with parchment or aluminum foil; reclosable quart-size freezer bag or pastry bag fitted with a number 6 (½-inch diameter) plain round pastry tube; pastry bag fitted with a number 12 (⁵/₁₆-inch diameter) decorating tube (2 teaspoons can be used in place of the bags and tubes).*

Place 2 oven racks in the upper and lower thirds of the oven.
Preheat oven to 350°F.

In a large saucepan, bring the water to a boil. Add the baking soda and nuts and boil for 3 minutes. (The water will turn black from the color in the skins.) Test a nut by running it under cold water. If the skin is not easy to remove with slight pressure from the fingers, boil the nuts another minute or so more. Drain, rinse, and peel them. Place the hazelnuts on a cookie sheet, and bake them, stirring occasionally, for 15 to 20 minutes or until golden brown. Cool completely. Turn off the oven.

In a food processor with the shredder disc, grate the nuts. Replace the shredder with the metal blade, add 1 tablespoon of the powdered sugar and the lemon zest and process until the nuts are ground very finely. Empty the mixture into a small bowl and set aside.

Electric Mixer Method

In a mixing bowl, beat the egg whites until frothy, add the cream of tartar, and beat at medium speed while gradually adding 1 tablespoon of the superfine sugar. When soft peaks form when the beater is raised, add 1 tablespoon of superfine sugar and increase the speed to high. When stiff peaks form when the beater is raised slowly, gradually beat in the re-maining superfine sugar and beat until very stiff and glossy. Sift the remaining powdered sugar over the meringue and fold it in, preferably using a large wire whisk.

Remove 1 cup of the meringue and stir it into the nut mixture. Place the remaining meringue in the reclosable bag with the larger tube. Place the nut mixture in the pastry bag with the smaller tube. Pipe 1-inch mounds of the meringue about 1 inch apart on the cookie sheets. Let the meringue mounds stand for about 10 minutes, until they are slightly firm. Using your index finger dipped in powdered sugar, or a tiny spoon, make a depression about ½ inch in diameter in the center of each mound and pipe the nut mixture into it. The opening will enlarge slightly to accommodate the filling. Alternatively, 2 teaspoons dipped in powdered sugar can be used to form and fill the balls.

Moisten your index finger with a little water and press the centers so that they are almost flush with the meringue. The centers will spread to about 3/4 inch in diameter and the meringue will spread to about 1¼ inches in diameter. Allow the puffs to dry for 1 hour or until set (when your fingertip touches the surface, the meringue stays intact). If any of the nut filling remains, pipe it into 1-inch mounds and bake it along with the puffs.

Preheat oven to 200°F.

Bake for about 1 hour or until completely set. The centers can be slightly sticky, as they will harden on cooling. For even baking, rotate the cookie sheets from top to bottom three quarters of the way through the baking period.

Use a small, angled metal spatula or pancake turner to transfer the puffs to wire racks to cool completely.

Store: In an airtight container at room temperature at low humidity.

Keeps: 2 months.

 ## Smart Cookie

- Superfine sugar makes a lighter meringue than granulated. It can be prepared easily in a food processor by processing granulated sugar for a few minutes or until it is as fine as sand. The addition of powdered sugar makes the meringue still lighter!
- For the best texture, use old egg whites (page 219).
- Make sure that the bowl, beater, and egg whites are free of grease, including even a speck of egg yolk, or the whites will not beat well.
- Fold in the powdered sugar with a wire whisk for the best incor-poration with the least amount of deflation of the beaten whites.
- For the stiffer nut mixture use a pastry bag because not all brands of reclosable freezer bags are strong enough.
- Do not use wax paper; the meringue may stick to it.
- Meringue mixtures should be piped shortly after preparing them. If you do not have enough cookie sheets for the whole batch, lay pieces of foil the size of your cookie sheet on the counter and pipe the meringue puffs onto the foil. When the first batch is baked, remove it from the cookie sheet and simply slip the cookie sheet under the foil of the next batch.
- To prevent cracking, do not open the oven door during the first three quarters of the cooking time.

Black and Whites

Makes about 1½ dozen
1½-inch rounds

These cookies are dramatically elegant and unusually delicious. The airy, sweet, and crispy almond-flavored meringue puff contains a fudgey chocolate counterpoint at its pistachio-coated center.

INGREDIENTS Do not make on a humid day	MEASURE volume	WEIGHT ounces	grams
2 large egg whites (room temperature)	¼ liquid cup	2 ounces	60 grams
cream of tartar	¼ teaspoon	•	•
superfine sugar	¼ cup	1.75 ounces	50 grams
pure almond extract	¼ teaspoon	•	•
powdered sugar	½ cup (lightly spooned into the cup)	2 ounces	57 grams

EQUIPMENT: *cookie sheets, non-stick or lined with parchment or aluminum foil; 2 reclosable quart-size freezer bags or pastry bags; plastic coupler for the smaller tube; piping tubes: number 6 (½-inch diameter) plain round pastry tube and number 12 (⁵/₁₆-inch diameter) plain round decorating tube (2 teaspoons can be used in place of the bags and tubes).*

Electric Mixer Method

In a mixing bowl, beat the egg whites until frothy, add the cream of tartar, and beat at medium speed while gradually adding ½ tablespoon of the superfine sugar. When soft peaks form when the beater is raised, add 1 tablespoon of the superfine sugar and increase the speed to high. When stiff peaks form when the beater is raised slowly, gradually beat in the remaining superfine sugar and beat until very stiff and glossy. Beat in the almond extract. Sift the powdered sugar over the meringue and

fold it in, preferably using a large wire whisk.

Place the meringue in the bag with the larger tube and close it securely. Pipe 1-inch mounds of the meringue about 1 inch apart on the cookie sheets. Alternatively, 2 teaspoons dipped in powdered sugar can be used to form the mounds. Allow the mounds to stand for 10 minutes.

Using your index finger dipped in powdered sugar, or a tiny spoon, make a depression about ½ inch wide in the center of each mound. Allow them to dry for 1 hour or until set (when your fingertip touches the surface, the meringue stays intact).

Place 2 oven racks in the upper and lower thirds of the oven.
Preheat oven to 200°F.

Bake for about 1 hour or until completely set. The centers can be slightly sticky, as they will harden on cooling. For even baking, rotate the cookie sheets from top to bottom and front to back three quarters of the way through the baking period.

Use a small, angled metal spatula or pancake turner to transfer the puffs to wire racks to cool completely.

Raise the oven temperature to 325°F.

Chocolate Fudge Topping

Break the chocolate into squares and place them, together with the butter, in the top of a double boiler set over very hot water (but no hotter than 160°F.). The water must not simmer or touch the bottom of the double-boiler insert. Stir occasionally until the chocolate is entirely melted. Return the pan to low heat if the water cools, but be careful that it does not get too hot.

Beat the egg yolk slightly and whisk it into the hot melted chocolate. Continue whisking the mixture, over the hot water, for 1 minute. Remove the upper container from the double boiler, dry any moisture that may have formed on its bottom, and scrape the mixture into a bowl. Allow the

Chocolate Fudge Topping

INGREDIENTS	MEASURE	WEIGHT	
	volume	ounces	grams
bittersweet or semisweet chocolate	1 (3-ounce) bar	3 ounces	85 grams
unsalted butter (softened)	2 tablespoons	1 ounce	28 grams
1 large egg yolk	1 tablespoon + 1/2 teaspoon	0.5 ounce	19 grams
shelled unsalted pistachio nuts	2 tablespoons	0.5 ounce	19 grams

mixture to cool to room temperature, stirring occasionally.

If your pistachio nuts are salted, rinse them in a strainer under hot tap water. Place the pistachios on a cookie sheet in the preheated 325°F. oven for 5 to 10 minutes or until, when scratched lightly with a fingernail, the skins separate from the nuts. With a large spoon, transfer the pistachios to a clean kitchen towel and wrap them with the towel. Allow them to sit for a few minutes. Use the towel to rub off as much peel as possible. Allow the nuts to cool to room temperature. Chop them medium coarsely and place them in a small custard cup.

When the puffs are completely cool, fill the second freezer or pastry bag with the Chocolate Fudge Topping and pipe it into the depressions (or use a tiny spoon or spatula).

To coat the chocolate with pistachio, hold the cookie between your thumb and first two fingers and invert it chocolate-side down into the nuts. The nuts will attach themselves to the chocolate.

Store: In an airtight container at room temperature at low humidity.

Keeps: For months. The texture of the chocolate filling is less good after about 2 weeks, but the taste is not affected.

 Smart Cookie

- Superfine sugar makes a lighter meringue than granulated. It can be prepared easily in a food processor by processing granulated sugar for a few minutes or until it is as fine as sand. (The addition of powdered sugar makes the meringue lighter still!)
- For the best texture, use old egg whites (page 219).
- Make sure that the bowl, beater, and egg whites are free of grease, including even a speck of egg yolk, or the whites will not beat well.
- Fold in the powdered sugar with a wire whisk for the best incorporation with the least amount of deflation of the beaten whites.
- Do not use wax paper; the meringue may stick to it.
- Meringue mixtures should be piped shortly after preparing them. If you do not have enough cookie sheets for the whole batch, lay pieces of aluminum foil the size of your cookie sheet on the counter and pipe the meringue puffs onto the foil. When the first batch is baked, remove it from the cookie sheet and simply slip the cookie sheet under the foil of the next batch.
- To prevent cracking, do not open the oven door during the first three quarters of the cooking time.
- The egg yolk contained in the chocolate topping gives it a nice gloss.

Chocolate-Dipped Melting Moments

Makes about 4 dozen
2¹/₂-inch cookies

Impossibly light yet buttery, crisper than the Mexican Wedding Cake cookies, the name says it all. Pack these delicate cookies in a beautiful container, such as the small hatbox shown in the photograph, nestled in a bed of crumpled colored tissue paper or tinsel for protection.

EQUIPMENT: *nonstick or buttered cookie sheets.*

Food Processor Method

In a medium bowl, whisk together the flour, cornstarch, and salt.

In a food processor with the metal blade, process the powdered sugar until very fine. Cut the butter into a few pieces and add it with the motor running. Process until smooth and creamy. Add the vanilla extract and pulse in. Scrape the sides of the bowl. Add the flour mixture and pulse in just until incorporated.

Electric Mixer Method

Soften the butter. In a medium bowl, whisk together the flour, cornstarch, and salt. In a mixing bowl, cream the butter and sugar until light and fluffy. Beat in the vanilla extract. On low speed, beat in the flour mixture until incorporated.

INGREDIENTS	MEASURE volume	WEIGHT ounces	grams
bleached all-purpose flour	³/₄ cup + 1 tablespoon (dip and sweep method)	4 ounces	114 grams
cornstarch	1 cup	4.25 ounces	120 grams
salt	¹/₈ teaspoon	•	•
powdered sugar	¹/₂ cup (lightly spooned into the cup)	2 ounces	57 grams
unsalted butter	1 cup	8 ounces	227 grams
pure vanilla extract	1 teaspoon	•	4 grams
Topping			
powdered sugar	³/₄ cup (lightly spooned into the cup)	3 ounces	85 grams
bittersweet or semisweet chocolate	2 (3-ounce) bars	6 ounces	170 grams

For Both Methods

Scrape the dough into a bowl and refrigerate it for at least 2 hours.

Place 2 oven racks in the upper and lower thirds of the oven.
Preheat oven to 375°F.
Divide the dough into 10 portions. One portion at a time, knead the dough between lightly floured hands until malleable.

On a lightly floured counter or pastry cloth, roll each dough portion back and forth, stretching to form ropes ¹/₂ inch in diameter. Cut the ropes into 2¹/₂-inch lengths and place them on the cookie sheets 1¹/₂ inches apart, curving them slightly into crescent shapes. Knead any leftover pieces of dough into the next portion.

Bake for 10 to 15 minutes or until just beginning to brown around the bottom edges. For even baking, rotate the cookie sheets from top to bottom and front to back halfway through the baking period.

Allow the cookies to cool on the sheets for a few minutes. Use a small, angled metal spatula or pancake turner to transfer the cookies to the powdered sugar and gently roll them in powdered sugar. The cookies are very fragile

when warm, but don't despair—you get to eat the broken pieces! Transfer the cookies to wire racks, and when cool, dip them a second time in the sugar.

To Dip Cookies in Chocolate

Break the chocolate into squares and place them in the top of a double boiler set over very hot water (but no hotter than 160°F.). The water must not simmer or touch the bottom of the double-boiler insert. Stir until the chocolate begins to melt. Return the pan to low heat if the water cools, but be careful that it does not get too hot. (The chocolate may be melted in a microwave oven *if stirred every 15 seconds.*) Remove the chocolate from the heat source before it is fully melted and stir, using residual heat to complete the melting. Keep the chocolate warm over a bowl of warm water (water must not exceed 120°F. and the bottom of the upper container must not touch the water).

Tilt the top part of the double boiler over the hot water so that all of the chocolate collects in one corner. (A large serving spoon placed between the two pans helps to hold the tilt.)

Lay sheets of aluminum foil or wax paper on the counter. Lightly brush away the powdered sugar from one end of each crescent and dip this end into the chocolate. Gently tap the chocolate-dipped end against the back of the stirring spoon to remove excess chocolate. Set the cookie onto the foil or wax paper and move it forward a tiny bit to cover any chocolate spread. (This makes a neater shape.) When the chocolate sets, it will dull and harden.

Store: In an airtight container, between sheets of wax paper, at room temperature.

Keeps: Several months. The appearance of the chocolate is less attractive after about 3 weeks. This does not affect the flavor.

Smart Cookie

- The traditional shape for these cookies is a ball. One-inch balls need to bake for about 10 minutes or until firm and golden.
- Allow the cookie sheet(s) to cool completely before using for the next batch.
- Distribute the cookies evenly around the cookie sheet. Avoid crowding the cookies into one section of the cookie sheet, leaving a large area bare.

Three-Nut Fingers

Makes 32 2-inch by
1¼-inch cookies

This simple oval cookie seems so innocent. But put it in your mouth and its dissolving texture with its fine crunch of nuts and intense depth of toasted nut flavor creates a close to obsessive craving.

EQUIPMENT: *nonstick or buttered cookie sheets.*

Place 2 oven racks in the upper and lower thirds of the oven.
Preheat oven to 350°F.

Place the nuts in separate piles on a cookie sheet and bake them, keeping the nuts separated but stirring occasionally, for 10 minutes or until the almonds are lightly browned. With a large spoon, transfer the hazelnuts to a clean kitchen towel and wrap them with the towel. Allow them to sit for a few minutes. Use the towel to rub off as much peel as possible. Cool all the nuts completely.

Food Processor Method

In a small bowl, whisk together the flour and salt.

In a food processor with the metal blade, process the sugar with the nuts until the nuts are

INGREDIENTS	MEASURE	WEIGHT	
	volume	ounces	grams
unblanched sliced almonds	½ cup	1.5 ounces	42 grams
pecan halves	⅓ cup	1.25 ounces	33 grams
whole hazelnuts	¼ cup	1.25 ounces	36 grams
bleached all-purpose flour	¾ cup + 1 tablespoon (dip and sweep method)	4 ounces	114 grams
salt	⅛ teaspoon	•	•
light brown sugar	2 tablespoons (firmly packed)	1 ounce	27 grams
unsalted butter	½ cup	4 ounces	113 grams
water	1½ teaspoons	•	7 grams
pure vanilla extract	½ teaspoon	•	2 grams
Topping			
superfine sugar	½ cup	3.5 ounces	100 grams

powder fine. Cut the butter into a few pieces and add it with the motor running. Process until smooth and creamy. Add the water and vanilla extract and process until incorporated, scraping the sides of the bowl. Add the flour and pulse in just until incorporated.

Electric Mixer Method

Soften the butter. Grate the toasted nuts powder fine. In a medium bowl, whisk together the flour, nuts, and salt. In a mixing bowl, cream the sugar and butter until light and fluffy. Beat in the water and vanilla extract until incorporated. On low speed, beat in the flour mixture until incorporated.

For Both Methods

Scrape the dough into a bowl. Measure the dough into a 1¼-inch cookie scoop or 2 level teaspoons. Shape the dough into datelike pieces (1¾ inches long by ¾ inch wide) and place them on the cookie sheets 1½ inches apart.

Bake for about 15 minutes or until lightly browned. For even baking, rotate the cookies sheets from top to bottom and front to back halfway through the baking period.

Allow the cookies to cool on the sheets for a few minutes. Use a small, angled metal spatula or pancake turner to lift the cookies from the sheets. Gently roll them in superfine sugar. Transfer the

cookies to wire racks, and when cool, dip them a second time in the sugar.

Store: In an airtight container at room temperature or in the freezer.

Keeps: 1 month at room temperature, several months frozen.

Smart Cookie

- To make superfine sugar, process granulated sugar in the food processor for a few minutes or until it is as fine as sand.
- Pecan halves are called for to ensure an accurate amount if you are using a measuring cup. Pecan pieces are fine to use if you weigh them.
- Allow the cookie sheet(s) to cool completely before using for the next batch.
- Distribute the cookies evenly around the cookie sheet. Avoid crowding the cookies into one section of the cookie sheet, leaving a large area bare.

Lora Brody's Chocolate Phantoms

Makes 5 dozen
1½-inch cookies

INGREDIENTS	MEASURE	WEIGHT	
	volume	ounces	grams
whole macadamia nuts	1½ cups	7 ounces	200 grams
bittersweet or semisweet chocolate	2⅔ (3-ounce) bars	8 ounces	227 grams
unsalted butter	2 tablespoons	1 ounce	28 grams
bleached all-purpose flour	3 tablespoons (dip and sweep method)	1 ounce	28 grams
baking powder	¼ teaspoon	•	•
2 large eggs	3 fluid ounces	3.5 ounces (weighed without the shells)	100 grams
sugar	½ cup	3.5 ounces	100 grams
pure vanilla extract	1 teaspoon	•	4 grams
semisweet chocolate chips	1⅓ cups	8 ounces	227 grams

A great name and a great cookie from a great lady. This recipe is from her book *Growing Up on the Chocolate Diet.* Everyone loves these very chocolatey candy cookies with their waxy-crunchy texture and distinctive flavor of macadamia nuts. Lora tells me she named them "phantoms" because they have a wonderful way of disappearing. Macadamia nuts are the most expensive of all nuts, making these cookies an impressively extravagant gift.

EQUIPMENT: *heavy cookie sheets,* preferably nonstick, or lined with parchment or aluminum foil (a must); 2 teaspoons.*

*This dough must be spooned into mounds soon after mixing or the chocolate cools and begins to set. Fifteen cookies will fit on a 10-inch by 15-inch cookie sheet so 4 of this size will be needed. If you do not have sufficient sheets, prepare extra sheets of parchment or aluminum foil the size of your cookie sheets. Measure out the dough onto these sheets. When the first batch of cookies has baked, carefully slip the parchment or foil with the baked cookies off the baking sheet onto a counter to cool completely. Cool the hot baking sheets under cold tap water. Carefully lift up the next parchment or foil sheet with the unbaked cookie dough on it and slide the cookie sheet under it.

Place 2 oven racks in the upper and lower thirds of the oven.
Preheat oven to 350°F.

Unsalted macadamia nuts are available in packages at health food stores. The bottled variety, however, does have salt listed in the ingredient list. If yours are salted, rinse the nuts in a strainer under hot tap water and recrisp them in a 350°F. oven for 5 to 10 minutes.

Break the bittersweet chocolate into squares and place them, together with the butter, in the top of a double boiler set over very hot water. The water must not simmer or touch the bottom of the double-boiler insert. Stir until the chocolate begins to melt. Return the pan to low heat if the water cools, but be careful that it does not get too hot. (The chocolate may be melted in a microwave oven *if stirred every 15 seconds.*) When melted, remove the chocolate from the heat source.

In a small bowl, whisk together the flour and baking powder.

In a mixing bowl, using a hand-held electric mixer set on high speed, beat the eggs, sugar, and vanilla extract until well blended (at least 15 seconds). On the lowest speed, add the melted chocolate mixture and beat until combined. Add the flour mixture and beat on low speed just until combined. With a rubber spatula, fold in the chocolate chips and nuts.

Use 2 teaspoons to drop the batter onto the prepared cookie sheets. Make the cookies very small, no bigger than a heaping measuring teaspoonful, about 1 inch wide, and mound each one as high as possible. Leave about 1½ inches between each mound.

Bake for 6 minutes, then rotate the cookie sheets from top to bottom and back to front and bake for 3 to 4 more minutes, until the tops are dry. The cookies should be very soft when removed from the oven. They will firm on cooling, but should remain moist and chewy.

Cool completely on the baking sheets and then peel them off.

Store: In an airtight container at room temperature.

Keeps: 2 days. The cookies remain delicious for weeks, but the texture becomes somewhat crystallized after 2 days.

Smart Cookie

- Heavy cookie sheets are best for these cookies in order to keep the chocolate bottoms from overbrowning.
- Allow the cookie sheet(s) to cool completely before using for the next batch.
- Distribute the cookies evenly around the cookie sheet. Avoid crowding the cookies into one section of the cookie sheet, leaving a large area bare.

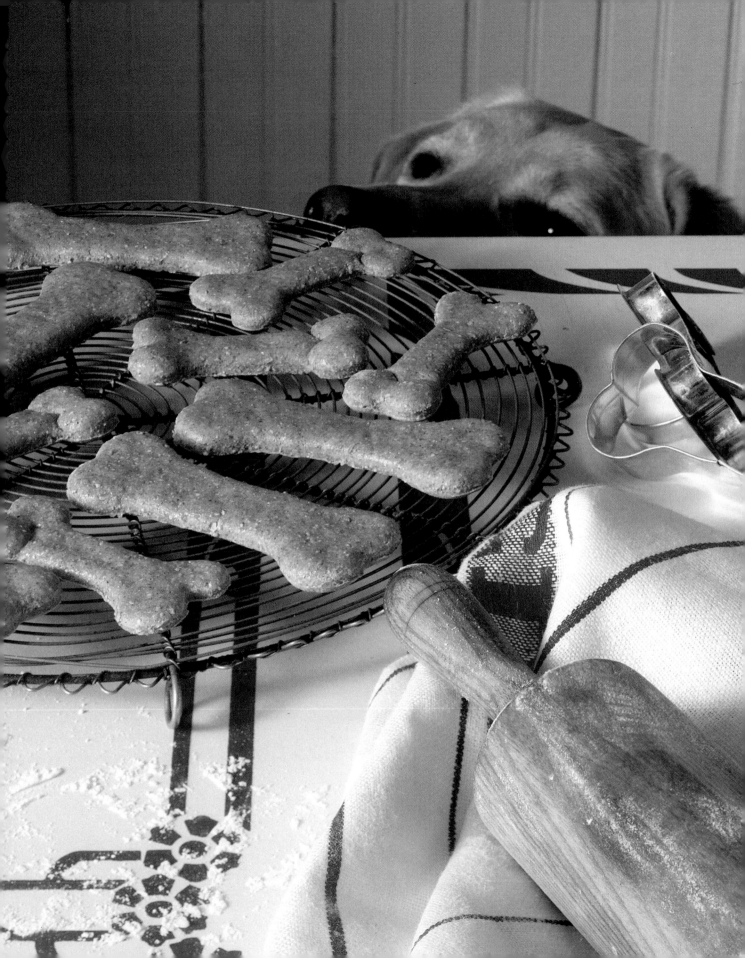

Bone à Fidos

Makes about 110 3½-inch long "bone" cookies, about 80 2½-inch round cookies

When we were growing up, all my brother, Michael, and I ever wanted for Christmas was *not* our two front teeth (our mother was a dentist so we were assured of them). We wanted a dog. First it was Lassie, then Rin Tin Tin. We begged and pleaded, but my mother (unreasonably, I thought at the time) did not want a dog in a New York City apartment. I eventually recovered from my disappointment, but my brother's interest matured into a profession. He now owns a very successful chain of stores in the San Francisco Bay area called Pet Food Express, specializing in all manner of food and equipment particularly geared to dog lovers.

He tells me that around Christmastime everyone buys special "cookies" for their beloved pets and that many people admit to a desire to make them from scratch. Actually, I'm not surprised. My father, who never has cooked for us, cooks for his dog on a regular basis. (He eventually wore

INGREDIENTS	MEASURE volume	WEIGHT pounds/ ounces	grams
dry yeast (1 envelope) *or*	2¼ teaspoons	0.25 ounce	7 grams
compressed fresh yeast	1 packed tablespoon	0.75 ounce	21 grams
warm water	¼ liquid cup	2 ounces	59 grams
sugar	pinch	•	•
all-purpose flour	3½ cups (dip and sweep method)	1 pound 1.5 ounces	500 grams
whole-wheat flour	2 cups (dip and sweep method)	11 ounces	312 grams
cracked wheat *or*	2 cups (dip and sweep method)	4.5 ounces	120 grams
cornmeal	1 cup (dip and sweep method)	5 ounces	115 grams
rye flour	1 cup (dip and sweep method)	5.25 ounces	145 grams
nonfat dry milk	½ cup (lightly spooned into the cup)	1.75 ounces	50 grams
kelp powder	4 teaspoons	•	•
beef or chicken broth	4 liquid cups	2 pounds	907 grams
Glaze (optional)			
1 large egg	3 tablespoons	1.75 ounces (weighed without the shell)	50 grams
milk	2 tablespoons	1 ounce	30 grams

down my mother's resistance by bringing home a russet Doberman puppy named Sean, who danced instead of walked and looked more like a graceful deer than like a dog.)

This cookie recipe was contributed by Barbara Vander-

bilt, who lives in Maine and makes them for her dog all year long. Their bone-hard texture and healthy ingredients make them ideal as a treat for your pet. I still don't have a dog myself. But if I did, these are the cookies I would make.

EQUIPMENT: *cookie sheets lined with parchment or aluminum foil; rolling pin; 3- to 3½-inch-long bone cutter or 2½-inch round cookie cutter.*

Place 2 oven racks in the upper and lower thirds of the oven.

Preheat oven to 300°F.

Sprinkle the dry yeast or crumple the compressed yeast over the water (110°F. if dry yeast, 100°F. if compressed yeast). Add a pinch of sugar and allow the yeast to sit in a draft-free spot for 10 to 20 minutes. The mixture should be full of bubbles. If not, the yeast is too old to be useful. Stir well to dissolve the yeast.

In a large bowl, place all the dry ingredients and stir to blend them. Add the yeast mixture and 3 cups of the broth. Using your hands, in the bowl, mix to form the dough, adding more broth if needed to make the dough smooth and supple. Half a batch at a time, knead the dough briefly on a lightly floured counter. (Keep the second batch of dough covered with a moist towel while shaping and cutting the first.)

Roll out the dough into an 18-inch by 13-inch by ¼-inch rectangle. Cut it into desired shapes, using a 3- to 3½-inch bone cutter or a 2½-inch round cookie cutter. Reroll the scraps. Repeat the procedure with the remaining dough.

For an attractive shine, lightly beat together the egg and milk. Brush the glaze on the cookies.

Bake for 45 to 60 minutes or until brown and firm. For even baking, rotate the cookie sheets from top to bottom three quarters of the way through the baking period.

Use a small, angled metal spatula or pancake turner to transfer the cookies to wire racks to cool completely.

Store: In an airtight container at room temperature.

Keeps: The dough must be used immediately. The baked cookies will keep for many months.

Smart Cookie

- Cracked wheat and kelp are available in most health food stores.
- Use 2 cups (5 ounces / 115 grams) of bran cereal (not flakes) in place of the cracked wheat, if desired.
- If your dog is large, make larger cookies.
- This recipe can be halved successfully.
- Allow the cookie sheet(s) to cool completely before using for the next batch.
- Distribute the cookies evenly around the cookie sheet. Avoid crowding the cookies into one section of the cookie sheet, leaving a large area bare.

Meringue Mushrooms

Makes about 2½ dozen
1½-inch mushrooms

INGREDIENTS Do not make on a humid day	MEASURE volume	WEIGHT ounces	grams
2 large egg whites (room temperature)	¼ liquid cup	2 ounces	60 grams
cream of tartar	¼ teaspoon	•	•
superfine sugar	½ cup + 1 tablespoon	4 ounces	113 grams

To my knowledge, it was the inimitable Maida Heatter who put meringue mushrooms on the culinary map, and I am very grateful to her for that, as well as for her many superb dessert books. Maida usually paints the bottoms of her mushroom caps with bittersweet chocolate, which is certainly a delicious option. I like to leave mine plain because I think they are even more realistic, especially if lightly dusted with earth-simulating cocoa. A fun way to pack them for giving is on a bed of crumpled green tissue paper in an attractive basket and wrapped with plastic wrap.

EQUIPMENT: *cookie sheet lined with parchment or aluminum foil; pastry bag or reclosable quart-size freezer bag, fitted with a coupler and a number 3 (¹⁄₁₆-inch diameter) round decorating tube; pastry bag or reclosable gallon-size freezer bag, fitted with a number 6 (½-inch diameter) round plain pastry tube.*

Electric Mixer Method

In a mixing bowl, beat the egg whites until frothy. Add the cream of tartar and beat at medium speed, gradually adding 2 tablespoons of superfine sugar. When soft peaks form when the beater is raised, add 1 tablespoon of superfine sugar and increase the speed to high. When stiff peaks form when the beater is raised slowly, gradually beat in the remaining superfine sugar and beat until very stiff and glossy.

Fill the pastry bags with the meringue mixture, placing about ¼ cup in the bag with the smaller tube and the remainder in the bag with the larger tube. Use the larger tube to pipe the caps and stems and the smaller tube to "glue" the pieces together.

To Pipe the Caps

Hold the bag upright with the tube slightly above the baking sheet. Squeeze with a steady, even pressure, gradually raising the tube as the meringue begins to build up but keeping the tip buried in the meringue. When you have achieved a well-rounded shape, stop the pressure as you bring the tip to the surface. Use the edge of the tip to shave off any point, moving it clockwise (fig. 1). Points can also be removed by pressing against them gently with a moistened fingertip.

To Pipe the Stems

Hold the bag upright with the tube touching the baking sheet. Squeeze with heavy pressure, keeping the tip buried in the meringue, until you build a cone ¾ inch high and wide enough at the base not to topple over (fig. 2). Allow the mushrooms to dry for 1 hour or until set (when your fingertip touches the surface, the meringue stays intact).

Place 2 oven racks in the upper and lower thirds of the oven.
Preheat oven to 200°F.

Bake for 45 minutes or until the mushrooms are firm enough to lift from the baking sheet. For even baking, rotate the cookie sheets from top to bottom and front to back three quarters of the way through the baking period.

With a sharp knife point, make a small hole in the underside of each cap. Use the smaller tube to pipe a tiny dab of meringue in the hole and attach the stem by inserting the pointed end (fig. 3).

Place the mushrooms, caps down, on the baking sheet and return them to the oven for 20 minutes or until thoroughly dry.

Store: In an airtight container at room temperature at low humidity.

Keeps: Indefinitely.

Smart Cookie

- Superfine sugar is easy to make in a food processor by processing granulated sugar for a few minutes or until it is as fine as sand.
- For the best texture, use old egg whites (page 219).

- Make sure that the bowl, beater, and egg whites are free of grease, including even a speck of egg yolk, or the whites will not beat well.
- Egg whites freeze beautifully for over 1 year and can be defrosted and refrozen. Whenever you have leftover egg whites, freeze them for a sunny day when you are in the mood to make a batch of meringue mushrooms.
- To prevent cracking, do not open the oven door during the first three quarters of the cooking time.
- Do not use wax paper; the meringue may stick to it.

- If you do not have enough cookie sheets for the whole batch, lay pieces of aluminum foil the size of your cookie sheet on the counter and pipe the mushrooms onto the foil. When the first batch is baked, remove it from the cookie sheet and simply slip the cookie sheet under the foil of the next batch.
- Distribute the cookies evenly around the cookie sheet. Avoid crowding the cookies into one section of the cookie sheet, leaving a large area bare.

1

2

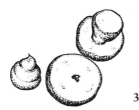

3

Meringue Mushrooms   82

Cookies for Sending

Cashew Puffies

Makes about 6 dozen
1³/₄-inch cookies

Quick and easy to make, this is the perfect puffy yet crunchy cookie for the cashew lover. The mellow quality of the nut is further enhanced by the mellowness of sour cream. Although they never last long in my house, these cookies keep well and hold up perfectly for shipping to far-off loved ones at Christmas.

EQUIPMENT: *nonstick, buttered, or greased cookie sheets.*

Place 2 oven racks in the upper and lower thirds of the oven.
   Preheat oven to 375°F.
   If the cashew nuts are salted, place them in a colander or strainer and rinse them under hot tap water. Crisp them for 10 minutes in a 350°F. oven. Cool completely and chop them coarsely.

INGREDIENTS	MEASURE	WEIGHT	
	volume	*ounces*	*grams*
unsalted roasted cashews, coarsely chopped	1¹/₃ cups	6.5 ounces	186 grams
bleached all-purpose flour	2 cups (dip and sweep method)	10 ounces	290 grams
baking powder	³/₄ teaspoon	•	3.7 grams
baking soda	³/₄ teaspoon	•	3.7 grams
salt	¹/₄ teaspoon	•	•
light brown sugar	³/₄ cup + 2 tablespoons (firmly packed)	6.75 ounces	190 grams
unsalted butter	¹/₂ cup	4 ounces	113 grams
1 large egg	3 tablespoons + ¹/₂ teaspoon	1.75 ounces (weighed without the shell)	50 grams
pure vanilla extract	1 teaspoon	•	4 grams
sour cream	¹/₂ cup	4.25 ounces	121 grams

Food Processor Method

In a small bowl, sift together the flour, baking powder, baking soda, and salt, then whisk to mix evenly. Add the cashews and set aside.

   In a food processor with the metal blade, process the sugar until it is very fine. Cut the butter into a few pieces and add it with the motor running. Process until smooth and creamy. Add the egg and vanilla extract and process until incorporated, scraping the sides of the bowl. Add the sour cream and process just until incorporated, scraping the sides of the bowl. Add the flour mixture and pulse in just until incorporated.

Electric Mixer Method

Soften the butter. In a small bowl, sift together the flour, baking powder, baking soda, and salt, then whisk to mix evenly. Add the cashews and set aside. In a mixing bowl, cream the butter and sugar until light and fluffy. Beat in the egg and vanilla extract and scrape the sides of the bowl. Beat in the sour cream until incorporated. At low speed, gradually beat in the flour mixture just until incorporated.

For Both Methods

Scrape the dough into a bowl.
   Drop the dough in heaping tea-spoons 1¹/₂ inches apart on the prepared cookie sheets.

   Bake for 10 to 15 minutes or until golden brown. For even baking, rotate the cookie sheets from top to bottom and front to back halfway through the baking period.

   Cool the cookies for a few minutes on the sheets. When they are firm enough to lift, use a small, angled metal spatula or pancake turner to transfer them to wire racks to cool completely.

Note: The mixer method results in a ¹/₄-inch higher, slightly airier cookie.

Store: In an airtight container at room temperature or in the freezer.

Keeps: 1 month at room temperature, several months frozen.

Smart Cookie

- Cashew nuts are difficult to chop evenly. Chopping by hand, with a long sharp knife, is the best method. It also works to crush the cashews under the flat side of a large chef's knife.

- Allow the cookie sheet(s) to cool completely before using for the next batch.

- Distribute the cookies evenly around the cookie sheet. Avoid crowding the cookies into one section of the cookie sheet, leaving a large area bare.

Cashew Puffies   86

Lemon Poppyseeds

Makes about 3 dozen
2-inch cookies

These crunchy-crackly-with-poppyseed little cookies are a sheer delight, and lemon zest gives them extra sparkle. I created them because the Lemon Poppyseed Pound Cake is one of my favorite cakes in *The Cake Bible,* and I wanted to capture the same special flavor in the texture of a cookie. These cookies are delicious with milk, tea, and espresso. Everyone adores them.

EQUIPMENT: *ungreased cookie sheets.*

INGREDIENTS	MEASURE volume	WEIGHT ounces	grams
bleached all-purpose flour	1 1/2 cups (dip and sweep method)	7.5 ounces	218 grams
poppyseeds	6 tablespoons	2 ounces	54 grams
salt	1/4 teaspoon	•	•
sugar	3/4 cup	5.25 ounces	150 grams
zest peeled from 3 medium lemons	2 tablespoons (finely grated)	•	12 grams
unsalted butter	1 cup	8 ounces	227 grams
2 large egg yolks	2 tablespoons + 1 teaspoon	1.25 ounces	37 grams
pure vanilla extract	2 teaspoons	•	8 grams
Topping			
blanched sliced almonds	1 cup	3 ounces	85 grams
Optional: powdered sugar for dusting			

Food Processor Method

In a small bowl, whisk together the flour, poppyseeds, and salt.

In a food processor with the metal blade, process the sugar with the zest until the zest is very fine. Cut the butter into a few pieces and add it with the motor running. Process until it is smooth and creamy. Add the egg yolks and vanilla extract and process until incorporated, scraping the sides of the bowl. Add the flour mixture and pulse in, just until incorporated.

Electric Mixer Method

Soften the butter. In a small bowl, whisk together the flour, poppyseeds, and salt. In a mixing bowl, cream the sugar and butter until light and fluffy. Beat in the egg yolks, vanilla extract, and zest, and scrape the sides of the bowl. At low speed, gradually beat in the flour mixture, just until incorporated.

For Both Methods

Scrape the dough into a bowl and refrigerate it for at least 1 hour.

In a food processor with the metal blade, process the almonds until very fine, almost to a powder. Do not overprocess, however, to a "butter." Transfer the chopped nuts to a small bowl.

Place 2 oven racks in the upper and lower thirds of the oven.
   Preheat oven to 350°F.
   Measure level tablespoons of dough and roll them between the palms of your hands to form balls. Drop each dough ball, *as soon as it is formed,* into the nuts and shake the bowl to twirl the ball around, coating it well with nuts. Place the nut-covered balls on cookie sheets, 2 inches apart.

Bake for 18 to 20 minutes or until the bottoms are browned. For even baking, rotate the cookie sheets from top to bottom and front to back halfway through the baking period.

Use a small, angled metal spatula or pancake turner to transfer the cookies to wire racks to cool completely.

If desired, sprinkle lightly with powdered sugar for an attractive finish.

Store: In an airtight container at room temperature or in the freezer.

Keeps: 2 months at room temperature, several months frozen.

Smart Cookie

- Use a vegetable peeler to peel the zest from the lemons, removing only the yellow portion and not the bitter white pith beneath.
- When rolling the balls of dough between the palms of your hands, the heat softens the dough temporarily so that the chopped almonds adhere well. For this reason, it is important to roll only 1 ball at a time. Do not use egg whites to make the nuts adhere; this results in cracks in the surface of the cookie.
- Allow the cookie sheet(s) to cool completely before using for the next batch.
- Distribute the cookies evenly around the cookie sheet. Avoid crowding the cookies into one section of the cookie sheet, leaving a large area bare.

Pfeffernüsse

Makes 14 dozen
1-inch cookies

It wouldn't be Christmas without this classic German cookie. Its name translates as "peppernut," which refers to the peppercorn. White pepper is traditionally used because it has the flavor of pepper with less of the sting. A white peppercorn is actually a black one with the outer hull removed. In medieval recipes for *pfeffernüsse,* the word *pepper* meant "spice," so many recipes evolved using different mixtures of spices.

This recipe also uses nuts, which result in a slightly softer texture; however, it is similar to the original recipes in that it contains no butter. This increases the cookies' shelf life at least to next Christmas! This cookie enables you to get a real head start on your Christmas baking. Be sure to age the cookies with a fresh slice of apple or they will be as hard as rocks. Their untraditional flat shape is easier to consume than the usual orbs.

PREPARE AT LEAST 2 WEEKS
BEFORE SERVING

EQUIPMENT: *nonstick or greased cookie sheets.*

Food Processor Method

In a medium bowl, whisk together the flour, baking powder, salt, pepper, cinnamon, and cloves.

INGREDIENTS	MEASURE volume	WEIGHT ounces	grams
bleached all-purpose flour	3 cups (dip and sweep method)	15 ounces	435 grams
baking powder	¼ teaspoon	•	•
salt	¼ teaspoon	•	•
white pepper	⅛ teaspoon	•	•
ground cinnamon	1 teaspoon	•	•
ground cloves	⅛ teaspoon	•	•
chopped candied lemon peel	½ cup	2.25 ounces	64 grams
unblanched sliced almonds	½ cup	1.5 ounces	43 grams
granulated sugar	1 cup	7 ounces	200 grams
3 large eggs	scant 5 fluid ounces	5.25 ounces (weighed without the shells)	150 grams
powdered sugar	1 cup (lightly spooned into the cup)	4 ounces	115 grams
1 apple slice	•	•	•

In a food processor with the metal blade, process the candied lemon peel, almonds, and granulated sugar until fine. Add the eggs and process until blended. Scrape the sides of the bowl. Add the flour mixture and process just until incorporated. The dough will be crumbly.

Electric Mixer Method

Grate the almonds finely. In a medium bowl, whisk together the flour, baking powder, salt, pepper, cinnamon, and cloves. In a mixing bowl, beat the eggs and granulated sugar until thick and light in color. Add the lemon peel and almonds and beat until blended. At low speed, gradually beat in the flour mixture just until incorporated.

For Both Methods

Scrape the dough onto plastic wrap, wrap tightly, and refrigerate for no more than 1 hour or it becomes difficult to roll. The dough is dry but holds together when rolled.

Place 2 oven racks in the upper and lower thirds of the oven.
Preheat oven to 350°F.

Roll the dough on a floured surface to ¼-inch thickness. Cut with a 1-inch round cookie cutter. Place the cookies about ½ inch apart on the cookie sheets. Reroll the scraps.

Bake for 15 minutes or until lightly browned. For even baking,

91   *Pfeffernüsse*

rotate the cookie sheets from top to bottom and front to back halfway through the baking period.

Use a small, angled metal spatula or pancake turner to transfer the cookies to wire racks to cool completely.

Place the powdered sugar in a bag. When cool, add the cookies to the bag, a few at a time, and shake them to coat well.

Store: In an airtight container with an apple slice. Allow the cookies to ripen and soften for at least 2 weeks.

Keeps: Many months.

Smart Cookie

- Allow the cookie sheet(s) to cool completely before using for the next batch.
- Distribute the cookies evenly around the cookie sheet. Avoid crowding the cookies into one section of the cookie sheet, leaving a large area bare.

Pfeffernüsse   92

Filbertines

Makes about 3½ dozen
1¾-inch cookies

*F*ilbert is another name for a hazelnut. These delicious butter cookies abound with the flavors of hazelnut and the uniquely fragrant spice cardamom. They are as delicious with an after-dinner liqueur as with a midafternoon glass of milk.

EQUIPMENT: *2 nonstick or buttered or greased cookie sheets; 1¼-inch cookie scoop, teaspoon, or tablespoon measure.*

INGREDIENTS	MEASURE volume	WEIGHT ounces	grams
unblanched whole hazelnuts	1 cup	5 ounces	142 grams
bleached all-purpose flour	1⅓ cups (dip and sweep method)	6.75 ounces	193 grams
baking soda	½ teaspoon	•	•
ground cardamom	½ teaspoon	•	•
salt	pinch	•	•
sugar	½ cup	3.5 ounces	100 grams
unsalted butter	8 tablespoons	4 ounces	113 grams
1 large egg	3 tablespoons + ½ teaspoon	1.75 ounces (weighed without the shell)	50 grams
pure vanilla extract	½ teaspoon	•	2 grams

Place 2 oven racks in the upper and lower thirds of the oven.
Preheat oven to 350°F.

Place the hazelnuts on a cookie sheet and bake them, stirring occasionally, for 10 minutes. Cool completely. Turn off the oven.

Food Processor Method

In a medium bowl, sift together the flour, baking soda, cardamom, and salt, then whisk to mix evenly.

In a food processor with the grater or shredder disc, grate the hazelnuts. Change to the metal blade and process the nuts until very fine but not powder fine. Remove half the nuts (about ¾ cup) to a small bowl and set aside. Add the sugar to the nuts remaining in the processor and process for about 1 minute or until the sugar

and nuts are very fine. Cut the butter into a few pieces and add it with the motor running. Process until smooth and creamy. Add the egg and vanilla extract and process until incorporated, scraping the sides of the bowl. Add the flour mixture and pulse in just until incorporated, scraping the sides of the bowl.

Electric Mixer Method

Soften the butter. Grate the hazelnuts very finely. In a medium bowl, sift together half the grated nuts, the flour, baking soda, cardamom, and salt, then whisk to mix evenly. In a mixing bowl, cream the sugar and butter until light and fluffy. Beat in the egg and vanilla extract until well blended. On low speed, beat in the flour mixture just until incorporated.

For Both Methods

Scrape the dough into a bowl and refrigerate it for at least 1 hour and preferably no longer than 3 hours.

Place 2 oven racks in the upper and lower thirds of the oven.
Preheat oven to 350°F.

Measure the dough into a 1¼-inch scoop, 2 level teaspoons, or 1 scant tablespoon and knead each piece by flattening it between your palms and then rolling it into a 1-inch ball. Roll each dough ball, as soon as it is formed, in the reserved chopped hazelnuts until it is well coated. Place the dough balls 2 inches apart on the prepared cookie sheets.

Bake for 15 minutes or until lightly browned and firm to the touch. For even baking, rotate the

cookie sheets from top to bottom and front to back halfway through the baking period.

Use a small, angled metal spatula or pancake turner to transfer the cookies to wire racks to cool completely.

Store: In an airtight container at room temperature or in the freezer.

Keeps: 1 month at room temperature, several months frozen.

 Smart Cookie

• The peel of the hazelnut is not removed for this cookie because it adds flavor intensity and an attractive speckle to the coating.

• Allow the cookie sheet(s) to cool completely before using for the next batch.

• Distribute the cookies evenly around the cookie sheet. Avoid crowding the cookies into one section of the cookie sheet, leaving a large area bare.

Mahogany Buttercrunch Toffee

Makes about 1 pound
(without the chocolate topping)

The classic combination of caramel, nuts, and chocolate is a sure pleaser.

Brown sugar makes the caramel here deeper in color and in flavor. The baking soda gives it a fine brittle shear and less sticky texture. People who have tasted this buttercrunch over the years have tried to persuade me to go into business producing it. This is a real holiday and year-round favorite.

INGREDIENTS Do not make on a humid day	MEASURE volume	WEIGHT ounces	grams
blanched sliced almonds	2 cups	6 ounces	170 grams
light brown sugar	1¼ cups (firmly packed)	9.5 ounces	270 grams
water	2 tablespoons	1 ounce	30 grams
unsalted butter	½ cup	4 ounces	113 grams
pure vanilla extract	1 teaspoon	•	4 grams
baking soda	¼ teaspoon	•	•
Topping			
bittersweet or semisweet chocolate, broken into squares or coarsely chopped	2 (3-ounce) bars	6 ounces	170 grams

EQUIPMENT: **nonstick, greased, or buttered cookie sheet.**

Place 2 oven racks in the upper and lower thirds of the oven.
Preheat oven to 350°F.

Place the almonds on a cookie sheet and bake them, stirring occasionally, for 10 to 12 minutes or until golden. Cool completely.

In a food processor with the metal blade, pulse the almonds until they are chopped very finely but not powder fine. Sprinkle half the nuts over a 7-inch by 10-inch area on the prepared cookie sheet. Place it near the range. Also have the vanilla extract and baking soda near the range.

In a heavy, medium-size saucepan, preferably with a nonstick lining, combine the brown sugar, water, and butter and, stirring constantly, bring to a boil. Stir often to prevent burning until the mixture reaches 285°F. (the soft-crack stage: Syrup dropped in ice water separates into threads that are hard but not brittle). Immediately remove the saucepan from the heat because the temperature will continue to rise to 290°F., and add the vanilla extract and baking soda. Pour the toffee mixture evenly in a 7-inch by 10-inch rectangle on top of the nuts.

Immediately scatter the chocolate squares over the hot toffee. Press the squares lightly with your fingers so they start melting. After about 5 minutes, the chocolate will be soft enough to spread with a long metal spatula in an even layer over the surface of the toffee. Dust the chocolate with the remaining chopped almonds.

Cool completely and break into irregular pieces.

Store: In an airtight container at room temperature.

Keeps: About 1 month, after which it is still delicious but the sugar starts to crystallize.

Smart Cookie

- The acidity in the brown sugar results in a creamier toffee. When baking soda is used, it combines with the acid in the brown sugar and separates the toffee into layers, resulting in a less sticky and finer texture.
- The higher the temperature reached by the toffee mixture, the crunchier the toffee.
- It is best not to use an enameled cast-iron saucepan because the temperature of the syrup continues to rise more quickly after removal from the heat.
- For a speedy cleanup, place all of the utensils in the saucepan, fill it with water, and bring it to a boil.

Chocolate Caramel Chews

The Ultimate Carmelitas

Makes 32 2-inch by
1¹/₂-inch bars

These are real crowd pleasers and always the first cookies to disappear. Their crunchy oat base is topped with walnuts and chocolate, which glistens brilliantly because during baking it becomes filmed with a thin layer of the caramel. Using your favorite chocolate and making your own caramel makes all the difference.

Caramel Topping

Have a long-handled ladle and a greased 2-cup heatproof measure ready near the range.

In a heavy, medium-size saucepan, preferably with a nonstick lining, combine the sugar and corn syrup and cook over medium-low heat, stirring constantly, until boiling. Stop stirring and continue boiling until the mixture caramelizes to a deep amber (a candy thermometer will read 370°F.). Immediately remove the pan from the heat and add the butter and cream, using the ladle to pour in the cream gradually to avoid spattering. Return the caramel to the

Caramel Topping

INGREDIENTS	MEASURE volume	WEIGHT ounces	grams
sugar	1 cup	7 ounces	200 grams
corn syrup	¹/₂ cup (use a greased liquid measuring cup)	5.75 ounces	164 grams
unsalted butter	1¹/₂ tablespoons	0.75 ounce	21 grams
heavy cream	³/₄ liquid cup	6 ounces	170 grams
pure vanilla extract	1 teaspoon	•	4 grams

Cookie Base

INGREDIENTS	MEASURE volume	WEIGHT ounces	grams
bleached all-purpose flour	1 cup (dip and sweep method)	5 ounces	145 grams
quick oats	1 cup	3 ounces	83 grams
light brown sugar	³/₄ cup (firmly packed)	5.75 ounces	163 grams
baking soda	¹/₂ teaspoon	•	•
salt	¹/₈ teaspoon	•	•
unsalted butter, melted	12 tablespoons	6 ounces	170 grams
bittersweet or semisweet chocolate, chopped into ¹/₂-inch pieces	2 (3-ounce) bars	6 ounces	170 grams
coarsely chopped walnuts	1 cup	4 ounces	114 grams

range and continue boiling on medium-high heat for about 1¹/₂ minutes or until a candy thermometer reads 240°F. or the caramel is reduced to 1¹/₂ cups (1 pound / 454 grams).

Immediately pour the caramel into the prepared cup and allow it to cool for at least 10 minutes or up to 1 hour (the caramel should still be pourable). Stir in the vanilla extract after 10 minutes.

EQUIPMENT: *9-inch by 13-inch baking pan, preferably metal (if using a glass pan, lower the oven temperature 25°F.), with only the*

sides buttered or greased to keep the caramel from sticking.

Cookie Base

Place 1 oven rack in the middle of the oven.
Preheat oven to 350°F.

Electric Mixer Method

In a large mixing bowl, at medium speed, beat together the flour, oats, brown sugar, baking soda, and salt for about 3 minutes or until well mixed. At low speed, beat in the melted butter.

Scrape the mixture into the prepared pan and pat it in to coat the bottom evenly.

Bake for 10 minutes. Remove the pan from the oven and evenly sprinkle on the chocolate pieces and walnuts. Drizzle the caramel mixture evenly on top and return the pan to the oven for 20 minutes more or until bubbling. (The caramel will bubble, coating most of the surface.)

Allow the chews to cool completely in the pan on a wire rack.

Use a small metal spatula or pancake turner to dislodge the sides and invert the chews onto a plastic wrap–covered cookie sheet. Reinvert it onto a cutting surface and cut it lengthwise into 4 strips (each about 2 inches wide) and then crosswise into 8 strips (about 1¹/₂ inches wide). Place on paper towels for at least 15 minutes to absorb the excess butter.

Store: In an airtight container at room temperature, or in the refrigerator or freezer, each layer separated by wax paper.

Keeps: About 3 weeks at room temperature, several months refrigerated or frozen.

 Smart Cookie

- The caramel can be made ahead and reheated in a microwave oven or in a pan of simmering water.

- This method of making caramel (first caramelizing the sugar, then caramelizing the sugar contained in the butter and cream) produces a very intense caramel because the sugar can be brought to a higher temperature and the tastes of the butter and cream do not get altered by long cooking.

- If the caramel is too dark or burned at 370°F. your thermometer is not accurate (page 246).

- Extra-bittersweet chocolate, when available, is excellent as a foil for the sweetness of the caramel.

- These cookies are at their very best within 6 hours of baking, while the chocolate is still soft. To obtain this texture with older cookies, simply put them on a cookie sheet in a 300°F. oven for 1 minute or so until the chocolate softens slightly.

Mother Bauer's Buttered Rum Cookies

Makes about 32 2-inch sandwiches

My friend Jeanne Bauer grew up in the Midwest and was blessed with a mother who baked wonderful Christmas cookies for family and friends. Although Mother Bauer had a full-time job outside the house, she spent evenings and weekends baking cookies. To this day, Jeanne has such loving memories of making Christmas cookies with her mother that never a year has gone by that she hasn't relived the tradition in her own home.

Mother Bauer's cookies are particular favorites of mine. They are divinely fragrant with butter, and soft and creamy yet crisp and crunchy all at the same time. This harmony is the result of a perfect marriage of rum buttercream filling and rum-flavored butter cookies. Perhaps the loveliest part of these sandwich cookies is the lingering perfumed flavor of buttered rum.

EQUIPMENT: *nonstick or buttered cookie sheets; floured pastry cloth and floured rolling pin sleeve, or lightly floured sheets of plastic wrap or wax paper; rolling pin; 2¹/₄-inch scalloped cutter (measured at its widest point); op-*

Cookie Base

INGREDIENTS	MEASURE *volume*	WEIGHT	
		ounces	*grams*
powdered sugar	¹/₂ cup (lightly spooned into the cup)	2 ounces	58 grams
blanched sliced almonds	¹/₃ cup	1 ounce	28 grams
unsalted butter	1 cup	8 ounces	227 grams
pure almond extract	¹/₂ teaspoon	•	2 grams
light rum	2 tablespoons	1 ounce	28 grams
bleached all-purpose flour	1²/₃ cups (dip and sweep method)	8 ounces	227 grams
salt	¹/₄ teaspoon	•	•

tional: *a number 6 plain round (¹/₂-inch diameter) pastry tube.*

Cookie Base

Food Processor Method

In a food processor with the metal blade, process the sugar with the almonds until the almonds are very fine. Cut the butter into a few pieces and add it with the motor running. Process until smooth and creamy. Add the almond extract and rum and process until incorporated, scraping the sides of the bowl. Remove the work bowl cover, add the flour and sprinkle the salt evenly on top. Pulse in the flour just until the dough starts to clump together.

Electric Mixer Method

Soften the butter. Grate the almonds finely. In a medium bowl, whisk together the flour, grated nuts, and salt. In a mixing bowl,

cream the sugar and butter until light and fluffy. Beat in the almond extract and rum until well blended. Scrape the sides of the bowl. On low speed, beat in the flour mixture until incorporated.

For Both Methods

Scrape the dough into a bowl and refrigerate it for at least 2 hours or overnight.

Place 2 oven racks in the upper and lower thirds of the oven.
Preheat oven to 375°F.

Working with a small amount of the dough at a time, briefly knead it until it is malleable but still well chilled, and roll it on the floured cloth to a ¹/₈-inch thickness. Cut out the cookies, using a small metal spatula to transfer them to the cookie sheets, 1 inch

apart. Reroll the scraps, chilling the dough as necessary.

For a decorative effect, if desired, use the pastry tube to cut out ½-inch holes in the center of half the cookies. These cookies with holes in the center will serve as the top portions of the sandwich cookies.

Bake for 8 to 10 minutes or until just beginning to become golden. For even baking, rotate the cookie sheets from top to bottom and front to back halfway through the baking period.

Use a small, angled metal spatula or pancake turner to transfer the cookies to wire racks to cool completely.

Buttered-Rum Cream Filling

Food Processor Method

In a food processor with the metal blade, process all the filling ingredients until smooth and creamy, scraping the sides of the bowl as needed. If necessary, add additional heavy cream by the droplets to soften the filling or additional powdered sugar by the teaspoon to make it more firm.

Electric Mixer Method

Soften the butter. In a mixing bowl, with the mixer at low speed, cream the butter and sugar until well mixed. Still at low speed, beat in the rum and heavy cream.

To Fill the Cookies

Use a small metal spatula to spread a rounded ½ measuring

Buttered-Rum Cream Filling

INGREDIENTS	MEASURE	WEIGHT	
	volume	*ounces*	*grams*
unsalted butter	3 tablespoons	1.5 ounces	43 grams
powdered sugar	1 cup (lightly spooned into the cup)	4 ounces	115 grams
light rum	¾ teaspoon	•	4 grams
heavy cream	2 teaspoons	•	10 grams

teaspoon of the buttercream on the underside of 1 of the whole cookie bottoms. Place a second cookie (if desired, one with a hole in it), bottom side against the buttercream, and press the 2 cookies together. Proceed this way for the remaining cookies.

Store: In an airtight container at room temperature or in the freezer.

Keeps: About 2 months unfilled, 3 weeks filled (the frosting becomes drier after this time but is still tasty).

 Smart Cookie

- Powdered sugar contains 3 percent cornstarch, which, in a frosting, is usually perceived as gritty. It works in the filling of this cookie because the pleasantly crunchy texture of the cookie prevents any perception of grittiness.

- A pastry cloth works best for rolling this delicate dough because the dough picks up just the amount of flour it needs and does not become too soft to transfer to the cookie sheets. If you are not using a pastry cloth, Saran Wrap is the ideal plastic wrap for rolling the dough because it lies very flat. Wax paper is the second choice. If the dough softens, simply slip the dough with the wrap onto a cookie sheet and refrigerate it until firm.

- Allow the cookie sheet(s) to cool completely before using for the next batch.

- Distribute the cookies evenly around the cookie sheet. Avoid crowding the cookies into one section of the cookie sheet, leaving a large area bare.

Jeanne Bauer's Maple Macadamia Bars

Makes 32 2-inch by 1¹/₂-inch bars

This is a soft and crumbly but crunchy with nuts, *fantastic* bar cookie with intriguing flavor. It is probably best described as candied nuts in a pastry crust. The small quantity of pure maple syrup adds a special tangy-sweet flavor that blends superbly with the flavor of the macadamia nuts. Jeanne advises making these cookies for people you *really* love because the large number of macadamia nuts in the filling are worth their weight in gold.

EQUIPMENT: *9-inch by 13-inch baking pan, preferably metal (if using a glass pan, lower the oven temperature 25° F.), lined entirely with aluminum foil and then buttered or greased; pennies, pie weights, dried beans, or rice; rolling pin.*

Crust

Food Processor Method

In a food processor with the metal blade, process the sugar for sev-

Crust

INGREDIENTS	MEASURE volume	WEIGHT ounces	WEIGHT grams
sugar	¹/₂ cup	3.5 ounces	100 grams
unsalted butter	8 tablespoons	4 ounces	113 grams
2 large egg yolks (cold)	2 tablespoons + 1 teaspoon	1.25 ounces	37 grams
pure vanilla extract	1 teaspoon	•	4 grams
bleached all-purpose flour	1¹/₂ cups (dip and sweep method)	7.5 ounces	213 grams

eral minutes, until it is very fine. Cut the butter into a few pieces and add it with the motor running. Process until smooth and creamy. Add the egg yolks and vanilla extract and process until incorporated, scraping the sides of the bowl. Add the flour and pulse in until the dough is crumbly. Do not overprocess it or try to form a ball.

Electric Mixer Method

Soften the butter. In a mixing bowl, cream the sugar and butter until light and fluffy. Beat in the egg yolks and vanilla extract and scrape the sides of the bowl. At low speed, gradually beat in the flour just until incorporated.

For Both Methods

Scrape the dough onto a piece of plastic wrap and use the wrap, not your fingers, to press the dough together to form a ball. Flatten the ball into a thick disc and roll it out into a 10-inch by 14-inch rectangle between 2 sheets of plastic wrap or wax paper. Slip it onto a cookie sheet and refrigerate for 15 minutes or until firm but still flexible.

Place 1 oven rack in the middle of the oven.
Preheat oven to 350°F.
Peel off the top piece of plastic wrap from the dough and invert the dough into the prepared baking pan. Peel off the bottom piece of plastic wrap. Don't worry if the pastry breaks. Simply press it evenly into the bottom of the pan. Press the edges of the dough up the sides of the pan, forming a ¹/₂-inch border. Press the tines of a fork along the border to form a design.

Tear off a piece of aluminum foil a little larger than the size of the pan and lay it on top of the dough. Place enough copper pennies or dried beans on top of the foil to hold it down and keep the crust from rising.

Bake for 15 minutes. Remove the foil and weights and bake for another 5 to 7 minutes or just until lightly golden.

While the crust is baking, make the filling.

Filling

Unsalted macadamia nuts are available in packages at health

Filling

INGREDIENTS	MEASURE	WEIGHT	
	volume	*ounces*	*grams*
macadamia nuts, *very* coarsely chopped	1¹/₂ cups	7 ounces	200 grams
dark brown sugar	1 cup (firmly packed)	8.5 ounces	240 grams
unsalted butter	5 tablespoons	2.5 ounces	71 grams
heavy cream	3 tablespoons	1.5 ounces	44 grams
corn syrup	3 tablespoons	2 ounces	62 grams
pure maple syrup	2 tablespoons	0.75 ounce	19 grams

food stores. The bottled variety does have salt listed in the ingredients list. If yours are salted, rinse them in a strainer under hot tap water and recrisp them in a 350°F. oven for 5 to 10 minutes.

Spread the macadamia nuts over the baked crust.

In a heavy, medium-size saucepan, preferably with a nonstick lining, combine the brown sugar, butter, heavy cream, corn syrup, and maple syrup. Bring the mixture to a boil over medium heat, stirring constantly. Stop stirring and allow the mixture to boil for 1 minute to dissolve the sugar.

Pour the mixture evenly over the nuts. Bake for 10 minutes. The filling will be bubbling.

Cool completely in the pan on a wire rack.

Remove the cookie from the pan by lifting out the aluminum foil. Invert onto a cookie sheet and peel off the foil. Reinvert onto a cutting surface and cut the cookie lengthwise into 4 strips (each about 2 inches wide) and then crosswise into 8 strips (about 1¹/₂ inches wide).

Store: In an airtight container at room temperature.

Keeps: 3 weeks (the sugar tends to crystallize slightly after a few days, but the cookies are still delicious).

Smart Cookie

- Saran Wrap is the ideal plastic wrap for rolling the dough because it lies very flat. Wax paper is the second choice.
- Copper pennies make great pie weights because copper is such an excellent heat conductor. It is superior to aluminum scrap that is marketed as pie weights for a higher price than the comparable weight of pennies. Dried beans or cherry pits also work to hold down the crust, although they don't conduct the heat well.

FROM
FIRST CLASS
PERSONAL
FRAGILE
FIRST CLASS
PERSONAL
FROM

Swiss Christmas Hazelnut Lebkuchen

Makes 29
2-inch-scant cookies

This is a cookie with an interesting history. Lebkuchen, which in German means the "cooking of life," is also known as *pain d'epices* in France. It is one of the world's oldest cookies, its origins going back to the honey and spice cakes of Mesopotamia around 2,000 B.C. Today, the mixtures are often prepared ahead (in olden days as much as a year in advance) to ripen in large vats until they lose their stickiness. The aging period produces fermentation that adds to their flavor and serves as leavening.

Daniel Eichenberger owns the largest and most popular confectionery in Berne, Switzerland. He makes twelve tons of lebkuchen a year in forty-five different varieties. His basement kitchen, located below his *konditorei,* resounds with the solid whack of antique wooden bear molds (the symbol of Berne) making their impressions on hundreds of rectangles of fragrantly spiced lebkuchen. In years gone by, bakers carved their own wooden molds during slow seasons.

At Christmastime the universal Berne favorite is the candylike lebkuchen prepared with hazelnuts and almonds instead of flour and very little candied fruit. My version is based on Herr Eichenberger's original recipe but contains a little flour to make it less sticky. Lebkuchen, however, will not hold an imprint unless more flour is added, and this would only spoil its unique sticky-chewy texture and pure nutty-candied flavor.

INGREDIENTS	MEASURE volume	WEIGHT ounces	grams
unblanched whole hazelnuts	1/2 cup	2.5 ounces	70 grams
unblanched whole almonds	1/4 cup	1.75 ounces	50 grams
bleached all-purpose flour	2 1/2 tablespoons (dip and sweep method)	0.75 ounce	22 grams
ground cinnamon	1/4 teaspoon	•	•
sugar	3/4 cup	5.25 ounces	150 grams
small mixed candied fruit	2 1/2 tablespoons	0.75 ounce	20 grams
lemon zest	1/2 teaspoon (finely grated)	•	•
honey	1 tablespoon	0.75 ounce	21 grams
1 large egg white	2 tablespoons	2 ounces	60 grams
29 blanched whole almonds	scant 1/4 cup	1.25 ounces	36 grams
Shiny Glaze *(optional)*			
gum arabic	4 1/2 teaspoons	0.5 ounce	14.6 grams
water	3 tablespoons	1.5 ounce	44 grams

PREPARE AT LEAST 2 WEEKS BEFORE SERVING

EQUIPMENT: *nonstick or greased and floured cookie sheets; 1 1/4-inch cookie scoop or teaspoon measure.*

Place 2 oven racks in the upper and lower thirds of the oven. Preheat oven to 350°F.

Place the nuts on a cookie sheet and bake them, stirring occasionally, for 10 minutes. Cool completely.

Raise oven to 400°F.

Food Processor Method

In a small bowl, whisk together the flour and cinnamon.

In a food processor with the metal blade, process the sugar, the hazelnuts and the unblanched almonds, candied fruit, and lemon zest until finely chopped. Add the honey, egg white, and flour and process until blended.

Electric Mixer Method or by Hand

Finely grate the nuts and, using a greased knife, chop the candied fruit. In a large bowl, whisk together the flour and cinnamon. Add the remaining ingredients, except the blanched whole almonds, and beat or stir them together until blended.

For Both Methods

Scrape the dough into a bowl. Measure the dough into a 1 1/4-inch scoop or 2 level teaspoons.

Roll the dough between the palms of your hands to form 1-inch balls. Place the balls 1 1/2 inches apart on the cookie sheets. Use a cookie press or the bottom of a tumbler, lightly oiled, to flatten the cookies (they should be 1 1/2 inches in diameter and 1/4 inch thick). Gently press a whole almond into the center of each cookie.

If desired, in a microwave oven or small saucepan, bring the gum arabic and water to a boil, stirring occasionally. Use this mixture either while hot or cool, to brush over the cookies before baking. The optional glaze stays liquid at room temperature.

Bake for 6 to 8 minutes or until golden brown. The cookies should still be slightly soft as they harden considerably on cooling. For even baking, rotate the cookie sheets from top to bottom and front to back halfway through the baking period.

For very crunchy cookies, allow the cookies to cool completely on the sheets. For softer, chewy cookies, allow them to cool for a few minutes on the sheets or just until firm enough to lift. Use a small, angled metal spatula or pancake turner to transfer them to wire racks to finish cooling.

Store: In an airtight container at room temperature.

Keeps: Several months.

Smart Cookie

- Gum arabic is a perfect glaze because an egg glaze tends to be absorbed by this type of lebkuchen dough. Gum arabic produces a very clear and flawlessly shiny glaze. It is available in candy-making supply houses such as Maid of Scandinavia and the Chocolate Gallery (page 229).
- Allow the cookie sheet(s) to cool completely before using for the next batch.
- Distribute the cookies evenly around the cookie sheet. Avoid crowding the cookies into one section of the cookie sheet, leaving a large area bare.

Swiss Christmas Hazelnut Lebkuchen   110

Tiny Fruitcake Gems

Makes 3¹/₂ dozen 1¹/₂-inch gems
(3 dozen 1³/₄-inch by
³/₄-inch gems if baked in
mini-muffin tins)

In America, fruitcake is so closely associated with Christmas that it almost becomes a necessary part of the celebration, even for those who don't like it! Here is a moist, flavorful, miniature version, which features more cake than candied fruit, that *everyone* loves. These gems keep for months, becoming ever more mellow, but they are also scrumptious right after baking. Get a head start on your holiday baking by making these in the fall. They are great for Thanksgiving feasts as well as Christmas and ship beautifully to loved ones who can't be home for the holidays.

INGREDIENTS	MEASURE volume	WEIGHT ounces	grams
unsifted cake flour without leavening	¹/₂ cup (dip and sweep method)	2.25 ounces	65 grams
ground cinnamon	¹/₄ teaspoon	•	•
salt	¹/₄ teaspoon	•	•
baking soda	¹/₈ teaspoon	•	•
dark brown sugar	¹/₄ cup (firmly packed)	2 ounces	60 grams
small mixed candied fruit	¹/₂ cup	2.25 ounces	64 grams
candied citron	2 tablespoons	1.25 ounces	35 grams
dried currants	¹/₄ cup	1.25 ounces	35 grams
pecan halves	¹/₄ cup	1 ounce	28 grams
Myers's dark rum	¹/₂ liquid cup	3.75 ounces	110 grams
unsalted butter	8 tablespoons	4 ounces	113 grams
1 large egg	3 tablespoons	1.75 ounces (weighed without the shell)	50 grams
unsulfured molasses (preferably Grandma's)	¹/₄ liquid cup (use a greased liquid measuring cup)	2.75 ounces	80 grams
milk	2 tablespoons	1 ounce	30 grams
pure vanilla extract	1 teaspoon	•	4 grams
Optional: 6 red and 6 green glacéd cherries, minced			

PREPARE AT LEAST 2 WEEKS
BEFORE SERVING

EQUIPMENT: *reclosable gallon-size freezer bag; 1³/₄-inch fluted tartlet tins with 1 tablespoon capacity, sprayed with Baker's Joy or greased and floured and set on a baking sheet (mini-muffin tins may also be used); ungreased cookie sheet.*

Place 1 oven rack in the middle of the oven.
Preheat oven to 325°F.
Set the tartlet tins on the baking sheet so they are not touching (use 2 baking sheets, if necessary, and rotate them during baking).

Food Processor Method

In a small bowl, sift together the flour, cinnamon, salt, and baking soda. Whisk or stir in the brown sugar.

In a food processor with the metal blade, process the candied fruit, citron, currants, and pecans until they are finely chopped. Add ¹/₄ cup of the rum and process to combine. Cut the butter into a few pieces and add it with the motor running. Process until blended. Add the egg, molasses, milk, and vanilla extract and process until well blended, scraping the sides of the bowl. Add the flour mixture and pulse in until incorporated.

Tiny Fruitcake Gems   112

Electric Mixer Method

Soften the butter. Finely chop the candied fruit, citron, currants, and pecans. Place the fruits and nuts in a small bowl and add 1/4 cup of the rum. Mix to combine. In a small bowl, sift together the flour, cinnamon, salt, and baking soda, then whisk together to combine evenly. In a mixing bowl, cream the sugar and butter until light and fluffy. Beat in the egg and add the flour mixture in 3 batches, alternating with the molasses and milk. Add the candied fruit mixture with the soaking rum and the vanilla extract and beat until blended.

For Both Methods

Scrape the batter into the bag and close it securely. Cut off a small piece from one of the corners of the bag. Pipe the batter into the tartlet molds, filling them not quite full. (Fill the mini-muffin pans a little less than half full.)

Bake for 15 to 17 minutes or until the batter just begins to shrink away from the sides of the molds and the tops spring back when lightly touched with a finger.

Unmold the gems onto greased or buttered wax paper or plastic wrap and sprinkle or brush the tops with the remaining rum. Set them so they are right side up and, if desired, place about 1/4 teaspoon of the minced glacéd cherries in the center of each one. Cool completely.

When cool, wrap each little gem in a small piece of plastic wrap.

Store: In an airtight container at room temperature. They are delicious immediately after baking, but the rum mellows even more when allowed to ripen for several weeks.

Keeps: Several months (at 4 months, they have the ideal flavor).

 Smart Cookie

- If you do not have enough tartlet molds to bake all the batter at one time, store the batter in the refrigerator and bake it in batches. Rinse out the molds after each batch and spray with Baker's Joy or grease and flour them. Baker's Joy contains both grease and flour and makes preparing these tiny fluted tins a breeze.

Cookies for
an Open House

David's Dreambars

Makes 50 2-inch by
1½-inch bars

This book would not be complete without a cookie or two from my incomparable friend and associate David Shamah. This spectacular contribution is not only delicious but easy to make. Everyone remembers similar bars from childhood, originally made with butterscotch morsels. David's recipe utilizes the more sophisticated flavors of three chocolates for the ultimate grown-up version. The ingredients, however, are undeniably expensive.

EQUIPMENT: *10-inch by 15-inch by 1-inch jelly roll pan, bottom and sides lined with heavy-duty aluminum foil.*

Place 1 oven rack in the middle of the oven.

Preheat oven to 350°F.

Break chocolate into individual squares and cut each in half, or chop the chocolate into ½-inch pieces. Mix the chocolate pieces together and set aside.

Melt the butter in the jelly roll pan in the preheating oven for 5 to 10 minutes. Spread the butter evenly over the bottom and sides of the pan by tilting the pan or using a pastry brush. Sprinkle the cracker crumbs over the butter,

INGREDIENTS	MEASURE volume	WEIGHT ounces	grams
bittersweet *or* semisweet chocolate*	2 (3-ounce) bars	6 ounces	170 grams
milk chocolate*	2 (3-ounce) bars	6 ounces	170 grams
white chocolate*	2 (3-ounce) bars	6 ounces	170 grams
unsalted butter	12 tablespoons	6 ounces	170 grams
cinnamon graham cracker crumbs (16 double cookies)	2 cups	7.75 ounces	220 grams
shredded coconut	1⅓ cups	4 ounces	113 grams
pecan halves	3 full cups	12 ounces	340 grams
sweetened condensed milk	1⅔ liquid cups	15 ounces	430 grams

*We both prefer Lindt Excellence, Milk, and Blancor.

mixing with a rubber spatula to moisten them. With your fingers, press the crumbs firmly and evenly onto the bottom and about ¾ inch up the sides of the pan. Strew the coconut evenly over the crumbs.

Reserve 1 scant cup (about 3.5 ounces/100 grams) of pecan halves. Chop the remaining pecans medium-coarsely and scatter them evenly over the coconut. Scatter the chocolate pieces in an even layer over the pecans. Slowly and evenly pour the condensed milk on top. Arrange the reserved pecan halves, smooth side up, in 5 long rows, starting 1 inch from each long edge and spacing them 1½ inches apart.

Bake for 10 minutes. Remove the pan from the oven and, using an angled spatula, press down the nuts so they adhere to the choco-

late. Return the pan to the oven and continue baking for 20 to 30 minutes or just until the milk bubbling up between the nuts in the center of the pan is pale golden. Do not overbake or the nuts and crust will be bitter.

Cool completely in the pan on a wire rack. Invert onto a large cookie sheet and peel off the aluminum foil. Reinvert onto a cutting surface and cut the cookie lengthwise into 5 strips (each about 2 inches wide), cutting in between the rows of pecans, and then crosswise into 10 strips (about 1½ inches wide).

Store: In an airtight container at room temperature or in the freezer.

Keeps: At least 2 weeks at room temperature, several months frozen. The texture is best up to 5 days at room temperature or frozen and defrosted.

Smart Cookie

- Half the mixture can be baked in an 8-inch square pan for 15 to 20 minutes.

- This recipe is also delicious with walnuts, which are more crunchy than pecans.
- Packaged shredded coconut is moister and gives a better texture to these cookies than does fresh coconut.

Ginger Pennies

Makes at least 25 dozen
³/₄-inch cookies

Mʏ first Christmas present and my first cookbook as a new bride was, at my request, *The Joy of Cooking*. It was from that book that I made my first cake (spice cake), my first bread (white bread), and my first pie (angel pie). Each was a great success; the book was everything its title promised. To this day, my favorite cookie recipe from *Joy* is for ginger thins, which inspired this recipe. These lovable little wafers are truly pennies from heaven: incredibly delicate, crispy, gingery, and addictive. Don't be tempted to make them too large as they will lose their unique daintiness.

INGREDIENTS	MEASURE volume	WEIGHT ounces	grams
bleached all-purpose flour	1¹/₂ cups (dip and sweep method)	7.5 ounces	215 grams
ground ginger	³/₄ teaspoon	•	•
ground cinnamon	³/₄ teaspoon	•	•
ground cloves	¹/₂ teaspoon	•	•
baking soda	¹/₂ teaspoon	•	•
salt	¹/₄ teaspoon	•	•
light brown sugar	1 cup (firmly packed)	7.75 ounces	217 grams
1 large egg	3 tablespoons	1.75 ounces (weighed without the shell)	50 grams
unsulfured molasses (preferably Grandma's)	¹/₄ liquid cup (use a greased liquid measuring cup)	2.75 ounces	80 grams
unsalted butter	12 tablespoons	6 ounces	170 grams

EQUIPMENT: *nonstick, lightly buttered, or greased cookie sheets; reclosable gallon-size freezer bag.*

*Place 2 oven racks in the upper and lower thirds of the oven.
Preheat oven to 325°F.*

Food Processor Method

In a medium bowl, sift together the flour, ginger, cinnamon, cloves, baking soda, and salt, then whisk together to mix evenly.

In a food processor with the metal blade, process the brown sugar, egg, and molasses. Cut the butter into a few pieces and add it with the motor running. Process until smooth, scraping the sides of the bowl as needed. Pulse in the flour mixture until well blended.

Electric Mixer Method

Soften the butter. In a medium bowl, sift together the flour, ginger, cinnamon, cloves, baking soda, and salt, then whisk together to mix evenly. In a mixing bowl, cream together the brown sugar, egg, molasses, and butter. On low speed, beat in the flour mixture until well blended.

For Both Methods

Scrape the mixture into the freezer bag, close it securely, and cut off a small piece of the corner of the bag. Pipe small dots, about ¹/₈ teaspoon in size (¹/₂-inch mounds), about 1 inch apart. Ignore the small peaks that form; they will melt and flatten as the cookies bake.

Bake for about 5 minutes or until browned. For even baking, rotate the cookie sheets from top to bottom and front to back halfway through the baking period.

Cool the cookies on the sheets for about 3 minutes, then slide them off onto wire racks to cool and crisp. Keep them separate as they are cooling or they will stick to one another.

Store: In an airtight container at room temperature at low humidity.

Keeps: Several months at low humidity.

Smart Cookie

- This practical recipe yields loads of cookies quickly and easily with ingredients most everyone has in the cupboard.

- When first removed from the oven, these cookies are very flexible. Cool them slightly on the cookie sheet to ensure a flat, even shape.
- Allow the cookie sheet(s) to cool completely before using for the next batch.

- Distribute the cookies evenly around the cookie sheet. Avoid crowding the cookies into one section of the cookie sheet, leaving a large area bare.

Swiss-Italian Mocha Meringues

Makes 1½ dozen 4-inch cookies

INGREDIENTS Do not make on a humid day	MEASURE volume	WEIGHT ounces	grams
Medaglia d'Oro instant espresso powder	2 teaspoons	•	2.5 grams
Optional: 4 drops red food coloring			
sugar	1¼ cups + 3 tablespoons	10 ounces	285 grams
water	½ teaspoon + ⅓ cup	2.75 ounces	80 grams
4 large egg whites (room temperature)	½ cup (use a liquid measuring cup)	4.25 ounces	120 grams
cream of tartar	½ teaspoon	•	•
unsweetened chocolate, melted and slightly cooled	2 (1-ounce) squares	2 ounces	57 grams

Several years ago I went to Switzerland at Christmastime to write an article for *The New York Times* about eating chocolate. The research would have been most enjoyable at any time of year. But being in Switzerland for Christmas was a magical experience because of the decorations. This is truely the land Irving Berlin must have had in mind when he wrote "White Christmas." The main motifs were stars and candles, and everything everywhere was white. The most enchanting decoration of all was on the Bahnhofstrasse (the main street of Zurich), where hundreds of strings of lights were suspended in long, dripping rows from overhead wires. All but unnoticed during the day, at twilight they were illuminated all at once into trails of twinkling stars against a deep blue evening sky.

One of my favorite chocolate discoveries, available in every *confiserie* in Zurich, was this S-shaped chocolate meringue cookie with a crispy exterior and fudgy center. It was made using chocolate Italian meringue, sometimes referred to as *neve nero,* "black snow" in Italian.

On my return to America, I succeeded in reproducing this Swiss classic, but it wasn't until my friend Corby Kummer suggested that the felicitous addition of coffee would make it less sweet, that this version was born.

EQUIPMENT: *2 14-inch by 17-inch baking sheets (or 2 smaller sheets), nonstick or lined with parchment or aluminum foil; large pastry bag or reclosable gallon-size freezer bag, fitted with a number 8 (¾-inch diameter) large star pastry tube.*

Electric Mixer Method

Stir the instant espresso into ½ teaspoon of boiling water and add the red food coloring, if desired, to make a paste. Set aside near the mixer. Have a 2-cup heatproof glass measure ready near the range.

In a small heavy saucepan, preferably with a nonstick lining, stir together 1¼ cups of sugar and the ⅓ cup of water. Heat, stirring constantly, until the sugar dissolves and the syrup is bubbling. Stop stirring and turn down the heat to the lowest setting. (If using an electric range, remove the pan from the heat.)

In a mixing bowl, beat the egg whites until foamy, add the cream of tartar, and beat until soft peaks form when the beater is raised. Gradually beat in the remaining 3 tablespoons of sugar until stiff peaks form when the beater is raised slowly.

Increase the heat and boil the syrup until a thermometer registers 248°F. to 250°F. (firm-ball stage). Immediately pour the syrup into the glass measure to stop the cooking.

If using an electric hand-held mixer, beat the syrup into the whites in a steady stream. Don't allow the syrup to fall on the beaters or they will spin the syrup onto the sides of the bowl. If using a stand mixer, pour a small amount of syrup over the whites with the mixer off. Immediately beat at high speed for 5 seconds. Stop the mixer and add a larger amount of syrup. Beat at high speed for 5 seconds. Continue with the remaining syrup. With the last addition, use a rubber spatula to remove the syrup clinging to the measure. Beat 1 minute.

Now comes the critical moment: Stop beating, disengage the beater attachment, and add the melted chocolate and coffee mixture (don't pour the coffee mixture on top of the chocolate or it will "seize"). Holding the beater with your hand, immediately beat for a few seconds *only until incorporated*. Transfer the mixture at once to the prepared bag and pipe immediately while still hot. If overbeaten, the mixture will be soft and the tube's ridges will not show.

Use a small spot of meringue at each corner of the pan to attach the parchment. Pipe large, high, tight S-shapes (see the photograph), allowing the mixture to fall from the bag. Avoid flattening it by having the decorating tip too low. From end to end, each S should measure 3½ inches. They will expand ½ inch when baked, so leave at least 1½ inches between the cookies (9 cookies will fit on each cookie sheet). Allow the cookies to dry for 2 hours or until set (when your fingertip touches the surface, the meringue stays intact).

Place 2 oven racks in the upper and lower thirds of the oven.
Preheat oven to 350°F.

Bake for 10 minutes. Lower the heat to 200°F. and bake without opening the oven door for 20 minutes. Check to see if the cookies can be removed easily from the sheet. They should be wet inside; they will continue to dry on removal from the oven and should be soft and chewy inside after cooling. If further baking is necessary, reverse the position of the cookie sheets from top to bottom and front to back. Bake up to 10 minutes longer.

Use a small, angled metal spatula or pancake turner to transfer the cookies to wire racks to cool completely.

Store: In airtight container at room temperature at low humidity.

Keeps: 1 week to 10 days at low humidity.

 ## Smart Cookie

- Baking sheets must be nonstick or lined with parchment or aluminum foil.

- A few drops of red food coloring give the chocolate a richer color.

- For maximum stability, the sugar syrup must reach 248°F. and not exceed 250°F. as higher temperatures will break down the egg whites. Use an accurate candy thermometer (page 246).

- For the best texture, use old egg whites (page 219).

- Make sure that the bowl, beater, and egg whites are free of grease, including even a speck of egg yolk, or the whites will not beat well.

- The melted chocolate should be warm (ideally 100°F.) when added to the meringue.

- Beating must be minimal after adding the chocolate. Pipe the mixture while still hot.

- Do not use wax paper; the meringue may stick to it.

- To prevent cracking, allow the cookies to dry at room temperature before baking and do not open the oven door during the early stage of baking.

- If you do not have enough cookie sheets for the whole batch, lay pieces of aluminum foil the size of your cookie sheet on the counter and pipe the meringues onto the foil. When the first batch is baked, remove it from the cookie sheet and simply slip the cookie sheet under the foil of the next batch.

- Distribute the cookies evenly around the cookie sheet. Avoid crowding the cookies into one section of the cookie sheet, leaving a large area bare.

- *Don't overbake the cookies.* They should be chewy, not dry, inside.

- Don't be afraid! These are easier than they sound; just follow all the instructions. They're well worth the effort!

Swiss-Italian Mocha Meringues 124

Lora Brody's Rugelach

Makes 4 dozen 2½-inch cookies

These are, without a doubt, the best rugelach I've ever tasted, and, to my mind, there is no point whatsoever in improving on perfection. From my friend Lora's wonderful book *Cooking with Memories,* this recipe was passed down to her from her mother.

One of the reasons these rugelach are so special is that the dough itself contains a little sugar, making it softer and more cozy and buttery than the usual. Then there is the extra zing of tartness from the apricot preserves and the sweet, sharp sting of lots of plump golden raisins. As I mentioned, perfection! As Lora warns: "Beware, you can't eat just one!"

EQUIPMENT: *cookie sheets lined with parchment or buttered; rolling pin.*

Food Processor Method

Into a food processor with the metal blade, place the cream cheese. Cut the butter into a few pieces and add it with the motor running. Process until smooth and creamy. Add the sugar and vanilla extract and process until incorpo-

Dough

INGREDIENTS	MEASURE volume	WEIGHT ounces	grams
cream cheese	1 (8-ounce) package	8 ounces	227 grams
unsalted butter	1 cup	8 ounces	227 grams
sugar	¼ cup	1.75 ounces	50 grams
pure vanilla extract	1 teaspoon	•	4 grams
bleached all-purpose flour	2 cups (sift into the cup and level off)	8 ounces	228 grams
salt* *(optional)*	¼ teaspoon	•	•

*Lora does not use salt in the dough. It is not strictly necessary because the cream cheese contains salt. I like a little extra.

rated, scraping the sides of the bowl. Add the flour and the optional salt and pulse in just until the dough starts to clump together.

Electric Mixer Method

Soften the cream cheese and butter. In a mixing bowl, cream the cream cheese and butter until blended. Beat in the sugar and vanilla extract. On low speed, beat in the flour and the optional salt until incorporated.

For Both Methods

Scrape the dough onto a piece of plastic wrap and press it together to form a ball. Divide the dough into 4 portions and cover each with plastic wrap. Refrigerate for 2 hours or overnight.

Filling

In a medium bowl, combine the sugars, cinnamon, raisins, and walnuts and stir with a spatula or fork until well mixed.

Remove the dough from the refrigerator and allow it to sit on the counter for about 15 minutes or until it is malleable enough to roll.

Place 2 oven racks in the upper and lower thirds of the oven.
Preheat oven to 350°F.

Using a floured rolling pin, on a lightly floured board, roll out each dough portion, one at a time, into a 9-inch circle to a ⅛-inch thickness, rotating the dough often to be sure that it isn't sticking. Using the back of a tablespoon, spread the dough evenly with 2 tablespoons of the apricot preserves. Sprinkle about ½ cup of the raisin-walnut filling over the preserves. Press the filling firmly and evenly over the dough. Using a sharp knife, cut the dough circle into 12 triangles or pieces of "pie."

Use a thin knife, if necessary, to loosen the triangles from the board. Starting at the wide end, roll up the triangle and bend the ends around to form a slight crescent shape. Place the rugelach, point underneath, about 1½

Filling

INGREDIENTS	MEASURE	WEIGHT	
	volume	*ounces*	*grams*
granulated sugar	1/4 cup + 2 tablespoons	2.5 ounces	75 grams
light brown sugar	1/4 cup (firmly packed)	2 ounces	54 grams
ground cinnamon	1/2 teaspoon	•	•
golden raisins	3/4 cup	3.75 ounces	108 grams
coarsely chopped walnuts	1 cup	3.5 ounces	100 grams
apricot preserves (well stirred)	1/2 cup	4 ounces	113 grams
Topping			
milk	1/4 liquid cup	2 ounces	60 grams
granulated sugar	2 tablespoons	0.75 ounces	25 grams
ground cinnamon	1 teaspoon	•	•

Smart Cookie

- If the raisins are not soft, soak them first in 1/2 cup of boiling water for 1 hour and drain them thoroughly.
- The apricot is stirred instead of strained because straining thins it too much and it tends to ooze out the sides of the rugelach.
- Unbaked rugelach dough freezes brilliantly. This is a great dough to have on hand in the freezer. Simply add on about 5 to 10 minutes to the baking time. The rugelach are especially delicious still warm from the oven and are at their best when freshly baked.
- The dough is chilled before baking to maintain the most even shape.
- Allow the cookie sheet(s) to cool completely before using for the next batch.
- Distribute the cookies evenly around the cookie sheet. Avoid crowding the cookies into one section of the cookie sheet, leaving a large area bare.

inches apart on the prepared baking sheets. Refrigerate, covered with plastic wrap, for at least 30 minutes or until firm.

Clean the work surface of excess filling before rolling out each batch.

For the topping, brush the rugelach with milk. In a small bowl, stir together the sugar and cinnamon, and sprinkle the rugelach with it.

Bake for 16 to 18 minutes or until lightly browned. For even baking, rotate the cookie sheets from top to bottom and front to back halfway through the baking period.

Use a small, angled metal spatula or pancake turner to transfer the cookies to wire racks to cool completely.

Store: In an airtight container at room temperature or in the freezer.

Keeps: 5 days at room temperature, 3 months frozen.

Cinnamon Cloud-Nine Crunchies

Makes 3 dozen 2½-inch cookies

This unassuming-looking cookie has much to recommend it, especially for the cinnamon lover. Its proportions of sugar, butter, and flour are much the same as the classic French *sablé,* but the added yeast and less sugar in the dough entirely change its texture.

The cinnamon-imbued cookie is crisp, slightly flaky, and altogether unusual. In fact, my daughter, Beth, says it is the only cookie she knows that is crunchy-crumbly and wonderfully dissolving all at the same time. This is a great cookie to set out with hot cocoa to welcome in carolers.

EQUIPMENT: *cookie sheets, non-stick or lined with aluminum foil.*

Proof the yeast in a small bowl by combining the water (ideally 100°F. for fresh yeast, a little warmer, 110°F., for dry yeast), ½ teaspoon of the sugar, and the yeast. If using fresh yeast, crumble it. Set aside in a warm, draft-free spot for 10 to 20 minutes. By that time, the mixture should be full of bubbles. If not, the yeast is too old to be useful.

INGREDIENTS	MEASURE	WEIGHT	
	volume	ounces	grams
warm water	⅓ cup	2.75 ounces	78 grams
sugar	1 cup	7 ounces	200 grams
fresh yeast *or*	2 packed teaspoons	0.5 ounce	14 grams
dry yeast	1½ teaspoons	•	5.5 grams
unsalted butter (cold)	1 cup	8 ounces	227 grams
sifted bleached all-purpose flour	2 cups (sift into the cup and level off)	8 ounces	228 grams
salt	⅛ teaspoon	•	•
pure vanilla extract	1 teaspoon	•	4 grams
Topping			
ground cinnamon	1 teaspoon	•	•

Food Processor Method

While the yeast is proofing, cut the butter into 1-inch cubes, wrap them in plastic wrap, and refrigerate.

In a food processor with the metal blade, process together the flour, salt, and 6 tablespoons of the sugar for a few seconds until mixed. Add the butter and pulse in until a coarse meal consistency. There should not be any large pieces of butter. Add the yeast mixture and vanilla extract and pulse just to combine.

Electric Mixer Method

Proof the yeast as above. While it is proofing, cut the butter into ½-inch cubes, wrap them in plastic wrap, and refrigerate. In a small mixing bowl, beat together 6 tablespoons of the sugar, the flour, and salt until mixed. Add the butter and beat on medium-low speed until a coarse meal texture is achieved. At low speed, beat in the yeast mixture and vanilla extract until well blended.

For Both Methods

Scrape the dough into a bowl, cover it tightly, and refrigerate for at least 1 hour or overnight.

Work with one quarter of the dough at a time, leaving the remainder refrigerated.

Place 2 oven racks in the upper and lower thirds of the oven.
Preheat oven to 350°F.

In a small dish, stir together the remaining sugar and the cinnamon.

Measure the dough into a 1¼-inch gently rounded scoop or 1 scant tablespoon and roll the dough between your palms to form 1-inch balls. The dough will be very soft and sticky. Drop each sticky ball as you form it into the sugar and immediately, while the dough is still soft from the heat of your hands, twirl the dish around to coat the dough all over. Roll the sugar-coated dough between your palms and roll it again in the sugar. The aim is to get as much sugar as possible on the outside of the dough ball.

Lift out the dough ball and place it on the cookie sheet, placing the dough balls 2 inches apart (15 will fit on a 10-inch by 15-inch sheet).

Bake for 20 to 25 minutes or until golden brown and baked through. (Cut one in half to see if any moist, unbaked dough re-

mains.) For even baking, rotate the cookie sheets from top to bottom and front to back halfway through the baking period. Avoid overcooking or the cinnamon becomes bitter.

Allow the cookies to cool completely on the sheets.

Store: In an airtight container at room temperature or in the freezer.

Keeps: 1 week at room temperature, several months frozen.

Smart Cookie

- There is no need to sift the flour if you have a scale and weigh it. Sifting is for accurate measure only in this recipe.
- Do not use rapid-rise yeast.

- Only a small amount of sugar is used in the dough to keep it crunchy and layered like pastry. It is therefore important to work as much sugar as possible into the outside of the dough ball.
- Do not use greased cookie sheets because the cookies may spread too much, making the edges too thin and brown.
- Allow the cookie sheet(s) to cool completely before using for the next batch.
- Distribute the cookies evenly around the cookie sheet. Avoid crowding the cookies into one section of the cookie sheet, leaving a large area bare.

"Lacey Susans"

Makes about 8 dozen
2½-inch cookies

My lively and generous friend Sue Zelickson, food columnist and radio personality in Minneapolis, created these divine cookies. Sue's theory is that no cookie can be either too rich or too thin, which is, quite possibly, the best description of what to anticipate in this cookie. It is buttery and crisply crunchy with caramelized sugar and the added pleasure of tiny bits of semisweet chocolate. Sue recommends molding them, while still hot, into dessert dishes, crumbling them over ice cream, or just eating them as they are.

Sue's "Lacey Susans" are so popular that she has recently marketed them as a mix. She donates the proceeds from this mix, produced by Canterbury Cuisine in Redmond, Washington, to the nonprofit Down Syndrome Congress. Naturally, this recipe is trademarked and top secret. But I have to admit, my interpretation comes very close to the original. If you have any doubts, send for the mix and decide for yourself.

INGREDIENTS	MEASURE volume	WEIGHT	
		ounces	grams
unbleached all-purpose flour	½ cup (dip and sweep method)	2.5 ounces	72 grams
baking soda	½ teaspoon	•	•
salt	pinch	•	•
granulated sugar	¼ cup	1.75 ounces	50 grams
light brown sugar	½ cup + 2 tablespoons (firmly packed)	4.75 ounces	135 grams
unsalted butter	12 tablespoons	6 ounces	170 grams
1 large egg	3 tablespoons + ½ teaspoon	1.75 ounces (weighed without the shell)	50 grams
pure vanilla extract	½ teaspoon	•	2 grams
mini-semisweet chocolate chips	⅓ cup	2 ounces	57 grams

EQUIPMENT: *cookie sheets, non-stick or lined with parchment or aluminum foil; reclosable quart-size freezer bag or ½ teaspoon measure.*

Place 2 oven racks in the upper and lower thirds of the oven. Preheat oven to 375°F.

Food Processor Method

In a food processor with the metal blade, process the flour, baking soda, salt, and sugars until evenly mixed. Cut the butter into a few pieces and add it with the motor running. Process until smooth and creamy. Scrape the sides of the bowl. Add the egg and vanilla extract and process just until incorporated, scraping the sides of the bowl.

Remove the blade, scraping off the batter with a spatula. Sprinkle the chocolate chips all over the surface of the batter. Use a spoon or spatula to mix in the chips.

Electric Mixer Method or by Hand

Soften the butter. In a large mixing bowl, sift together the flour, baking soda, salt, and sugars, then whisk together to mix evenly. Add the butter, egg, and vanilla extract and beat or stir with a large wooden spoon until smooth. Stir in the chocolate chips.

For Both Methods

Scrape the batter into the freezer bag and close it securely. The batter will be very soft. Cut off a small piece of the corner of the bag and pipe the mixture onto the cookie sheets. Make the cookies very small, only a level ½ tea-

spoon amount (¹/₂-inch-wide mounds), and 3 inches apart because they spread a great deal. The ¹/₂ teaspoon and your index finger can be used instead of the bag, but piping the cookies is much speedier. (Fifteen cookies will fit on a 10-inch by 15-inch sheet.)

Bake for 4 to 6 minutes or until well browned and bubbling (the cookies will firm up on standing). Watch the cookies carefully toward the end of the baking period as once they start to brown they go fast. For even baking, rotate the cookie sheets from top to bottom and front to back halfway through the baking period.

Allow the cookies to cool on the sheets for 2 to 3 minutes or just until they can be lifted with a metal small, angled spatula or pancake turner. Start by lifting around the edges first. Transfer the cookies to paper towels to absorb the excess butter.

Store: In an airtight container at room temperature at low humidity. Layer the cookies between sheets of wax paper to ensure crispness.

Keeps: 1 week at low humidity. The batter keeps for months refrigerated.

Smart Cookie

- These cookies have many virtues: They are inexpensive and easy to make with easy-to-find ingredients; there is no rolling or cutting of dough, and the cookies bake so quickly that you get about 100 cookies in less than 1 hour.
- There is no need to cool baking sheets between batches.
- Distribute the cookies evenly around the cookie sheet. Avoid crowding the cookies into one section of the cookie sheet, leaving a large area bare.

Grandmother Schorr's Moravian Spice Crisps

Makes almost 9 dozen
2 1/2-inch cookies

INGREDIENTS	MEASURE volume	WEIGHT ounces	grams
bleached all-purpose flour	1 1/3 cups (dip and sweep method)	6.75 ounces	194 grams
baking soda	1 1/4 teaspoons	•	6 grams
ground cinnamon	3/4 teaspoon	•	•
ground ginger	1 teaspoon	•	•
ground cloves	1/2 teaspoon	•	•
solid white vegetable shortening	1/4 cup	1.75 ounces	50 grams
light brown sugar	1/3 cup (firmly packed)	2.5 ounces	72 grams
unsulfured molasses (preferably Grandma's)	1/2 cup (use a greased liquid measuring cup)	5.5 ounces	161 grams

$\mathcal{M}$y husband and I usually spend Christmastime in our mountain house in Hope, New Jersey, a charming town settled by the Moravians of Bohemia over two hundred years ago. I first went to Hope twenty-three years ago to visit the Goodbodys, who own a farm just outside of Hope to which they humorously refer as "the beyond Hope farm." Coincidentally, when my dear friend Shirley Corriher informed me that her son had married into a Moravian family, my cookie imagination took over. "I hope you can get me a good recipe for Moravian cookies," I prompted.

Shirley's response: "I *sure* can. Ted's mother-in-law, Bonnie Wagner, has one that has been in her family for over two hundred years and was given to her by her grandmother!" Just the kind of recipe with a history that is dearest to my heart.

This recipe produces the most impossibly thin, crisply firm yet delicate spice cookies imaginable. The flavor, which almost defies description, is both peppery and gingery and quite special enough to be compatible with the uniqueness of the texture.

The original recipe called for lard, but vegetable shortening is a healthy substitution and makes absolutely no difference in the flavor or texture. Bonnie's recipe makes close to nine hundred cookies, which take an entire day to roll out. Here I am offering a more manageable quantity.

Bonnie continues to make these cookies as she always has. She rolls out her cookies with a marble rolling pin on a flour sack that she's had since childhood. She says it's a lot of work, but it just wouldn't be Christmas without these cookies, and she'd hate to disappoint the children.

EQUIPMENT: *nonstick or greased cookie sheets; floured pastry cloth and floured rolling pin sleeve; rolling pin; round (2 5/8-inch diameter) scalloped cutter.*

Food Processor Method

In a small bowl, sift together the flour, baking soda, cinnamon, ginger, and cloves, then whisk together to mix evenly.

In a food processor with the metal blade, process the shortening and sugar until creamy, scraping the sides of the bowl. With the motor running, add the molasses and process until incorporated. Scrape the sides of the bowl. Add the flour mixture and process until

it is incorporated and starts to clump together.

Electric Mixer Method

In a small bowl, sift together the flour, baking soda, cinnamon, ginger, and cloves, then whisk together to mix evenly. In a large mixing bowl, beat the shortening and sugar until creamy, scraping the sides of the bowl. With the mixer at medium speed, beat in the molasses until incorporated. Scrape the sides of the bowl. With the mixer at low speed, gradually add the flour, beating until it is incorporated. If the motor starts to strain, stir in the remainder of the flour with a wooden spoon.

For Both Methods

Scrape the dough onto a counter and knead the dough lightly, adding more flour if the dough is very sticky. It should be slightly sticky, firm but malleable.

Wrap the dough with plastic wrap and place it in an airtight container or heavy-duty storage bag. Allow it to rest overnight or up to 3 days at room temperature so that it will be less sticky and easier to roll.

Place 2 oven racks in the upper and lower thirds of the oven.

Preheat oven to 325°F.

Working with half the dough at a time, roll each half as thinly as possible into a rectangle, about 10 inches by 15 inches. The dough will be so thin you can see your fingers behind it.

Cut out the cookies, pressing firmly so that each one is completely separated from the dough.

Transfer the cut cookies to the cookie sheets, placing them about 1/4 inch to 1/2 inch apart.

Bake for about 8 to 10 minutes or until golden brown. Do not make them too dark or they will be bitter. For even baking, rotate the cookie sheets from top to bottom and front to back halfway through the baking period.

Allow the cookies to cool on the sheets for about 30 seconds. When they are firm enough to lift, use a small, angled metal spatula or pancake turner to transfer the cookies to wire racks to cool completely.

Gather up the remaining dough scraps and add water as necessary if they have become dry. A plant mister works well for this. Reroll the scraps until all the dough has been used or freeze the dough, wrapped airtight, for up to 3 months.

Store: In an airtight container at room temperature.

Keeps: Many months.

 ## Smart Cookie

- The original recipe used 1 1/2 teaspoons each of cinnamon, ginger, and cloves for this quantity of dough. I found this a bit intense for the delicate texture of the cookie. If you like more of a "spicy bite," increase the spices accordingly.
- Allow the cookie sheet(s) to cool completely before using for the next batch.
- Distribute the cookies evenly around the cookie sheet. Avoid crowding the cookies into one section of the cookie sheet, leaving a large area bare.

Chocolate-Pistachio Marzipan Spirals

Makes 2 dozen
2½-inch by 1-inch by
½-inch slices

Lora Brody, friend and author of *Cooking with Memories,* developed these spirals from two recipes in *The Cake Bible:* pistachio marzipan and ganache. It was my fondest hope that people would use my recipes to create their own specialties in this way, and I am delighted to report that the silky-rich chocolate ganache, rolled together with chewy pistachio marzipan, is a combination that tastes every bit as good as it looks. Thank you, Lora.

These candies are terrific to have on hand to serve with espresso to friends who drop in with holiday gifts and wishes.

EQUIPMENT: *rolling pin; plastic wrap (preferably Saran Wrap).*

Pistachio Marzipan

If your pistachio nuts are salted, rinse them in a strainer under hot tap water. Place the pistachios on a cookie sheet in a 325°F. oven for 5 to 10 minutes or until the skins

Pistachio Marzipan

INGREDIENTS	MEASURE	WEIGHT	
	volume	ounces	grams
shelled unsalted pistachio nuts	¼ cup	1.25 ounces	38 grams
powdered sugar	¾ cup (lightly spooned into the cup)	3 ounces	86 grams
corn syrup	1 tablespoon + 1 teaspoon	1 ounce	27 grams
glycerine *or* light vegetable oil (not peanut oil)	½ teaspoon	•	3 grams
Optional: a dab of green paste food coloring or a few drops of liquid green food coloring			

separate from the nuts when scratched lightly with a fingernail. With a large spoon, transfer the nuts to a clean kitchen towel and wrap them with the towel. Allow them to sit for a few minutes. Use the towel to rub off as much peel as possible. Cool to room temperature.

In a food processor with the metal blade, process the nuts until a smooth paste forms. Add the sugar and process until it is well mixed. Add the corn syrup and glycerine and process about 20 seconds or until well blended. The mixture will appear dry, but a small amount pressed between your fingers should hold together. If it seems too dry, add more corn syrup, ¼ teaspoon at a time, with the motor running. If you wish to deepen the color, add the optional food coloring. Process until the marzipan has a smooth, doughlike consistency. Knead it briefly by hand until the color is uniform.

The marzipan can be used at once, but it is much easier to work with if it is allowed to rest over-

night at room temperature, tightly covered with plastic wrap.

Ganache

Break the chocolate into pieces and chop it finely, or process it in a food processor with the metal blade until finely chopped.

In a small saucepan, heat the cream and corn syrup to a full boil. Remove the saucepan from the heat, immediately add the chocolate, and cover the pan. Allow it to sit for 1 to 2 minutes to melt the chocolate. Then stir the mixture until it is smooth and uniform in color. Cool to room temperature. (To speed cooling, you can transfer the ganache to a bowl.)

While the ganache is cooling, roll the marzipan between 2 sheets of plastic wrap into a 12-inch by 6-inch by ¹⁄₁₆-inch rectangle.

When the ganache is at room temperature, remove the top sheet of plastic wrap covering the marzipan and spread the ganache on top, leaving ¼ inch bare along 1

Ganache

INGREDIENTS	MEASURE	WEIGHT	
	volume	ounces	grams
bittersweet or semisweet chocolate	1 (3-ounce) bar	3 ounces	85 grams
heavy cream	3 tablespoons	1.5 ounces	44 grams
corn syrup	1/2 teaspoon	•	3.5 grams

Topping

INGREDIENTS	MEASURE	WEIGHT	
	volume	ounces	grams
shelled unsalted pistachio nuts, chopped medium coarsely	3 tablespoons	1 ounce	28 grams
1 large egg white, lightly beaten	2 tablespoons	2 ounces	30 grams

long edge. (An angled metal spatula works well to spread the ganache.) Using the bottom sheet of plastic wrap, slip the marzipan onto a cookie sheet. Refrigerate until the chocolate dulls and is barely tacky to the touch (about 10 minutes).

Use your fingers to roll the marzipan. Start with the long end that is covered with ganache. Roll it about 1/4 inch and press down on top of it to make it adhere tightly. Continue rolling until you have reached the other end. If a little ganache squishes out, wipe it away so that the outside of the roll is only the marzipan.

Topping

If the pistachio nuts are salted, rinse the nuts in a strainer under hot tap water. Place the pistachios on a cookie sheet in a 325°F. oven for 5 to 10 minutes to recrisp them. Cool to room temperature and chop them medium coarsely.

Brush the marzipan roll with the egg white (only about 2 teaspoons will be necessary to coat it) and roll it in the chopped pistachios.

Place the roll on a cookie sheet lined with plastic wrap and refrigerate for at least 1 hour before cutting the roll into slices. You may also freeze the roll, tightly wrapped in plastic wrap, and cut it when frozen. To cut beautiful slices, use a serrated knife, dipped in hot water, to cut 1/2-inch-thick diagonal slices. Wipe the blade clean after each slice.

Store: In an airtight container in the refrigerator or freezer. If storing the uncut roll, wrap it first in plastic wrap and, when firm, in 2 layers of aluminum foil.

Keeps: Several weeks refrigerated, several months frozen.

 Smart Cookie

- Glycerine is a combination of fat and oil that keeps the marzipan soft and chewy.
- Saran Wrap is the ideal plastic wrap for rolling the marzipan because it lies very flat. Wax paper is the second choice.

David Shamah's Jumbles

Makes about 3 dozen
2½-inch cookies

A fabulous cross between Toll House chocolate chip cookies and chunky candy bars, David's jumbles are moist with sweet, tangy pockets of raisins, but they are not *too* sweet because they have so many nuts and so little batter (just enough to hold the delicious ingredients together). In fact, these cookies are so chock-full of wonderful textures and flavors that I just can't keep away from them as long as I know they're around.

EQUIPMENT: *ungreased cookie sheets.*

INGREDIENTS	MEASURE volume	WEIGHT ounces	grams
pecan halves	¾ cup	2.5 ounces	75 grams
unblanched whole almonds	1¼ cups	8.5 ounces	239 grams
bleached all-purpose flour	1 cup + 2 tablespoons (dip and sweep method)	5.5 ounces	160 grams
baking soda	1 teaspoon	•	5 grams
salt	¼ teaspoon	•	•
granulated sugar	½ cup	3.5 ounces	100 grams
light brown sugar	¼ cup (firmly packed)	2 ounces	54 grams
unsalted butter	8 tablespoons	4 ounces	113 grams
1 large egg	3 tablespoons + ½ teaspoon	3.5 ounces (weighed without the shell)	100 grams
pure vanilla extract	¾ teaspoon	•	3 grams
semisweet chocolate chips	1 cup	6 ounces	170 grams
raisins	1½ cups	7.5 ounces	216 grams

Place 2 oven racks in the upper and lower thirds of the oven.

Preheat oven to 375°F.

Place the pecans on 1 cookie sheet and the almonds on another. Bake them, stirring occasionally, for about 7 minutes or until they begin to have a toasted aroma. Do not bake them until the almond skins begin to crack. Cool completely. Chop each separately in very coarse pieces.

Food Processor Method

In a small bowl, sift together the flour, baking soda, and salt, then whisk together to mix evenly.

In a food processor with the metal blade, process the sugars until very fine. Cut the butter into a few pieces and add it with the motor running. Process until it is smooth and creamy. Add the egg and vanilla extract and process until incorporated, scraping the sides of the bowl. Add the flour mixture and pulse in just until incorporated.

In a large bowl, stir together the chocolate chips, raisins, pecans, and almonds. Empty the batter into the bowl and mix together evenly with a large spoon or spatula.

Electric Mixer Method

Soften the butter. Into a small bowl, sift together the flour, baking soda, and salt, then whisk together to mix evenly. In a mixing bowl, cream the sugars and butter until light and fluffy. Beat in the egg and vanilla extract until well blended. On low speed, beat in the flour mixture until incorporated. In a large bowl, stir together the chocolate chips, raisins, pecans, and almonds. Empty the batter into the bowl and mix together evenly with a large spoon or spatula.

For Both Methods

Drop the batter by rounded tablespoons (1¹/₂-inch balls) onto the cookie sheets, 1¹/₂ inches apart.

Bake for 12 to 15 minutes or until golden brown and barely soft. For even baking, rotate the cookie sheets from top to bottom and front to back halfway through the baking period.

Allow the cookies to cool for a few minutes on the sheets. When the cookies are firm enough to lift, use a pancake turner to transfer them to wire racks to cool completely.

Store: In an airtight container at room temperature or in the freezer.

Keeps: 1 month at room temperature, several months frozen.

Smart Cookie

- Because this cookie is chock-full of nuts, chocolate, and raisins and very little dough—just enough to hold it together—the relatively large amount of baking soda is needed to puff up the dough around the other ingredients.
- The dry ingredients are sifted together because baking soda has a tendency to lump.
- If the raisins are dry, sprinkle them with some hot water or a mixture of hot water and brandy and allow them to sit, covered with plastic wrap, for at least 30 minutes to soften.
- Allow the cookie sheet(s) to cool completely before using for the next batch.
- Distribute the cookies evenly around the cookie sheet. Avoid crowding the cookies into one section of the cookie sheet, leaving a large area bare.

Marion Bush's Cranberry-Chocolate Chippers

Makes 2½ dozen
2-inch cookies

INGREDIENTS	MEASURE	WEIGHT	
	volume	*ounces*	*grams*
walnut halves	½ cup	1.75 ounces	50 grams
bleached all-purpose flour	1 cup + 2 tablespoons (dip and sweep method)	5.5 ounces	160 grams
baking soda	½ teaspoon	•	•
zest from 1 large orange, removed in lengthwise strips with a vegetable peeler	2 scant tablespoons (finely chopped)	•	10 grams
granulated sugar	¼ cup + 2 tablespoons	2.5 ounces	75 grams
light brown sugar	¼ cup + 2 tablespoons (firmly packed)	3 ounces	82 grams
unsalted butter	8 tablespoons	4 ounces	113 grams
1 large egg	3 tablespoons + ½ teaspoon	1.75 ounces (weighed without the shell)	50 grams
pure vanilla extract	¼ teaspoon	•	•
fresh cranberries	1½ cups	5.25 ounces	150 grams
semisweet chocolate chips	1 cup	6 ounces	170 grams

When I was growing up, I felt like a triplet because my best friends were twin cousins my age. They had curly red hair, bright blue eyes, and I adored them. As children they were roly-poly food enthusiasts who had to encourage the then-skinny me to taste what I considered to be suspicious foodstuffs (which, regrettably, included almost everything except butter, silky-smooth baby applesauce, lamb chop bones, and ice cream in Dixie cups). Interestingly enough, we all eventually shared the same passionate obsession with food. Sue teaches baking to friends and neighbors and brings her magnificent breads to holiday dinners. Marion started a company called Wild Harvest, which supplies many of New York's top restaurants with wild edibles from mushrooms to clover. These delightfully tangy cranberry and chocolate chip Toll House variations are her creation. Her young daughter, Alexandra, has been making them by hand since she could sit up straight enough to hold a wooden spoon. She tells me that when she grows up she is going to be a pastry chef. She must think we're having a lot of fun. And she's absolutely right!

EQUIPMENT: *ungreased cookie sheets.*

Place 2 oven racks in the upper and lower thirds of the oven. Preheat oven to 375°F.

Place the walnuts on a cookie sheet and bake them, stirring occasionally, for about 10 minutes or until lightly browned. Cool completely.

Food Processor Method

In a small bowl, sift together the flour and baking soda, then whisk together to mix evenly. Set aside.

In a food processor with the metal blade, process the orange zest and sugars until they are well mixed. Cut the butter into a few pieces and add it with the motor running. Process until smooth and creamy. Add the egg and vanilla extract and process just until incorporated, scraping the sides of the bowl. Add the cranberries and pulse to chop them coarsely, scraping the sides of the bowl to ensure uniformity. Pulse in the flour mixture and walnuts, just until the flour is incorporated. The nuts will be coarsely chopped.

Scrape the batter into a bowl and stir in the chocolate chips with a rubber spatula or wooden spoon.

Electric Mixer Method

Soften the butter. Coarsely chop the cranberries and walnuts. In a small bowl, sift together the flour and baking soda, then whisk together to mix evenly. Set aside. In a mixing bowl, cream the sugars and butter until light and fluffy. Beat in the egg, orange zest, and vanilla extract until blended, scraping the sides of the bowl. On low speed, gradually beat in the flour mixture just until incorporated. Add the walnuts, cranberries, and chocolate chips and beat just until blended.

For Both Methods

Drop the batter by rounded tablespoons, 2 inches apart, onto the cookie sheets.

Bake for 20 minutes. The cookies should still be soft. For even baking, rotate the cookie sheets from top to bottom and front to back halfway through the baking period.

Allow the cookies to cool on the sheets for a few minutes. When they are firm enough to lift, use a small, angled metal spatula or pancake turner to transfer the cookies to wire racks to cool completely.

Store: In an airtight container at room temperature or in the freezer.

Keeps: 1 month at room temperature, several months frozen.

Smart Cookie

- When removing the zest from the orange, remove only the orange portion and not the bitter white pith beneath.
- Use only fresh cranberries. Frozen cranberries bleed their juices into the dough, and the cookies have a tendency to burn on the outside before cooking thoroughly.
- The food processor method for making this cookie dough is especially effective because the batter does not turn pink.
- These cookies are also delicious without the chocolate.
- Allow the cookie sheet(s) to cool completely before using for the next batch.
- Distribute the cookies evenly around the cookie sheet. Avoid crowding the cookies into one section of the cookie sheet, leaving a large area bare.

Aunt Margaret's Star-Spangled Meringues

Makes about 15 3-inch stars or about 4 dozen 1³/₄-inch kisses

INGREDIENTS Do not make on a humid day	MEASURE volume	WEIGHT ounces	grams
granulated sugar	¹/₂ cup + 1 tablespoon	4 ounces	113 grams
unsweetened chocolate	•	2 ounces	57 grams
powdered sugar	1 cup (lightly spooned into the cup)	4 ounces	115 grams
4 egg whites (room temperature)	¹/₂ liquid cup	4.25 ounces	120 grams
cream of tartar	¹/₂ teaspoon	•	•

The best cook on my mother's side of the family has always been my aunt Margaret. The division of holiday-dinner responsibilities, however, was always clear, consistent, and fairly fair: Aunt Florence did Christmas, Aunt Margaret Thanksgiving, and my mother took care of the family teeth and, on rare occasions, made a Seder. It simply was never questioned.

At one of these holiday dinners Aunt Margaret took me aside and imparted some special wisdom: finely ground bitter chocolate is a fantastic way to temper the sweetness of meringue and also adds an attractive speckle. I harbored this pleasant tidbit for years and finally decided to try it. The results are delightful—everything she promised. If you are not adept at piping, simply spoon the mixture into small mounds resembling kisses. This one is too good to miss.

EQUIPMENT: *2 cookie sheets lined with parchment or aluminum foil; optional: 3-inch (measured from point to farthest point) star cutter; large nylon pasty bag or reclosable gallon-size freezer bag with a* number 6 (¹/₂-inch diameter) large star pastry tube.

If you are making star-shaped meringues, place the star cutter on the aluminum foil and, with the tip of a knife (or a pencil, if you are using parchment), lightly mark the 5 points as a piping guide. Leave about 3 inches between star markings.

In a food processor with the metal blade, process the granulated sugar for several minutes, until it is as fine as sand. Empty it into a small bowl and set aside.

Process the chocolate and powdered sugar until the chocolate is powder fine. Keep the chocolate in a cool place or refrigerate it until you are ready to add it to the meringue. (This will keep it from melting into the meringue and turning it brown.)

Electric Mixer Method

In a mixing bowl, beat the egg whites until frothy. Add the cream of tartar and beat at medium speed, gradually adding 2 table-spoons of the processed sugar. When soft peaks form when the beater is raised slowly, add another tablespoon of the sugar and increase the speed to high. When stiff peaks form when the beater is raised slowly, gradually beat in the remaining sugar and beat until the meringue is very stiff and glossy. Use a large whisk or spatula to fold the chocolate mixture into the meringue until evenly incorporated.

Scoop the mixture into the prepared bag and pipe the stars, following the marked guides. Or, hold the bag so that the tube is pointing straight down, a little above the surface of the cookie sheet, and pipe out 1³/₄-inch ridged mounds resembling stars (or simply spoon the mixture into small mounds). Allow the stars to dry for 30 minutes or until set

(when your fingertip touches the surface, the meringue stays intact).

Place 2 oven racks in the upper and lower thirds of the oven.
   Preheat oven to 200°F.
   Bake for 2 hours or until crisp throughout but not beginning to color. (If you choose to make small mounds, check after 1 hour.) For even baking, rotate the cookie sheets from top to bottom three quarters of the way through the baking period.
   Use a small, angled metal spatula or pancake turner to transfer the cookies to wire racks to cool completely.

Store: In an airtight container at room temperature at low humidity.

Keeps: Many months at low humidity.

Smart Cookie

- Superfine sugar makes a lighter meringue than granulated. It can be prepared easily in a food processor by processing granulated sugar for a few minutes or until it is as fine as sand. The addition of powdered sugar makes the meringue lighter still!
- For the best texture, use old egg whites (page 219).
- Make sure that the bowl, beater, and egg whites are free of grease, including even a speck of egg yolk, or the whites will not beat well.
- Fold in the powdered sugar and cocoa with a wire whisk for the best incorporation with the least amount of deflation of the beaten whites.
- Do not use wax paper; the meringue may stick to it.

- Distribute the cookies evenly around the cookie sheet. Avoid crowding the cookies into one section of the cookie sheet, leaving a large area bare.
- Meringue mixtures should be piped shortly after preparing them. If you do not have enough cookie sheets for the whole batch, lay pieces of aluminum foil the size of your cookie sheet on the counter and pipe the meringue onto the foil. When the first batch is baked, remove it from the cookie sheet and simply slip the cookie sheet under the foil of the next batch.
- To prevent cracking, do not open the oven door during the first three quarters of the baking time.
- Bound with thin ribbon in a crisscross manner, the stars make an unusual and attractive tree ornament.

Bûchettes
de Noël

Makes about ³/₄ pound
(340 grams) *bûchettes*

Bûche de Noël is a classic French Christmas cake whose name translates as "yule log." These *bûchettes,* meaning "little logs," are intended to be mini-versions of this classic made with, instead of cake, the crispest, lightest, cocoa meringue. They are a perfect accompaniment to hot chocolate, coffee, tea, eggnog, Cognac, or even milk.

EQUIPMENT: *2 cookie sheets lined with parchment or aluminum foil, reclosable quart-size freezer bag or pastry bag; number 6 (¹/₂-inch diameter) large star pastry tube.*

Electric Mixer Method

In a small bowl, whisk together the powdered sugar and cocoa.

In a mixing bowl, beat the egg whites until frothy, add the cream of tartar, and beat at medium speed while gradually adding 1 tablespoon of the superfine sugar. When soft peaks form when the beater is raised, add 1 tablespoon of superfine sugar and increase the speed to high. When stiff peaks form when the beater is raised slowly, gradually beat in the remaining superfine sugar and beat until very stiff and glossy. Sift the cocoa mixture over the meringue and fold it in, preferably using a large wire whisk or a large rubber spatula.

INGREDIENTS	MEASURE	WEIGHT	
	volume	*ounces*	*grams*
powdered sugar	1 cup (lightly spooned into the cup)	4 ounces	115 grams
unsweetened cocoa (preferably Dutch-processed)	2 tablespoons	0.5 ounces	12 grams
4 large egg whites (room temperature)	¹/₂ liquid cup	4.25 ounces	120 grams
cream of tartar	¹/₂ teaspoon	•	•
superfine sugar	1 tablespoon + ¹/₂ cup	4 ounces	113 grams

Spoon the mixture into the bag fitted with the tube. Hold the bag at a slight angle away from you, with the tube several inches above the sheet. Starting at the top of the sheet, squeeze the meringue with steady pressure, allowing it to drop from the tube. Leave about ¹/₂ inch between the lines of meringue. Don't worry if the lines are nubbly or not straight; it adds to their charm.

Allow the *bûchettes* to dry for 1 hour or until set (when your fingertip touches the surface, the meringue stays intact).

Place 2 oven racks in the upper and lower thirds of the oven.
Preheat oven to 200°F.

Bake for about 1 hour or until completely set. The centers can be slightly sticky as they will harden on cooling. For even baking, rotate the cookie sheets from top to bottom three quarters of the way through the baking period.

Cool completely before carefully removing the meringue strips from the cookie sheets. Break them into pieces about 4 inches long.

Store: In an airtight container at room temperature at low humidity.

Keeps: For many months at low humidity.

Smart Cookie

- Superfine sugar makes a lighter meringue than granulated. It can be prepared easily in the food processor by processing granulated sugar in a food processor for a few minutes or until it is as fine as sand. The addition of powdered sugar makes the meringue lighter still!
- For the best texture, use old egg whites (page 219).
- Make sure that the bowl, beater, and egg whites are free

of grease, including even a speck of egg yolk, or the whites will not beat well.

- Fold in the powdered sugar and cocoa with a wire whisk for the best incorporation with the least amount of deflation of the beaten whites.
- Do not use wax paper; the meringue may stick to it.
- Pipe the *bûchettes* at even intervals on the cookie sheet to avoid creating a large empty area on the sheet.
- Meringue mixtures should be piped shortly after preparing them. If you do not have enough cookie sheets for the whole batch, lay pieces of foil the size of your cookie sheet on the counter and pipe the bûchettes onto the foil. When the first batch is baked, remove it from the cookie sheet and simply slip the cookie sheet under the foil of the next batch.
- To prevent cracking, do not open the oven door during the first three quarters of the cooking time.

Cookies for Holiday Dinner Parties

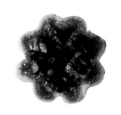

Savory Cheese Dollars

Makes 4 dozen
1½-inch hors d'oeuvres

INGREDIENTS	MEASURE	WEIGHT	
	volume	*ounces*	*grams*
bleached all-purpose flour	1 cup (sift into the cup and level off)	4 ounces	114 grams
salt	⅛ teaspoon	•	•
black pepper, freshly ground	sprinkling	•	•
cayenne pepper	pinch	•	•
grated sharp Cheddar cheese	1 cup	4 ounces	113 grams
unsalted butter	8 tablespoons	4 ounces	113 grams

My first job in food was at Reynolds Metals Company working for Eleanor Lynch, director of consumer information. In those days there was no test kitchen, so Eleanor would give me recipes to test at home. She was eventually responsible, together with her friend Cecily Brownstone of the Associated Press, for encouraging me to go back to school and get my degrees in food. Eleanor was a spirited, loving woman who wanted to change the world. She certainly had a major effect on mine.

Cheese Dollars was my favorite of Eleanor's recipes. Easy to make, they store well at room temperature, and are deliciously full flavored. These buttery, cheesy, crunchy hot hors d'oeuvres can be served hot with wine or drinks but are equally pleasing served at room temperature. And, this is a great dough to have on hand for unexpected holiday entertaining.

EQUIPMENT: *ungreased cookie sheets.*

Food Processor Method

In a small bowl, whisk together the flour, salt, and peppers.

In a food processor with the metal blade, process the cheese and butter (cut into small chunks if it is refrigerator-cold) until well mixed. Add the flour mixture and pulse in until blended.

Electric Mixer Method

Soften the butter and Cheddar cheese. In a small bowl, whisk together the flour, salt, and peppers. In a mixing bowl, cream the cheese with the butter until well mixed. On low speed, add the flour mixture and beat until well blended.

For Both Methods

Scrape the dough onto a piece of plastic wrap and refrigerate for about 1 hour or until firm. Form the dough into three 1-inch-diameter rolls. Wrap each roll in plastic wrap (and then aluminum foil if freezing) and refrigerate up to 3 days or freeze up to 3 months until shortly before serving.

Place 2 oven racks in the upper and lower thirds of the oven.
Preheat oven to 425°F.

If the dough has been frozen, remove it from the freezer and let it rest for a few minutes or until it is easy to slice. Slice the dough into ¼-inch slices. Place the slices about ½ inch apart on the cookie sheets.

Bake for 8 to 10 minutes or until very lightly browned. For even baking, rotate the cookie sheets from top to bottom and front to back halfway through the baking period.

Use a small, angled metal spatula or pancake turner to transfer the cookies to wire racks. Serve immediately or at room temperature.

Store: In an airtight container at room temperature.

Keeps: 1 month. Unbaked dough keeps 3 days refrigerated, 3 months frozen.

Smart Cookie

- There is no need to sift the flour if you have a scale and weigh the flour. Sifting is for accurate measure only in this recipe.

- Allow the cookie sheet(s) to cool completely before using for the next batch.
- Distribute the cookies evenly around the cookie sheet. Avoid crowding the cookies into one section of the cookie sheet, leaving a large area bare.

Savory Cheese Dollars   156

Pecan Tassies

Makes 4 dozen
1⅝-inch tassies

The Beranbaum family prefers these sticky, chewy tassies to the larger pecan pie, especially after a filling holiday dinner party. The soft, buttery cream cheese pastry blends perfectly with the sticky, buttery pecan filling. An important advantage of these cookies is that they can be made up to 2 weeks before the party and stored at room temperature, not using up valuable refrigerator or freezer space.

EQUIPMENT: *1¾-inch ungreased fluted tartlet tins with 1 tablespoon capacity; cookie sheets; reclosable quart-size freezer bag.*

Cream Cheese Pastry

Food Processor Method

Cut the butter into 1-inch cubes, wrap them in plastic wrap, and refrigerate.

In a food processor with the metal blade, process the flour and salt, just to mix them. Add the butter and cream cheese and pulse in until the dough starts to clump together.

Electric Mixer Method

Slightly soften the butter and cream cheese. In a mixing bowl, cream together the butter and cream

Cream Cheese Pastry

INGREDIENTS	MEASURE volume	WEIGHT ounces	grams
unsalted butter	8 tablespoons	4 ounces	113 grams
bleached all-purpose flour	1 cup (dip and sweep method)	5 ounces	145 grams
salt	¼ teaspoon	•	•
cream cheese	1 (3-ounce) package	3 ounces	85 grams

Pecan Filling

INGREDIENTS	MEASURE volume	WEIGHT ounces	grams
1 large egg, lightly beaten	3 tablespoons + ½ teaspoon	1.75 ounces (weighed without the shell)	50 grams
golden refiner's syrup *or* dark corn syrup	½ cup (use a greased liquid measuring cup)	6 ounces	170 grams
dark brown sugar	⅓ cup (firmly packed)	2.75 ounces	80 grams
unsalted butter, melted	2 tablespoons	1 ounce	28 grams
pure vanilla extract	1 teaspoon	•	4 grams
salt	pinch	•	•
pecan pieces *or* coarsely chopped pecans	1 cup	4 ounces	114 grams

cheese until blended. On low speed, beat in the flour and salt just until incorporated.

For Both Methods

Scrape the dough onto a piece of plastic wrap and shape the dough into a smooth ball. Measure the dough into rounded teaspoons and roll them between the palms of your hands into balls. Place them in the tartlet tins. If the dough becomes too soft to hold its shape, refrigerate it briefly. Use a floured index finger knuckle to press the dough against the sides of the tin. Be careful not to let the tin show through as the filling will stick to it.

Set the dough-lined tins, at least ½ inch apart, on cookie sheets and refrigerate them while making the filling.

Pecan Tassies   158

Chocolate Lace Topping (optional)

INGREDIENTS	MEASURE volume	WEIGHT ounces	grams
bittersweet or semisweet chocolate	²/₃ (3-ounce) bar	2 ounces	57 grams
flavorless vegetable oil	2 teaspoons	•	4.5 grams

ner of the bag. Let the chocolate mixture stand at room temperature until cooled and slightly thickened. Drizzle the chocolate over the tops of the cooled tassies.

Store: In an airtight container at room temperature.

Keeps: 2 weeks at room temperature.

Pecan Filling

Place 1 oven rack in the middle of the oven.

Preheat oven to 350°F.

In a medium bowl, combine the filling ingredients except for the pecans and stir them together until well blended. Stir in the pecans.

Spoon about 1 heaping teaspoon of filling into the pastry, filling it but not touching any exposed area of the tin.

Bake for 20 minutes or until set but still soft in the centers. For even baking, rotate the cookie sheet from front to back halfway through the baking period.

Allow the tassies to cool on the cookie sheets on wire racks. The tassies unmold more easily when cool. A small metal cuticle pusher is ideal to slip between the edge of the pastry and the fluted sides of the tin.

Chocolate Lace Topping

Break the chocolate into squares and place them, together with the oil, in the top of a double boiler set over very hot water (but no hotter than 160°F.). The water must not simmer or touch the bottom of the double-boiler insert. Stir until the chocolate begins to melt. Return the pan to low heat if the water cools, but be careful that it does not get too hot. (The chocolate may be melted in a microwave oven *if stirred every 15 seconds.*) Remove the chocolate from the heat source before it is fully melted and stir, using residual heat to complete the melting.

Dry any moisture that formed on the bottom of the chocolate container. Pour the melted chocolate into a reclosable quart-size freezer bag, close it securely, and cut off a small piece from one cor-

 ## Smart Cookie

- If you like a crispy top and pastry, allow the tassies to cool in the turned-off oven for 10 minutes. My personal preference is for a softer pastry.
- Refiner's syrup, available as Lyle's Golden Syrup in specialty stores such as Dean & DeLuca (page 229), is a by-product of sugar refining. It can be used in place of corn syrup and, to my taste, is a more delicious sweetener.
- If you only have 12 tartlet tins, it's fine to bake this recipe in batches. Be sure to stir the filling between batches so that it does not separate.
- If you prefer to make larger tassies, this recipe can be baked in 2 mini-muffin tins to make 2 dozen tassies. Increase the baking time to 25 to 30 minutes.

Praline Truffle Cups

Makes 3 dozen 1-inch bonbons

There's always room for a few exquisitely satisfying bonbons, even after the most lavish of holiday dinners. They are the ideal accompaniment to espresso. No one, however, will be disappointed if you serve these crisp, paper-thin cups of bittersweet chocolate with their creamy melting chocolate-hazlenut centers as dessert. These candies are easy to make, though a little time-consuming, and well worth the effort.

EQUIPMENT: *36 1-inch foil bonbon cups; small, clean, dry paintbrush; reclosable gallon-size freezer bag.*

Break 5 ounces of the chocolate into squares and place them in the top of a double boiler set over very hot water (but no hotter than 160°F.). The water must not simmer or touch the bottom of the double-boiler insert. Stir until the chocolate begins to melt. Return the pan to low heat if the water cools, but be careful that it does not get too hot. (The chocolate may be melted in a microwave oven *if stirred every 15 seconds.)* Remove the chocolate from the heat source before it is fully melted and stir, using residual heat to complete the melting. Keep the chocolate warm over a bowl of warm water (water must not exceed 120°F.).

INGREDIENTS	MEASURE volume	WEIGHT ounces	grams
extra bittersweet, bittersweet, *or* semisweet chocolate	3 (3-ounce) bars	9 ounces	255 grams
heavy cream	1/2 liquid cup	4 ounces	116 grams
unsalted butter (softened)	2 teaspoons	•	10 grams
praline paste*	2 tablespoons	1.5 ounces	40 grams
Frangelico liqueur	4 teaspoons	•	•

*Praline paste is available in specialty food stores such as Maison Glass (page 229).

Using a small paintbrush, coat the inside of the bonbon cups with the chocolate. Use all of the chocolate or spoon the excess onto a piece of aluminum foil and, when it hardens, reserve it for another use. Be sure to coat the cups completely, with no foil showing through. Two thin coats are best. Refrigerate the coated cups for at least 15 minutes.

Reheat the water in the bottom of the double boiler.

Break up the remaining 4 ounces of chocolate into the same double boiler top, set it over the hot water, and melt, stirring often. Gradually stir in the cream, then the butter and the praline paste, stirring until smooth.

Remove the top container from the lower one and stir in the liqueur. Spoon the chocolate mixture into the freezer bag, close it securely, and allow the mixture to cool to room temperature.

Cut a small corner from the bag and pipe the chocolate mixture into the chocolate-lined cups.

Refrigerate for at least 2 hours or until completely firm.

Serve in the foil cups or carefully peel away the foil. The truffle cups are good at room temperature, but I love the flavor and texture even better when they are chilled.

Store: In an airtight container at room temperature or in the refrigerator.

Keeps: 3 days at room temperature, 3 weeks refrigerated.

 ### Smart Cookie

- Chocolate picks up other flavors. Beware of uncovered garlic or other incompatible aromas in your refrigerator.
- When melting the chocolate, even a drop of water will cause it to seize and become unworkable.

The Ultimate Lemon Butter Bar

Makes 1½ dozen 2⅔-inch by 1⅓-inch bars

Ihis classic cookie combines two of my favorite sweets: buttery-tender Scottish shortbread and satiny lilting English lemon curd. The problem has always been getting a firm enough topping and avoiding a soggy shortbread base. The special technique discovered for this recipe virtually guarantees success.

The clean, refreshing flavor of lemon makes these the perfect sweets to follow a rich Christmas goose.

EQUIPMENT: *8-inch by 8-inch by 2-inch baking pan, preferably metal (if using a glass pan, lower the oven temperature 25° F.), bottom and 2 sides lined with an 8-inch by 16-inch strip of heavy-duty aluminum foil.*

Shortbread Base

Food Processor Method

Cut the butter into 1-inch cubes, wrap it, and refrigerate.

In a food processor with the metal blade, process the sugars for 1 minute or so, until the sugar is very fine. Add the butter and pulse in until the sugar disappears. Add the flour and pulse in until there are a lot of little moist crumbly

Shortbread Base

INGREDIENTS	MEASURE	WEIGHT	
	volume	*ounces*	*grams*
unsalted butter (cold)	8 tablespoons	4 ounces	113 grams
powdered sugar	2 tablespoons	0.5 ounce	14 grams
granulated sugar	2 tablespoons	0.75 ounce	25 grams
bleached all-purpose flour	1¼ cups (dip and sweep method)	6.25 ounces	180 grams

pieces and no dry flour particles remain.

Dump the mixture into a plastic bag and press it together. Remove the dough from the plastic bag and knead it lightly until it holds together.

Electric Mixer Method or by Hand

In Scotland, it is said that the best shortbread is mixed with the fingers and that each woman's fingers lend something distinctive and special to the finished cookie. I find that the texture is more delicate when the dough is mixed with the fingers rather than in a machine. For either method, use superfine sugar for the best texture and be sure to soften the butter.

In a medium bowl, whisk together the sugars. In a large bowl, cream the butter with the sugars until light and fluffy. With your fingers or with the electric mixer, mix in the flour until incorporated. If using the mixer, add the flour in 2 parts.

For Both Methods

Place 1 oven rack in the middle of the oven.

Preheat oven to 325°F.

Pat the dough into the prepared pan. Use a fork to prick the dough all over.

Bake for about 50 minutes or until the edges are lightly browned and the top is pale golden (do not brown).

While the shortbread is baking, prepare the Lemon Curd Topping.

Lemon Curd Topping

Have a strainer, suspended over a bowl, ready near the range.

In a heavy noncorrodible saucepan, beat the egg yolks and sugar with a wooden spoon until well blended. Stir in the lemon juice, butter, and salt. Cook over medium-low heat, stirring constantly, for about 6 minutes, until thickened and resembling hollandaise sauce, which thickly coats a wooden spoon but is still liquid enough to pour. (A candy thermometer will read 196°F.) The mixture will change from translucent to opaque and begin to take on a yellow

color on the back of a wooden spoon. It must not be allowed to boil or it will curdle. (It will steam above 140°F. Whenever steaming occurs, remove the pan briefly from the heat, stirring constantly to prevent boiling.)

When the curd has thickened, pour it at once into the strainer. Press it with the back of a spoon until only the coarse residue remains. Discard the residue. Stir in the lemon zest.

When the shortbread is baked, remove it from the oven, lower the temperature to 300°F., pour the lemon curd on top of the shortbread, and return it to the oven for 10 minutes.

Cool the lemon curd–topped shortbread completely in the pan on a wire rack. Refrigerate the pan for 30 minutes to set the lemon curd completely before cutting into bars. Place the powdered sugar in a strainer and tap the strainer with a spoon to sprinkle a thick, even coating, entirely covering the lemon.

Run a small metal spatula between the sides of the pan and the pastry on the 2 sides without the aluminum foil. Use the foil to lift out the lemon curd–covered shortbread onto a cutting surface. Use a long, sharp knife to cut the shortbread first in thirds, then in half the other way, and then each half in thirds. Wipe the blade after each cut.

The powdered sugar will start to be absorbed into the lemon curd after several hours, but it can be reapplied before serving.

Store: In an airtight container at room temperature, or in the refrigerator or freezer.

Lemon Curd Topping

INGREDIENTS	MEASURE	WEIGHT	
	volume	*ounces*	*grams*
4 large egg yolks	2 full fluid ounces	2.5 ounces	74 grams
sugar	³/₄ cup	5.25 ounces	150 grams
lemon juice, freshly squeezed (about 2¹/₂ large lemons)	3 fluid ounces (use a liquid measuring cup)	3.25 ounces	94 grams
unsalted butter (softened)	4 tablespoons	2 ounces	57 grams
salt	pinch	•	•
lemon zest	2 teaspoons (finely grated)	•	4 grams
powdered sugar for dusting	2 tablespoons	0.5 ounce	14 grams

Keeps: 3 days at room temperature, 3 weeks refrigerated (individually wrapped in plastic wrap to prevent drying), or 3 months frozen.

Smart Cookie

- Cooking the topping before pouring it onto the shortbread ensures crispness as opposed to the usual pastiness of the pastry.
- Returning the curd to the oven, where it will be exposed to heat without stirring, causes the yolk to rebond, making it firm enough to cut after cooling.
- If each lemon is heated about 10 seconds in a microwave oven on high power and rolled around while pressing on it lightly, it will release a significantly greater quantity of juice.
- An aluminum pan should not be used to prepare the lemon curd because it will react with the egg yolks, turning them chartreuse.
- Sugar raises the coagulation point of the egg yolk. It also protects it from premature coagulation during the addition of the lemon juice. If the juice were added directly to the unprotected yolk, the yolk would partially coagulate and, when strained, a large percentage of it would be left behind in the strainer. Be sure to mix the sugar well with the egg yolks before adding the juice.

Chocolate-Orange Paradise Bars

Makes 1½ dozen 1⅓-inch by 2⅔-inch bars

Since I adore lemon butter bars, one day I started to fantasize about what an orange version would taste like. Since orange and chocolate are such a divine combination, it didn't take long to devise a chocolate shortbread base. The fudgy, crumbly chocolate shortbread is so heavenly with the creamy orange curd it seemed inevitable to crown it with still more orangy chocolate—silky-smooth Grand Marnier ganache—laced over the top. These bars are lovely served as dessert or any time at all.

EQUIPMENT: *8-inch by 8-inch by 2-inch baking pan, preferably metal (if using a glass pan, lower the oven temperature 25° F.), bottom and 2 sides lined with an 8-inch by 16-inch strip of heavy-duty aluminum foil; reclosable quart-size freezer bag.*

Chocolate Shortbread Base

Food Processor Method

Cut the butter into 1-inch cubes, wrap it, and refrigerate.

Chocolate Shortbread Base

INGREDIENTS	MEASURE volume	WEIGHT ounces	grams
unsalted butter (cold)	8 tablespoons	4 ounces	113 grams
powdered sugar	2 tablespoons	0.5 ounce	14 grams
granulated sugar	2 tablespoons	0.75 ounce	25 grams
unsweetened cocoa (preferably Dutch-processed)	¼ cup (lightly spooned into the cup)	0.75 ounce	23 grams
bleached all-purpose flour	1 cup (dip and sweep method)	5 ounces	145 grams

In a food processor with the metal blade, process the sugars with the cocoa for 1 minute or so, until very fine. Add the butter and pulse in until the butter and sugars are well combined. Add the flour and pulse in until there are a lot of little moist crumbly pieces and no dry flour particles remain.

Dump the mixture into a plastic bag and press it together. Remove the dough from the plastic bag and knead it lightly until it holds together.

Electric Mixer Method or by Hand

In Scotland, it is said that the best shortbread is mixed with the fingers and that each woman's fingers lend something distinctive and special to the finished cookie. I find that the texture is more delicate when the dough is mixed with the fingers rather than in a machine. For either method, use superfine sugar for the best texture and be sure to soften the butter.

In a medium bowl, whisk together the sugars and cocoa. In a large bowl, cream the butter with the cocoa mixture until light and fluffy. With your fingers or with the electric mixer, mix in the flour until incorporated. If using the mixer, add the flour in 2 parts.

For Both Methods

Place 1 oven rack in the middle of the oven.

Preheat oven to 325°F.

Pat the dough into the prepared pan. At first the dough will be dry and crumbly, but the heat of your hands quickly makes it blissfully soft and supple. Use a fork to prick the dough all over.

Bake for 1 hour.

While the shortbread is baking, prepare the Orange Curd Topping.

Orange Curd Topping

Pour the orange juice into a greased 4-cup heatproof measure. Microwave it on high power until it is reduced to 2 tablespoons. This will take about 15 minutes. Watch closely toward the end as the juice gets very syrupy and reduces quickly. (Or reduce the juice in a

Orange Curd Topping

INGREDIENTS	MEASURE	WEIGHT	
	volume	ounces	grams
orange juice, freshly squeezed (3 large oranges)	1 cup (use a liquid measuring cup)	8.5 ounces	242 grams
unsalted butter (softened)	4 tablespoons	2 ounces	57 grams
4 large egg yolks	2 full fluid ounces	2.5 ounces	74 grams
sugar	½ cup	3.5 ounces	100 grams
salt	pinch	•	•
zest from 3 large oranges, removed in lengthwise strips with a vegetable peeler	2 tablespoons (finely chopped)	•	12 grams

Orange Ganache Lace Topping

INGREDIENTS	MEASURE	WEIGHT	
	volume	ounces	grams
bittersweet chocolate, finely chopped	⅓ (3-ounce) bar	1 ounce	28 grams
heavy cream	2 tablespoons	1 ounce	30 grams
Grand Marnier	1½ teaspoons	•	•

Orange Ganache Lace Topping

In a small bowl, place the chopped chocolate.

In a microwave oven or saucepan, bring the heavy cream to the boiling point. Pour it on top of the chocolate and stir until smooth. Cool to room temperature and stir in the Grand Marnier.

Pour the mixture into a reclosable quart-size freezer bag and close it securely. Set aside.

When the orange curd–covered shortbread has cooled, cut off a small corner from the bag. Drizzle swirls of chocolate over the top of the orange curd. (You will not need all of the topping. Any left-over topping is delicious on ice cream.)

Run a small metal spatula between the sides of the pan and the pastry on the 2 sides without the aluminum foil. Before the chocolate drizzle sets, use the foil to lift out the orange curd–covered shortbread onto a cutting surface. Use a long, sharp knife to cut the shortbread first in thirds, then in half the other way, and then each half in thirds. Wipe the blade after each cut.

Store: In an airtight container at room temperature, or in the refrigerator or freezer.

Keeps: 3 days at room temperature, 3 weeks refrigerated (individually wrapped in plastic wrap to prevent drying), or 3 months frozen.

saucepan over high heat stirring occasionally.) Stir the butter into the concentrated orange juice.

In a heavy noncorrodible saucepan, beat the egg yolks and sugar with a wooden spoon until well blended. Stir in the orange mixture, salt, and orange zest. The mixture will be very thick. Cook over low heat, stirring constantly, for about 3 minutes or until it pools up on the surface when dropped from a spoon. (A candy thermometer will read 155°F. to 160°F.) It must not be allowed to boil or it will curdle. (It will steam above 140°F. Whenever steam occurs, remove the pan briefly from the heat, stirring constantly to prevent boiling.)

When the curd has thickened, pour it at once into a bowl.

When the shortbread is baked, remove it from the oven, lower the temperature to 300°F., pour the orange curd on top of the shortbread, and return it to the oven for 5 minutes.

Cool completely in the pan on a wire rack. While it is cooling, prepare the Orange Ganache Lace Topping.

Smart
Cookie

- Cooking the topping before pouring it onto the shortbread ensures crispness as opposed to the usual pastiness of the pastry.
- Returning the curd to the oven, where it will be exposed to heat without stirring, causes the yolk to rebond, making it firm enough to cut after cooling.
- If each orange is heated about 10 seconds in a microwave oven on high power and rolled around while pressing on it lightly, it will release a significantly greater quantity of juice.
- A microwave oven is ideal for reducing the orange juice as the saucepan method may caramelize the juice slightly, affecting the color of the finished curd.
- An aluminum pan should not be used to prepare the orange curd because it will react with the egg yolks, turning them an off color.
- Sugar raises the coagulation point of the egg yolk. It also protects it from premature co-agulation during the addition of the orange juice. If the juice were added directly to the un-protected yolk, the yolk would partially coagulate. Be sure to mix the sugar well with the egg yolks before adding the juice.
- Blood orange curd makes an appealing variation because of its beautiful pink color. To make blood orange curd, reduce 1 cup of blood orange juice to only $1/4$ cup of juice as it is more acidic and will thicken the curd more than ordinary orange juice.

Chocolate-Orange Paradise Bars   168

Chocolate Moist Madeleines

Makes 3 dozen
3-inch madeleines

Although madeleines are traditionally dry and spongy and were designed to be dipped in tea, it's great not to have to. So these chocolate madeleines have been created as intensely chocolate, *moist* little cakes but still retain the classic shell shape. If you are an inveterate Proustian madeleine dunker, simply allow them to dry out for a day or two and these too will be perfectly suitable for that ritual. Incidentally, chocolate madeleines are also splendid when served with after-dinner coffee, Cognac, or other spirits.

INGREDIENTS	MEASURE volume	WEIGHT ounces	grams
unsweetened cocoa (Dutch-processed)	3 tablespoons + 1½ teaspoons	0.75 ounce	21 grams
boiling water	3 tablespoons	1.5 ounces	44 grams
3 large eggs	scant 5 fluid ounces	5.25 ounces	150 grams (weighed without the shells)
pure vanilla extract	1½ teaspoon	•	6 grams
sifted cake flour (not self-rising)	1¼ cups (sift into the cup and level off)	4.5 ounces	125 grams
sugar	¾ cup + 2 tablespoons	6 ounces	175 grams
baking powder	¾ teaspoon	•	3.7 grams
salt	¼ teaspoon	•	•
unsalted butter (softened)	13 tablespoons	6.5 ounces	184 grams

EQUIPMENT: *buttered madeleine molds; reclosable gallon-size freezer bag.*

Place 2 oven racks in the upper and lower thirds of the oven. Preheat oven to 350°F.

Electric Mixer Method

In a medium mixing bowl, whisk together the cocoa and water until smooth. Allow the mixture to cool to room temperature, then lightly whisk in the eggs and vanilla extract.

In a large mixing bowl, combine the remaining dry ingredients and mix on low speed for 30 seconds to blend. Add half the chocolate mixture and the butter to the dry ingredients. Mix on low speed until the dry ingredients are moistened. On medium speed (high speed if using a hand-held mixer), beat for 1 minute to aerate and develop the structure. Scrape the sides of the bowl. Gradually add the remaining chocolate mixture in 2 batches, beating for 20 seconds after each addition to incorporate the ingredients and strengthen the structure. Scrape the sides of the bowl.

Scrape the batter into the freezer bag, close it securely, and cut off a small piece from one of the corners of the bag. Pipe the batter into the prepared molds, filling them not quite full. Leave the remaining batter in the bag, refrigerated, for the following batches.

Bake for 10 to 12 minutes or until a tester inserted in the center comes out clean and the madeleines spring back when pressed lightly in the centers. For even baking, rotate the molds from top to bottom and front to back halfway through the baking time.

Unmold the madeleines onto wire racks to cool completely.

Syrup

In a small pan, stir together the sugar and water. Bring to a full rolling boil. Cover immediately and remove the pan from the heat. When cool, swirl in the Kahlúa.

If desired, brush the madeleines on both sides with the syrup.

Syrup (optional)

INGREDIENTS	MEASURE	WEIGHT	
	volume	*ounces*	*grams*
sugar	2 tablespoons	1 ounce	25 grams
water	¼ cup	2 ounces	60 grams
Kahlúa	1 tablespoon	•	17 grams

Wrap each one separately in plastic wrap. For the most attractive appearance, store them without the syrup and brush on the syrup a day or so before you plan to serve them.

Store: In an airtight container at room temperature, or in the refrigerator or freezer.

Keeps: 3 days without syrup, 1 week with syrup, at room temperature; 2 weeks refrigerated; 3 months frozen.

 Smart Cookie

- If you do not have enough madeleine molds to bake all the batter at one time, store the batter in the refrigerator and bake it in batches. Rinse out the molds after each batch and butter them.
- If you are planning to use the madeleines to dunk, omit the syrup; madeleines should be a little dry so that they act like sponges. The syrup helps to preserve the moistness and will greatly extend their keeping qualities, which is helpful if you are planning to give them as gifts.
- The syrup allows the cookies to keep over 1 week at room temperature. If you are planning to eat them the same day or the next, omit the syrup or use only a sprinkle of Kahlúa. The subtle coffee flavor accentuates the chocolate.

Maple Walnut Sablé Sandwiches

Makes about 2 dozen 3-inch leaf
sandwiches or about 3¹/₂ dozen
3-inch heart sandwiches

The *sablé*, which means "sand" in French, is a cookie found in every *boulangerie* in France. Because the least amount of flour possible has to be added, they are a bit painstaking to make, but the fragile, buttery results are extraordinary. Delicious served plain, they are elevated to a glorious new stature when pressed around the classic New England flavors of maple and walnut. These are truly a labor of love, but, boy, are they worth it!

INGREDIENTS *Do not make these cookies in warm weather or in a hot kitchen*	MEASURE volume	WEIGHT ounces	grams
unsalted butter (cold)	1 cup	8 ounces	227 grams
cake flour (not self-rising)	¹/₂ cup (dip and sweep method)	2.25 ounces	65 grams
bleached all-purpose flour	1¹/₂ cups (dip and sweep method)	7.5 ounces	215 grams
salt	¹/₄ teaspoon	•	•
sugar	³/₄ cup	5.25 ounces	150 grams
toasted walnuts*	¹/₄ cup	1 ounce	25 grams
2 large egg yolks	2 tablespoons + 1 teaspoon	1.25 ounces	37 grams
pure vanilla extract	2 teaspoons	•	8 grams

*Although not necessary, toasting brings out the flavor of nuts. In a small toaster oven or regular oven, toast the nuts at 350°F. for about 10 minutes and allow them to cool completely.

EQUIPMENT: *buttered cookie sheets, refrigerated; plastic wrap or a floured pastry cloth and floured rolling pin sleeve; 3-inch maple leaf or 3-inch scalloped heart cookie cutter.*

Cut the butter into 1-inch cubes, wrap in plastic wrap, and refrigerate.

In a small bowl, whisk together the flours and salt.

In a food processor with the metal blade, process the sugar and walnuts until they are powder fine. Add the butter and process until well blended. Add the egg yolks and vanilla extract and pulse in until incorporated, scraping the sides of the bowl. Add the flour mixture and pulse in just until incorporated.

Scrape the dough onto a counter and smear it 2 or 3 times using the palm of your hand. The dough will be very soft. Scrape the dough onto a piece of plastic wrap and refrigerate it for 2 hours until well chilled, but preferably no longer than 3 hours.

Place 2 oven racks in the upper and lower thirds of the oven.

Preheat oven to 350°F.

Roll out the dough on a floured pastry cloth or well-floured surface to a ¹/₈-inch thickness. Slide the dough onto the chilled cookie sheets, cover with plastic wrap, and refrigerate for at least 15 minutes or until firm enough to make cutouts.

Cut out the dough with the cookie cutter and remove the scraps between the desired shapes with a small metal spatula. (Or roll out the dough between 2 sheets of plastic wrap, cut out the dough with a cookie cutter, remove the scraps of dough between the desired shapes with a small metal spatula, and refrigerate the dough for 15 minutes or until firm enough to peel off the plastic.) If

the cookie cutter is not perfectly symmetrical, flip over half the cookies before placing them on the cookie sheets so that you will be able to make perfectly shaped sandwiches.

Gather up the scraps, wrap them in plastic wrap, press them into a thin disc, and place the disc in the freezer to quick-chill before rerolling the dough.

With the dull back of a knife, mark lines resembling veins on the cookies.

Bake for 8 to 10 minutes or until *barely* beginning to brown around the edges. For even baking, rotate the cookie sheets from top to bottom and front to back halfway through the baking period.

Use a small, angled metal spatula or pancake turner to transfer the cookies to wire racks to cool completely. They are fragile when hot.

Maple Walnut Buttercream Filling

Have ready a greased or buttered 1-cup heatproof glass measure near the range.

In a small bowl, beat the egg yolks with a hand-held electric mixer until they are pale yellow in color. Set aside.

In a small saucepan (preferably with a nonstick lining), on low heat, bring the sugar and maple syrup to a boil, stirring constantly. Stop stirring and allow the syrup to come to a rolling boil (the entire surface will be covered with large bubbles). *Immediately trans-*

Maple Walnut Buttercream Filling

INGREDIENTS	MEASURE	WEIGHT	
	volume	*ounces*	*grams*
2 large egg yolks	2 tablespoons + 1 teaspoon	1.25 ounces	37 grams
sugar	¹/₄ cup	2 ounces	50 grams
pure maple syrup	2 tablespoons + 2 teaspoons	1 ounce	25 grams
unsalted butter (softened)	12 tablespoons	6 ounces	170 grams
maple flavoring	¹/₂ teaspoon	•	•
toasted walnuts,* chopped very finely but not powder fine	¹/₄ cup	1 ounce	25 grams

*Although not necessary, toasting brings out the flavor of nuts. In a small toaster oven or regular oven, toast the nuts at 350°F. for about 10 minutes and allow them to cool completely.

fer the syrup to the glass measure to stop the cooking.

Beat the syrup into the egg yolks in a steady stream, avoiding pouring the syrup on the beaters. Continue beating until the mixture is *completely* cool. Beat in the butter by the tablespoon until the buttercream is smooth and creamy. On low speed, beat in the maple flavoring and walnuts.

To Fill the Cookies

These cookies are so fragile that they need the support of a flat work surface. Do not hold them in your hand while spreading them with the buttercream.

Place half of the cookies top sides down on the work surface. Use a rounded teaspoon of filling for leaf-shaped cookies, 2 level measuring teaspoons of filling for heart-shaped cookies. Using a small angled metal spatula, spread the buttercream on the cookies. (If

desired, the buttercream can be piped onto the cookie bottoms using a number 8 [³/₈-inch diameter] small decorating tube.) Place a second cookie bottom side against the buttercream and press the 2 cookies together gently.

Store: Unfilled cookies: In an airtight container at room temperature or in the freezer.

Filling: In an airtight container at room temperature, or in the refrigerator or freezer.

Filled cookies: In an airtight container at room temperature, or in the refrigerator or freezer.

Keeps: Unfilled cookies: Several weeks at room temperature, several months frozen.

Filling: 1 day at room temperature, 1 week refrigerated, 8 months frozen.

Filled cookies: 1 day at room temperature, about 1 week refrigerated, 1 month frozen. Refrigerated or frozen, filled cookies lose some of their crispness but still taste wonderful.

 Smart
Cookie

- The less flour worked into the dough, the more tender the cookie. Nuts are added for a more tender texture rather than for their flavor.
- Don't overmix the dough after the flour has been added or it will toughen.

- The dough can be made with an electric mixer or using your fingers, but the food processor works best. It makes possible the least amount of handling and heat transfer from your hands, makes the finest grind of nuts and sugar, and produces the most delicate *sablés*.
- If the kitchen is hot, work with only part of the dough at a time and refrigerate the rest.
- The maple leaf cutters are available through Hammer Song (page 249).
- If you are using plastic wrap to roll out the dough, Saran Wrap is the ideal plastic wrap for rolling the dough because it lies very flat. Wax paper is the second choice.
- If the dough cracks while rolling it, cut it in quarters and allow it to soften until it is more malleable before continuing.
- Allow the cookie sheet(s) to cool completely before using for the next batch.
- Distribute the cookies evenly around the cookie sheet. Avoid crowding the cookies into one section of the cookie sheet, leaving a large area bare.
- The maple flavoring adds an attractive color and slightly intensifies the maple flavor in a very pleasant way.

Linzer Squares and Thumbprints

Makes 16 2-inch
squares plus about 3 dozen
thumbprint cookies

This favorite Austrian pastry also makes wonderful cookies. I love making them as squares because that shape offers the best balance of jam to dough; round thumbprint cookies are also very attractive and more crunchy. An egg white has been added to some of the dough to make it possible to pipe a decorative lattice, which is so much easier than trying to roll and cut this tender, nutty pastry. The egg white also contributes a crisper upper crust, creating a greater variety of textures.

My tart, homemade raspberry jam makes the most extraordinary Linzer cookies, but they are also excellent with your favorite commercially made jam.

INGREDIENTS	MEASURE volume	WEIGHT ounces	grams
unblanched whole hazelnuts	1 cup	5 ounces	142 grams
unsalted butter (cold)	1 cup	8 ounces	227 grams
bleached all-purpose flour	2 cups (dip and sweep method)	10 ounces	290 grams
sugar	2/3 cup	4.5 ounces	132 grams
baking powder	1 teaspoon	•	5 grams
ground cinnamon	1 teaspoon	•	•
salt	1/4 teaspoon	•	•
2 large eggs, separated yolks	2 tablespoons + 1 teaspoon	1.25 ounces	37 grams
whites, lightly beaten	1/4 liquid cup	2 ounces	60 grams
pure vanilla extract	1 teaspoon	•	4 grams
lemon zest	1 tablespoon (finely grated)	•	6 grams
Cordon Rose Raspberry Conserve (recipe follows) or seedless raspberry jam	1 cup	10.5 ounces	300 grams
Nut Coating (optional for cookies)			
unblanched hazelnuts, chopped finely	2/3 cup	3.25 ounces	94 grams
Optional: powdered sugar for dusting			

EQUIPMENT FOR THE SQUARES: *8-inch by 8-inch by 2-inch baking pan, preferably metal (if using a glass pan, lower the oven temperature 25°F.), bottom and 2 sides lined with an 8-inch by 16-inch strip of heavy-duty aluminum foil, well buttered or greased; pastry bag, fitted with a coupler and number 12 (5/16-inch diameter) decorating tube (a reclosable freezer bag is not strong enough for this stiff dough).*

EQUIPMENT FOR THE COOKIES: *2 nonstick, buttered, or greased cookie sheets; reclosable quart-size freezer bag or pastry bag, fitted with a coupler and a number 12 (5/16-inch diameter) round decorating tube or 1/4 teaspoon measuring spoon.*

Place 2 oven racks in the upper and lower thirds of the oven.

Preheat oven to 350°F.

Place the hazelnuts on a cookie sheet and bake them, stirring occasionally, for 10 to 12 minutes or

until they turn golden where the skins crack. Cool to room temperature.

Food Processor Method

Cut the butter into 1-inch cubes, wrap in plastic wrap, and refrigerate.

In a food processor with the metal blade, process the nuts with $1/2$ cup of the flour until the nuts are fine but not powder fine. Add the rest of the flour, the sugar, baking powder, cinnamon, and salt and process for a few seconds until evenly mixed. Pulse in the butter until mixture has the consistency of fine crumbs. Add the egg yolks, vanilla extract, and lemon zest and pulse just until the dough begins to hold together (do not allow it to form a ball).

Electric Mixer Method

Finely grate the nuts. Soften the butter. In a medium bowl, whisk together the flour, baking powder, cinnamon, salt, and lemon zest. In a mixing bowl, cream the butter and sugar about 3 minutes or until light and fluffy. Beat in the egg yolks, then the vanilla extract. At low speed, gradually beat in the flour mixture just until the dough begins to hold together.

For the Squares

Remove 1 cup of the dough and press it into the prepared pan. Spread $2/3$ cup of the jam to within $1/4$ inch of the edges. Set aside.

Add 3 tablespoons of the egg whites to the dough remaining in the food processor or mixer and pulse or beat until it is incorporated. (Set aside the remaining egg whites for the cookies.)

Scrape 1 cup of the dough into the pastry bag and close it securely. Pipe the mixture to form a lattice on top of the raspberry filling. Pipe the first line down the center, dividing the square in half. Now pipe 2 more lines, dividing the square into quarters. Then pipe 4 more lines, each between the existing lines, dividing the square into eighths. There will be 7 lines.

Turn the square 1 turn and repeat the process, adding 7 more lines. Next pipe a border line around the 4 edges of the square.

Bake for 30 to 35 minutes or until the dough is golden brown and the jam bubbling.

Cool completely in the pan on a wire rack.

To unmold, run a small metal spatula between the sides of the pan and the pastry on the 2 sides without the aluminum foil. Use the foil to lift out the whole square and slide it off the foil onto a cutting surface. Use a long, serrated knife to cut 2-inch squares. For the most attractive squares, first cut the square in half right in the middle of the center lattice line. Then cut into quarters, always cutting in the middle of the piped lattice line (not on either side). Turn the square 1 turn and cut it into quarters following the same directions, forming the 2-inch squares.

For the Cookies

Measure the remaining dough into a $1 1/4$-inch scoop or 2 level teaspoons and roll it between the palms of your hands to form 1-inch balls. If you are using the optional nut coating, roll each ball in the reserved egg whites. Lightly flour your hands, if necessary, to prevent sticking. Roll each ball in the chopped nuts.

Place the balls $1 1/2$ inches apart on the cookie sheets. Use your floured index finger to create depressions in the center of each ball. Fill each depression with $1/4$ teaspoon of the remaining jam, using the reclosable bag or the spoon.

Bake for 20 minutes or until the cookies begin to brown lightly. For even baking, rotate the cookie sheets from top to bottom and front to back halfway through the baking period.

Use a small, angled metal spatula or pancake turner to transfer the cookies to wire racks to cool completely.

If desired, dust the cookies with powdered sugar.

Store: In an airtight container at room temperature or in the refrigerator.

Keeps: 1 week at room temperature, 2 weeks refrigerated. The cookie squares, made with jam, will keep for several weeks refrigerated. The thumbprints become dry.

Smart Cookie

- In this particular dough, the dark skin of the hazelnuts adds a pleasant taste.
- For the squares, if you wish to dust them with powdered sugar after baking, as shown in the photograph, you also will need to pipe or spoon a little extra jam into the openings of the lattice after dusting.
- Allow the cookie sheet(s) to cool completely before using for the next batch.
- Distribute the cookies evenly around the cookie sheet. Avoid crowding the cookies into one section of the cookie sheet, leaving a large area bare.

Cordon Rose Raspberry Conserve

Makes 1 quart
(4 half-pint jars + ½ cup)
(2.5 lbs/1 kilogram 157 grams)

INGREDIENTS	MEASURE	WEIGHT	
	volume	pounds/ounces	kilograms/grams
sugar	2 cups + 2 tablespoons	15 ounces	425 grams
water	1 liquid cup + 2 tablespoons	9.25 ounces	266 grams
raspberries	3 quarts	3 pounds	1 kilogram 361 grams

This super-concentrated conserve is the very essence of raspberry. Its exceptional tartness makes it perfect to add to other sweets. It will spoil you for life. To use as a spread for toast, you may want to add extra sugar to taste.

In a large-diameter pot, combine the sugar and water and bring to a boil, stirring constantly. Boil for 1 minute. Add 3 to 4 cups of the berries (so that they are in a single layer) and boil for 1 minute. Remove with a slotted spoon or skimmer to a colander suspended over a bowl to catch the syrup. Reduce the syrup in the pot to 2 cups and repeat the procedure with more berries. From time to time return the syrup that drains from the cooked berries to the pot. Skim the white foam from the surface.

When the last batch of raspberries is completed, boil the syrup down to 2 cups (the temperature will be 210°F.) and reserve. Sieve the berries to remove most of the seeds. (When condensing raspberries to this degree, leaving all the seeds would be excessive; however some seeds lend a nice texture to the conserve. I use the colander and the sieve attachment on my KitchenAid, which has large enough holes to allow a few seeds

to pass through. You can also use a food mill fitted with the finest disc.) You should have 2 cups of raspberry pulp and ²/₃ cup of seeds.

Add the sieved berries to the reserved syrup and simmer for 10 minutes or until reduced to 4 cups. Fill canning jars which have been rinsed in boiling water, leaving ³/₈ inch of head space. Screw on the caps and place them in a water bath, covered, for 10 minutes after the water comes to a boil. Remove and allow to cool before checking the seal.

Jars in the water bath must be sitting on a rack to allow the water to flow all around them, and the water must be high enough to cover them by 1 inch. They must be upright to expel any air inside the jars, producing a vacuum which seals the jars. If this process is eliminated, be sure to store the conserve in a cool, dry area away from light as there are no preservatives in it to prevent mold from forming. (If mold does form, scrape it off and reboil the conserve.) The conserve takes 2 days in the jar to thicken.

Note: Half-pint jars can hold only 7 fluid ounces because of the ³/₈-inch head space required on top.

Refrigerate extra for up to 2 weeks.

Store: I have stored this conserve for as long as 4 years. The flavor does not deteriorate, but after 2 years the color deepens and is less bright.

 ## Smart Cookie

- *Formula:* 1 pound berries/5 ounces sugar/3 ounces water. A large unlined copper pot is traditional for jam-making because the faster the berries and syrup cook, the better the flavor and gelling. Be sure to use a pot with a large diameter to speed evaporation of the syrup.
- Raspberry growers do not recommend washing raspberries and assure us of no harmful effects. If washed, cook berries as soon as possible
- The conserve can be prepared using raspberries frozen without sugar. Allow them to defrost in a colander, reserving the juice. Add the juice to the sugar syrup and proceed as with fresh berries. The flavor will be indistinguishable from conserve prepared with fresh berries.

Mini-Cheesecakes with Lemon Curd or Cranberry Topping

Makes 2 dozen 1³/₄-inch cheesecakes

These little cakes are sensational. Creamy and tangy, for some mystical reason they are even more seductive tasting than a chunk of cheesecake and a lot more appropriate after a holiday dinner party.

Lemon Curd Topping is the perfect flavor complement, but the Cranberry Topping is a festive variation. These cheesecakes are small enough for your guests to try both, so make some of each.

EQUIPMENT: *2 1³/₄-inch by 1-inch mini-muffin pans (12 depressions in each pan), sprayed with non-stick vegetable cooking spray or greased or buttered; teaspoon or reclosable quart-size freezer bag; baking sheets.*

Place 2 oven racks in the upper and lower thirds of the oven.
Preheat oven to 375°F.

In a medium bowl, stir together the graham cracker crumbs and butter until evenly mixed.

Spoon 2 rounded teaspoons of the crumb mixture into each depression of the prepared pans and press into the bottoms and up the sides.

Cheesecakes

INGREDIENTS	MEASURE volume	WEIGHT ounces	grams
graham cracker crumbs (8 double cookies)	1 cup	3.75 ounces	110 grams
unsalted butter, melted	4 tablespoons	2 ounces	56 grams
cream cheese	1 (8-ounce) package	8 ounces	227 grams
sugar	¹/₃ cup	2.25 ounces	66 grams
1 large egg	3 tablespoons + ¹/₂ teaspoon	1.75 ounces (weighed without the shell)	50 grams
sour cream	2 tablespoons	1 ounce	30 grams
pure vanilla extract	¹/₂ teaspoon	•	2 grams
lemon juice, freshly squeezed	2 teaspoons	•	10 grams

Food Processor Method

In a food processor with the metal blade, process the cream cheese and sugar for about 30 seconds or until smooth. Add the egg and pulse in. Scrape the sides of the bowl. Add the sour cream, vanilla extract, and lemon juice and process for a few seconds or until uniformly mixed.

Electric Mixer Method

Soften the cream cheese. In a mixing bowl, beat the cream cheese and sugar about 3 minutes until very smooth, preferably with a whisk beater. Beat in the egg, scraping the sides of the bowl. Add the vanilla extract and lemon juice and beat until incorporated. Add the sour cream and beat just until the mixture is blended.

For Both Methods

Fill each graham cracker–lined depression almost to the top with the batter, using a spoon or a reclosable quart-size freezer bag with a piece cut off one of the corners of the bag.

Set the mini-muffin pans on baking sheets in the oven. Bake for 10 minutes. For even baking, rotate the pans from top to bottom and front to back halfway through the baking period. The cakes will puff up but deflate on cooling, leaving shallow hollows perfect for filling with the toppings.

Cool completely in the pans on wire racks. Refrigerate for at least 3 hours.

Lemon Curd Topping

Have a strainer, suspended over a bowl, ready near the range.

In a heavy noncorrodible saucepan, beat the egg yolks and sugar with a wooden spoon until well blended. Stir in the remaining ingredients except the lemon zest. Cook over medium-low heat, stirring constantly for about 4 minutes, until thickened and resembling a thin hollandaise sauce, which thickly coats a wooden spoon but is still liquid enough to pour. (A candy thermometer will read 196°F.) The mixture will change from translucent to opaque and begin to take on a yellow color on the back of a wooden spoon. It must not be allowed to boil or it will curdle. (It will steam above 140°F. Whenever steam occurs, remove the pan briefly from the heat, stirring constantly to prevent boiling.)

When the curd has thickened, pour it at once into the strainer. Press it with the back of a spoon until only the coarse residue remains. Discard the residue. Stir in the lemon zest.

Spoon 1 level measuring teaspoon of lemon curd onto each little cheesecake.

Lemon Curd Topping

INGREDIENTS	MEASURE volume	WEIGHT ounces	grams
2 large egg yolks	2 tablespoons + 1 teaspoon	1.25 ounces	37 grams
sugar	1/4 cup + 2 tablespoons	2.5 ounces	75 grams
lemon juice, freshly squeezed	3 tablespoons (use a liquid measuring cup)	1.75 ounces	47 grams
unsalted butter (softened)	4 tablespoons	2 ounces	57 grams
salt	pinch	•	•
lemon zest	2 teaspoons (finely grated)	•	4 grams

Cranberry Topping

INGREDIENTS	MEASURE volume	WEIGHT ounces	grams
water	1/4 liquid cup	2 ounces	60 grams
sugar	1/4 cup + 2 tablespoons	2.75 ounces	75 grams
cranberries (fresh or frozen)	1 cup	3.5 ounces	100 grams
cornstarch	2 1/2 teaspoons	•	6 grams

Cranberry Topping

In a small saucepan, combine all the topping ingredients and bring to a boil, stirring constantly. Stop stirring, reduce the heat, and simmer for 1 minute, swirling the pan occasionally. The mixture will be thickened but pourable. Allow it to cool to room temperature.

Use a small spoon to place about 4 berries with the glaze onto each of the cheesecakes.

To Unmold the Chilled Cheesecakes

Fill the sink with a few inches of hot tap water. Carefully dip each pan into the water for about 30 seconds, being careful not to allow the water to get to the top of the pan.

Use a small metal spatula to slip in between the sides of the cakes and the pan to pop out the cakes. There is no need to run the spatula around the sides; the hot water makes unmolding easy.

Store: In an airtight container in the refrigerator.

Keeps: 1 week.

Smart Cookie

- Make lots of these; they really are addictive.

Brandy Snaps Filled with Whipped Cream

Makes 2 dozen 4-inch by
1-inch rolled cookies

For a sweeping finale to a grand holiday dinner, you can't find a fancier cookie than brandy snaps. I first tasted the packaged variety in England and wondered what all the fuss was about. Homemade, they are a very different matter indeed. These are crunchy, buttery, with a faint taste of caramel and a mysterious undertone of brandy.

EQUIPMENT: *2 nonstick or buttered or greased cookie sheets; 1-inch diameter greased dowel, broom handle, or cannoli mold.*

Place 2 oven racks in the upper and lower thirds of the oven.
Preheat oven to 350°F.

INGREDIENTS	MEASURE	WEIGHT	
	volume	*ounces*	*grams*
unsalted butter	10.5 tablespoons	5.25 ounces	150 grams
golden refiner's syrup *or* light corn syrup	2/3 cup (use a greased liquid measuring cup)	8 ounces	224 grams
light brown sugar	1/4 cup (firmly packed)	2 ounces	54 grams
ground ginger	1 1/4 teaspoons	•	•
salt	pinch	•	•
bleached all-purpose flour	1 cup (dip and sweep method)	5 ounces	145 grams
brandy	4 teaspoons	•	•

Whipped Cream Filling

INGREDIENTS	MEASURE	WEIGHT	
	volume	*pounds/ ounces*	*grams*
heavy cream	2 liquid cups	1 pound	464 grams
sugar	1 tablespoon	0.5 ounce	12 grams
brandy	2 teaspoons	•	•
pure vanilla extract	1 teaspoon	•	4 grams

In a heavy saucepan, combine the butter, syrup, sugar, ginger, and salt. Bring the mixture to a boil, stirring often. (Or place these ingredients in a 4-cup heatproof measure or bowl and microwave on high power for about 3 minutes or until boiling.)

Remove the container from the heat and whisk in the flour and brandy. Keep the batter warm and

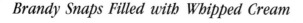

fluid by setting the container in a pan of hot water.

Drop the batter by the tablespoon onto the prepared cookie sheets. They will spread to about 4 inches, so bake only 4 at a time per sheet.

Bake for 7 to 10 minutes or until the cookies are a deep golden brown. For even baking, rotate the cookie sheets from top to bottom and front to back halfway through the baking period.

Allow the cookies to cool on the sheets for about 1 minute or until they can be lifted without wrinkling but are still flexible. Use a small, angled metal spatula or

pancake turner to lift the cookies from the sheets.

Roll each cookie tightly around the 1-inch dowel, pressing down firmly on the seam for a few moments. After it is rolled, place each cookie seam side down on a wire rack to cool. If cookies become too rigid to roll, return them briefly to the oven.

Repeat with the remaining batter. It is not necessary to cool the cookie sheets between batches.

Store: In an airtight container at room temperature.

Keeps: 1 week.

Note: You can fill the brandy snaps with whipped cream up to 2 hours ahead if you are refrigerating them or 1 hour ahead if they will be held at room temperature. Any further ahead and the brandy snaps will lose their lovely crispness. The cream can be whipped several hours ahead, refrigerated, and lightly rebeaten before using it.

EQUIPMENT: *reclosable gallon-size freezer bag or pastry bag, fitted with a number 8 large star pastry tube.*

Whipped Cream Filling

In a large mixing bowl, place all the filling ingredients and refrigerate for at least 15 minutes. (Chill the beater alongside the bowl.) Beat until stiff peaks form when the beater is raised.

Spoon the whipped cream into the bag and pipe it into the brandy snaps.

 Smart Cookie

- Refiner's syrup, available as Lyle's Golden Syrup in specialty stores such as Dean & DeLuca (page 229), is a by-product of sugar refining. It can be used in place of corn syrup and, to my taste, is a more delicious sweetener.
- Distribute the cookies evenly around the cookie sheet. Avoid crowding the cookies into one section of the cookie sheet, leaving a large area bare.
- Because the cookie is so sweet, no sugar is added to the filling.
- For a delicious, more tart filling variation, omit the sugar and brandy. Beat 1 cup of Lemon Curd Topping (page 164) that has been thinned with 1 tablespoon of water into the whipped cream at the point when the beater marks are beginning to show distinctly in the whipped cream.

185   *Brandy Snaps Filled with Whipped Cream*

Notre Dame Gingerbread Cathedral

A Christmas cookie book would be incomplete without a gingerbread house, and the most awe-inspiring "house" is a cathedral. A cathedral such as the one pictured is an ambitious project that takes about a week to complete, although it is possible to start making the gingerbread components several months ahead. It is also possible to use some of the elements in this design for inspiration and to construct your own design on a smaller or even grander scale.

Most people won't make this elaborate a structure, as all the details make it labor-intensive. But I am offering the complete instructions for this cathedral, ideal for craftspeople with impassioned souls and genius in their fingertips, people like Helen Raffels and Slobodan Saramandic, who designed it with me and constructed it. It is also perfect as a project for students or to enjoy with friends. However, I put this cathedral in the book for everyone who simply loves to dream.

BEFORE EMBARKING ON THIS PROJECT, READ THROUGH THE ENTIRE RECIPE AND PROCEDURES.

EQUIPMENT/MATERIALS:* $1/2$-inch-thick Fome-Cor® or plywood: 20 inches by 30 inches for the base; $3/16$-inch-thick Fome-Cor: 2 sheets, 20 inches by 30 inches, for substructure side pieces; $1/16$-inch-thick illustration board: 3 sheets, 20 inches by 30 inches, for substructure curved pieces and roof, patterns, and baking strips; surface for cutting out templates (cardboard or professional cutting board); hot glue gun and glue sticks or white glue for the substructural frame; masking tape for the cardboard substructure; ruler with metal edge; pushpins; craft or utility/matte knife for cutting Fome-Cor; graph paper (guidelines for icing decorations); aluminum foil, plastic wrap, wax paper, reclosable quart- and gallon-size freezer bags; paper towels; heavy cookie sheets; wire cooling racks; smooth table or countertop for rolling and drying dough; cutting surface (pastry board or acrylic cutting board); long rolling pin; small X-Acto razor saw; X-Acto knife with 10 or more no. 11 blades; terry cloth dish towel (the size of your cookie sheet); water spritzer; airtight containers for storing baked pieces; spatulas: large pancake type, small angled, artist's palette knife; paintbrushes: number 7 or number 8 square tip for cleanup of excess flour on candy windows, numbers 1 and 3 pointed tip for gilding; nail or dull side of knife blade for etching stone markings; tweezers for attaching star decorations; food processor; large hammer for pulverizing candies; small cups or disposable containers for the pulverized candies; tiny spoon such as a $1/8$ measuring teaspoon for filling window openings with candies; pastry bag or reclosable quart-size freezer bag, fitted with a coupler; Wilton or Ateco decorating tubes: no. 14 star for around rose windows, on frieze, front door sides, middle of buttresses; no. 18 star for roof crest and stars along lower roof edge; no. 3 round for front frieze; no. 5 round for dots around steeple window and on front frieze; no. 86 ruffle for borders along edges of roof (this also comes in a left-handed version); no. 172 drop flower (closed star) for front roof facade; no. 44 flat basketweave for edge of front steps; no. 46 flat basketweave for roof tiles; small fluorescent lighting fixture.

*Available at cake-decorating and artist supply stores.

Ingredients Shopping List

For 11 batches of Gingerbread

11 pounds bleached all-purpose flour

3 pounds dark brown sugar

3 pounds unsalted butter

6 (12-ounce) jars unsulfured molasses

2 ounces (about $3/4$ cup) baking soda

2 ($1/2$- to 2-ounce) jars ground ginger

1 jar *each* ground cinnamon, nutmeg, and cloves

For 4 batches of Royal Icing

1 dozen large egg whites *or* $3/4$ cup (3 ounces) meringue powder*

4 pounds powdered sugar

2 jars brown paste food coloring*

1 jar copper paste food coloring*

For Stained-glass Windows and Gilding

Life Saver roll candies: 30 rolls of multiflavored, 6 rolls of cherry

$1/2$ bag Brach's blue Mint Coolers or liquid blue food color

1 small jar gold petal dust*

100 proof vodka (a miniature bottle is more than enough)

To Make the Templates

Enlarge the drawings for the pattern pieces to full size, where 1 square equals 1 inch. This is most easily accomplished by photocopy, but it can also be done by drawing a grid.

Transfer the drawings onto illustration board or other heavy cardboard and use an X-Acto knife to cut them out. These templates will be used for the substructural frame and for the gingerbread dough cutouts.

To Build the Structural Supports

The base

A rigid $1/2$-inch-thick plywood or Fome-Cor 20-inch by 30-inch base is necessary to enable the cathedral to be moved after it has been constructed. The surface area that extends beyond the perimeter of the cathedral can be covered, as shown in the photograph, with pieces of baked gingerbread scraps, scored to resemble stones, and/or with fake snow, which is available in hobby or crafts stores. In order to position a light inside the cathedral, cut a slot in the middle of the base large enough to accommodate a fluorescent light fixture (it should be about $1/2$ inch larger than the light fixture).

The substructural frame

Refer to the drawings for the substructural frame.

Because the cathedral has 2 roofs at different levels, it is nec-

*Available through Maid of Scandinavia or the Chocolate Gallery, page 229 (the gold petal dust from the Chocolate Gallery is the most intense).

essary to build a simple frame that supports the roofs as they are placed in position against the side and back walls. This frame consists of 5 separate pieces that are glued together and then glued down to the base. The 4 side pieces are made of $3/16$-inch Fome-Cor and the 2 back pieces are made of thinner $1/16$-inch illustration board. The back pieces need to be scored in order to bend them into the curved shape at the back of the cathedral. For additional stability for the upper roof, I recommend using the Fome-Cor scored in the middle for the 2 main sections of the roof and the 2 small gables.

Use the templates to draw the frame directly onto the Fome-Cor and illustration board.

For the lower-level sides (make 2): Draw a 15-inch by $3^5/8$-inch rectangle on the Fome-Cor. Draw the outline of the windows. Use an X-Acto knife to cut out the windows, making the openings slightly larger than the cutouts so that they will not be visible when covered with the gingerbread panels.

For the upper-level sides (make 2): Draw a 15-inch by 9-inch rectangle on the Fome-Cor. Draw the outline for all window openings. Cut out the rectangles from the bottom. They are larger than the bottom-level window openings so that the support does not obstruct the light or become visible through the bottom windows. Cut out the windows, making the openings slightly larger than the cutouts.

For the back lower level: Draw a 15-inch by $3^5/8$-inch rectangle on the illustration board. Draw the outline for the windows and also the dotted vertical lines. Use an X-

Acto knife to cut out the windows, making the openings slightly larger than the cutouts. Also with the X-Acto knife, score the cardboard along each of the vertical lines so that it still holds together but can be bent cleanly at each line. After bending it in place, run a piece of masking tape along each line for extra stability.

For the back upper level: Draw a 7-inch by 9-inch rectangle on the illustration board. Draw the outline for all window openings and also the dotted vertical lines. Cut out the rectangles from the bottom. Cut out the windows, making the openings slightly larger than the cutouts. Also with the X-Acto knife, score the cardboard along each of the vertical lines so that it still holds together but can be bent cleanly at each line. After bending it in place, run a piece of masking tape along each line for extra stability.

For the roof: Place templates 9, 10, and 11 on the Fome-Cor and outline them. Flip them over to make a mirror image right alongside the first outline so that the center line becomes the peak of the roof. Use an X-Acto knife to cut them out and to score each one down the center line so that it still holds together but can be bent cleanly to form the peak of the roof. After bending it in place run a piece of masking tape along each line for extra stability.

Attaching the substructural frame to the base

Using a glue gun, white glue, or masking tape, attach the lower 2 sides to the lower back and the upper 2 sides to the upper back. You now have 2 frames: a high inner one and a low outer one. Position the inner frame on the

1/2-inch-thick base so that the 2 sides are spaced 4 1/2 inches apart. Use scraps or cut small rectangles of Fome-Cor and attach them to either side of the frame at the base in several places to serve as stabilizing feet.

Position the outer frame and secure it in the same way. (Use the width of template 3 or 3A to determine the exact distance between the inner and outer frames; it should be about 3 1/4 inches.)

Finally, attach the 2 main roof pieces to the top of the inner frame and the 2 small gabled roof pieces to the 2 large ones.

To Prepare for Rolling and Drying the Gingerbread Dough

For rolling

For the most even gingerbread, it is best to roll out the dough on a heavy cookie sheet without sides (so they don't interfere with the rolling pin). A piece of aluminum foil is placed under each piece of dough so that the rolled and shaped dough can be transferred to another sheet to bake.

Cut about 50 7-inch by 9-inch pieces of aluminum foil.

Cut 2 12-inch by 1 1/4-inch strips of 1/16-inch-thick illustration board to lie on either side of the dough on the cookie sheet and serve as tracks for the rolling pin. This will establish an even thickness of the dough during rolling.

Dampen a terry cloth towel with water, wring it out, and place it on a table or countertop. Place the cookie sheet on top of the towel. (The damp towel keeps the cookie sheet from sliding.) Spritz the center of the sheet with water and spread a piece of the prepared foil in the center, smoothing it with your hand.

For drying

The baked dough must be cooled on a flat surface. If you have enough cookie sheets, the dough can be cooled on the sheet on a wire rack, but be sure to loosen it from the foil before it cools completely. The dough can also be cooled for a few minutes on the sheet and then transferred to a counter lined with wax paper to finish cooling.

Gingerbread

Make 11 batches of this recipe.

Prepare 2 hours or up to 1 week ahead of baking, or you can make them as you need them.

EQUIPMENT: *heavy cookie sheets.*

Food Processor Method

In a medium bowl, sift together the flour, salt, baking soda, and spices. Whisk to combine well.

In a food processor with the metal blade, process the brown sugar until fine. Cut the butter into a few pieces and add it with the motor running. Process until smooth and creamy. Add the molasses and process until incorporated, scraping the sides of the bowl. Add the flour mixture and pulse in just until the dough begins to clump together.

Electric Mixer Method

Soften the butter. In a small bowl, sift together the flour, salt, baking soda, and spices. Whisk to combine well. In a mixing bowl, cream together the sugar and butter until fluffy. Add the molasses and beat until blended. On low speed, gradually beat in the flour mixture until incorporated.

For Both Methods

Scrape the dough onto a sheet of plastic wrap and use the wrap, not your fingers, to press it together to form a thick flat disc. Wrap it well and refrigerate for at least 2 hours or up to 1 week.

INGREDIENTS	MEASURE volume	WEIGHT	
		ounces	grams
bleached all-purpose flour	3 cups (dip and sweep method)	15 ounces	425 grams
salt	1/4 teaspoon	•	•
baking soda	1 teaspoon	•	5 grams
ground ginger	2 teaspoons	•	•
ground cinnamon	1 teaspoon	•	•
grated nutmeg	1/2 teaspoon	•	•
ground cloves	1/4 teaspoon	•	•
dark brown sugar	1/2 cup (firmly packed)	4.25 ounces	120 grams
unsalted butter	8 tablespoons	4 ounces	113 grams
unsulfured molasses (preferably Grandma's)	1/2 cup (use a greased liquid measuring cup)	5.5 ounces	161 grams

Place 1 oven rack in the middle of the oven.

Preheat oven to 350°F.

Place 1 piece of the foil on a cookie sheet and sprinkle it lightly with flour. Place the illustration-board strips on either side of the foil.

Working with pieces of dough about the size of an orange, roll out the dough, being sure to have the rolling pin resting on the illustration-board strips to ensure an even thickness. Use all the fresh dough first and keep the scraps covered to prevent drying. (When only the scraps remain, knead them together and use them to roll out more pieces. When the dough has been rolled out more than three times, the texture becomes less smooth and even.)

Trim the dough with a small metal spatula so that there is about a 1-inch margin around the perimeter of each template. (Don't use a knife; it will cut through the foil.) Leave the dough on the foil and transfer it to another cookie sheet for baking.

Repeat this process with the remaining dough. When all the template pieces plus extras have been baked, roll out the remaining dough and bake it in large free-form pieces for use as the stone surface around the base of the cathedral.

Bake only 1 cookie sheet with a maximum of 4 pieces on it at a time to ensure even baking. Distribute the pieces evenly on the cookie sheet. Avoid crowding pieces into one section of the cookie sheet, leaving a large area bare.

Bake for 8 to 10 minutes or until the pieces are firm to the touch and just beginning to color around the edges. Do not press the pieces in the middle, as the indentations may remain. For even baking, rotate the cookie sheet from front to back halfway through the baking period.

Cool the cookies on the sheet for a few minutes. When they are firm enough to lift, use a small, angled metal spatula or pancake turner to loosen the cookies from the foil and transfer them to the wax paper–lined counter to cool completely. Allow the cookie sheet

to cool completely, then wipe the foil with a paper towel before using it for the next batch.

The baked dough cuts most evenly when not too dry, so cut window openings, etc., soon after cooling. If desired, shortly before assembling, you may bake the cathedral pieces once more for a few minutes to harden them and enhance the etching marks. (The pieces containing the "stained glass" will be rebaked during the candy melting process.)

Store: In an airtight container at room temperature.

Keeps: For months.

Smart Cookie

- If the unbaked dough dries, moisture can be restored by placing the dough on a wire rack suspended over a pan of hot (not simmering) water for 1 to 2 minutes.
- Little imperfections on the dough surface contribute to an overall stonelike effect. Don't strive to make all the pieces identical or perfect except in thickness.
- Bake extra Gothic window dough pieces for experimentation with the stained-glass window procedure and in case of breakage.

Royal Icing

Make 4 batches of this recipe.

INGREDIENTS *Do not make on a humid day*	MEASURE *volume*	WEIGHT	
		ounces	*grams*
3 large egg whites	3 fluid ounces	3 ounces	90 grams
powdered sugar	4 cups (lightly spooned into the cup)	1 pound	460 grams
brown paste food coloring	1 teaspoon	•	•
copper paste food coloring	a small dab (less than 1/8 teaspoon)	•	•

In a large mixing bowl, place the egg whites and sugar and beat, preferably with the whisk beater, at low speed until the sugar is moistened. Beat at high speed until very glossy and stiff peaks form when the beater is lifted (5 to 7 minutes). The tips of the peaks should curve slightly. (If necessary, for intricately precise decorations such as the tiny stars, ruffles, and roof tiles, more powdered sugar can be added.) Add the food colorings and beat in until uniform in color.

Store: In an airtight container at room temperature. Rebeat lightly as needed.

Keeps: 3 days.

Royal Icing with Meringue Powder:
Replace the egg whites with 3 tablespoons of meringue powder and 3 fluid ounces (6 tablespoons) of warm water (this is approximately the amount of water contained in the eggs). Proceed as for basic Royal Icing. Store in an airtight container at room temperature for up to 2 weeks. Rebeat as needed.

To Cut and Assemble Baked Pieces

When connecting pieces to form units, always take care to have the attractive top side of the dough facing outward.

Select and assemble the baked dough pieces. Hold the appropriate template in place and, with the X-Acto knife, carefully cut around the outline, trimming off the uneven excess dough. For templates with straight sides, such as the square windows, a small X-Acto razor saw works best.

When cutting openings for the windows, scrap pieces of baked dough the same size or slightly larger can be placed on the cutting board beneath the dough to be cut. This provides an ideal cushion to achieve clean cuts. Hold the templates for the windows in place on the dough surface with plastic-topped pushpins. Pierce holes near the corner edges where they will not show on the finished structure.

Gothic Windows (template 5): With the small saw or X-Acto knife, trim the 4 straight sides of the window pieces. Hold the template in place and, with the X-Acto knife, carefully cut out the dough from the center of the window along the mullion (Y-shaped) edges and along the window sides. It works best to start at the inside point of the stem and cut outward to the edge, then to cut the other side of the Y, the lower portion of the mullion, and finally the window edges. When cutting, hold the knife blade in a vertical position and use an up-and-down motion to draw the blade through the dough. Proceed slowly and do not attempt to cut through the first time around. Repeat the cutting motions until the dough slips out easily. Set each piece aside and go on to the next, cutting 18 in all.

Use a nail to etch stone lines on the window pieces as shown in the photograph.

Narrow rear windows, rose windows, and quatrefoil openings on the pediments (templates 13, 1, 6, 2, 3, and 3A): Follow the same procedure as for the Gothic windows.

Front door and arches (templates X, Y, Z, and 4A): The front door is composed of 3 recessed arches and a stained-glass center panel. For this panel (template Z), follow the same procedure as for the Gothic windows. Cut dough from templates X, Y, and 4A. Assemble these pieces after making the stained-glass door section in piece Z.

To assemble the door and arches, start with the largest piece, 4A. Set it right side down on the counter. Set piece X right side up on the counter and pipe dots of tinted Royal Icing around the outer edges. Invert it over piece 4A so that the arches line up evenly. Each arch is slightly smaller than the one before it.

Set piece Y right side up on the counter and pipe dots of tinted Royal Icing around the outer edges. Invert it over piece X so that the arches line up evenly.

Set piece Z right side up on the counter and pipe dots of tinted Royal Icing around the outer edges. Invert it over piece Y so that the stained-glass portion is centered in the arch. Allow the pieces to dry for at least 1 hour.

Steps (templates 20 and 21): Attach pieces 20 and 21 to each other with a small amount of tinted Royal Icing, placing the wider one (21) on the bottom, as shown in the photograph. With the number 44 pastry tube, pipe a narrow band of icing along the edges of the steps. Let the icing dry for a few minutes before scoring it with a nail. Test a small edge before scoring. If the icing is not dry enough, it will pull away from the edge. If it dries too long, the marks won't sink in or the icing will crack. Just before placing the door in position on the cathedral, insert the steps beneath.

Pilasters (templates 5A and 5C): Each pilaster is composed of 2 side pieces (template 5A) and 1 front piece. You will need to cut 18 pieces for the left sides of the pilasters and then flip the pattern piece and cut 18 more mirror-image pieces for the right sides.

You will also need 18 front strips (template 5C).

Assemble the 3 pieces for each pilaster so that the underside of the front strip is placed directly on top of the shorter cut edges of the side pieces. Etch stone lines with a nail.

Caps for the ends of pilasters and flying buttresses: Cut 4 strips of baked dough 9 inches by 3/4 inch and then cut the strips into 3/4-inch lengths. For the 2 shorter caps on the front top strip flanking the main rose window, cut one 3/4-inch length in half.

Buttresses (templates 7, 7A, and 7B): Using template 7, cut 14 pieces, then flip over the template and make another 14. Cut 14 dough strips using template 7A for the tops and 14 dough strips using template 7B for the fronts of the buttresses. Sandwich together the 2 opposing buttresses, back to back, with tinted Royal Icing to make pairs. Allow to dry for at least 1 hour. Etch in stone lines with a nail. Use icing to attach the strips to the tops and fronts of the buttresses and then place the caps, as in the photograph. Etch stone lines into the strips with a nail.

Steeple (templates 16 and 17, 18 and 19): Cut 2 pieces of each template. Cut the 3 quatrefoil openings (these are vents, not stained-glass windows). Attach pieces cut from templates 16 and 17 at right angles. Repeat with the other 2 corresponding pieces and then attach them together with tinted Royal Icing to form the square tower section. Allow it to dry for at least 1 hour.

Assemble the 4 spire sections cut from templates 18 and 19 in the same manner and allow the spire

to dry for at least 1 hour. Attach the spire to the tower with icing.

Roof (templates 8, 8A, 9, 10, 11, 14, and 15): Cut 8 pieces of template 8, 2 pieces each of templates 9 and 10, 4 pieces of template 11, 5 pieces each of templates 14 and 15, and 14 strips of template 8A, for each section between the pieces of lower roof.

To Make the Stained Glass

First, assemble all the windows and the door: This includes the main rose window (template 1); 2 side rose windows (template 6); 19 Gothic windows (template 5); 3 quartrefoil shapes for the top of the main rose window (template 2) and the top of the side rose windows (template 6); and 2 windows at the sides of the front door (template X). ·

Place 1 oven rack in the center of the oven.

Preheat oven to 350°F.

Line cookie sheets with aluminum foil.

Pulverize the candy.

Pulverize no more than 6 Life Saver candies of a single color at a time as they become sticky. Use a food processor with the metal blade or place the candies in a re-closable quart-size freezer bag, close it, place it on a chopping board, and hammer the candies until they are crushed very finely. Place each color of crushed candies into its own small disposable cup.

Fill and bake the cookie windows

Place the 4 Gothic windows on 1 cookie sheet. Place each rose window in the center of a separate cookie sheet.

Use the tiny spoon or the tip of a sharp paring knife to place the pulverized candies in the window openings (fill each rose window just before baking). The windows should be overfull, slightly "heaped," as the candy will melt down. (If the openings are smaller than those shown, the pulverized candy should then be flush with the surface of the cookie as the candies do not melt as well.) If you wish, refer to the photograph as a guide for placing the colors in the rose windows. For the Gothic windows, green is at the base, followed by yellow and then red at the top. Blue may be added at the end. For blue, use pulverized Brach's blue Mint Coolers or make blue candies yourself. Add a few drops of the liquid blue food coloring to the pale yellow pulverized candy, stir with a stainless steel or disposable spoon, and allow it to dry for a few hours in a cool place before placing it in the cookie opening. Use the square-tipped brush to brush away any excess candy from the cookie dough.

Bake for 4 to 5 minutes or until the candy bubbles up. Watch carefully that the candy does not begin to brown.

Cool completely on the sheet on a wire rack. When completely cool, the foil will peel away easily from the back of the windows. Place each cookie on wax paper and store at room temperature, uncovered.

 **Smart Cookie**

- If not enough candy was placed in the openings and holes ap-

pear, add more pulverized candy and rebake, watching carefully to prevent browning.

To Make Royal Icing Decorations

Fit the pastry bag or a reclosable quart-size freezer bag (cut off a small piece from one corner of the freezer bag) with a coupler, fill the bag about half full, and close it tightly. To prevent the icing from hardening in the tube, use a small damp cloth to keep the tip covered when not in use.

Roof: Attach the number 46 flat basketweave tube to the coupler. Assemble all the roof pieces. Set aside the pieces from template 15. (These will be decorated after they are placed in their final position on the cathedral.) Place a small square of wax paper beneath each roof piece and pipe short bands to resemble tiles, starting at the bottom of the piece and working up in vertical lines. For a more realistic look, stagger the tiles so that they do not all begin and end at the same spot. Allow the piping to dry overnight before placing the roof pieces on the cathedral.

Stars: (These decorations will keep for years so they can be made at your convenience.) Attach the number 14 star tube to the coupler. Tape a few sheets of wax paper to the counter so that they lie flat. Pipe about 400 stars onto the wax paper. (These go very quickly.) Allow them to dry until they are easy to remove from the wax paper. Turn the stars upside down and dry the bottom sides completely. This will take a few hours. If you are not planning to use them for several weeks, store

them in an airtight container at room temperature.

When ready, attach the stars with dots of tinted Royal Icing to decorate the perimeters of the rose windows, the sides of the front door, along the frieze above the front door, and in the middle of the buttresses.

Ruffles for roof-edge decoration: Attach the number 86 (or 87 for left-handed work) to the coupler. Place a few sheets of wax paper on the counter. Slide graph paper underneath to serve as a piping guide. Tape the wax paper in place. Pipe about 20 10-inch lines of ruffles onto the wax paper. Allow the ruffles to dry completely (this will take a few hours) before cutting them into lengths to use above the windows along the upper-roof edge.

Frieze atop front door: Attach the number 3 round tube to the coupler. Have ready the number 5 round tube. Decorate the baked dough piece from template 4B as shown in the photograph, using the number 3 round tube to pipe the lines and the number 5 round tube to pipe the dots. When the icing is dry, attach stars, using little dots of Royal Icing.

Large stars and rosettes: Attach the number 172 drop flower (closed star) to the coupler. Have ready the number 136 decorative flower tube. Tape a few sheets of wax paper to the counter so that they lie flat. Pipe about 12 stars and 12 rosettes from each tube onto the wax paper. Allow them to dry until they are easy to remove from the wax paper. Turn them upside down and dry the bottoms completely (this will take a few hours).

Steeple: Attach the number 18 star tube to the coupler. Have ready the number 5 round tube. Decorate with stars piped directly in 2 long rows onto each of the 4 corners where the sides meet, as shown in the photograph. Use the number 5 round tube to pipe dots around the quatrefoil openings as shown. Use a small amount of tinted Royal Icing and your fingers to mold a cone shape atop the steeple. Use a palette knife or spatula to smooth 4 flat faces. Allow the steeple to dry for several hours before placing it on top of the roof.

To Attach and Assemble All Pieces and Royal Icing Trims

Use tinted Royal Icing as glue for all pieces. Start at one end of the lower level and attach the Gothic window panels to the substructure, working around the side, back, and around the other side. Trim 5/16 inch from each of the 2 long sides of the lower roof pieces to make room for the 5/8-inch-wide strips that lie in between them. Attach the lower roof pieces, alternating them with the strips so that the center of each strip falls right in between the joined edges of the window panels. The top edge of the strip will start flush with the top edge of the roof panel and the bottom will extend past it to form a cap for the pilaster. Allow to dry at least 4 hours before attaching the next level.

Again starting with the same side Gothic window panel, repeat the process with the upper side and back panels. Attach the upper roof pieces starting with 4 large ones, add the gables, and finally attach the small wedge shapes that

form the back roof. Mount the steeple on top of the roof.

Have a champagne toast— you're halfway there!

Position the steps as indicated in the photograph and attach them to the base with a small amount of the icing. Set the fully assembled front-door panel in place so that it fits over the steps. Attach the 2 front side panels adjacent to it. Allow to dry for 2 hours.

Attach the main upper rose window by placing the bottom edge against the top edge of the door panel. Attach the pediment (triangular piece, template 2) on top of it. Allow to dry for 2 hours.

Attach the frieze over the doorway.

Attach all the pilasters to the bottom level. Attach 2 of the 4 front strips (template 4C) over the pilasters on either side of the door and attach the remaining 2 on top of them. Attach the 2 front strips (template 4D) on top of the bottom 2 strips on either side of the rose window. Attach the 2 small caps to the upper strips.

Attach the buttresses. Attach the strips (template 5B) under the buttresses.

Surround the base of the cathedral with etched scraps of baked gingerbread dough, notching them where necessary to fit flush around the pilasters.

Proceed with the finishing trims, decorations, and gilding.

Finishing decorations
Pipe all finishing decoration with a number 18 star tube.

Upper rounded back end of roof: Finish piping the tiles on this small section.

Roof crest: With a small palette knife or metal spatula, fill the empty space along the crest of the

roof with tinted Royal Icing. Use the spatula to smooth it flush. Allow it to dry for 1 hour. Pipe a row of shells along the crest.

Stars along lower roof edge: Pipe stars directly onto the structure as shown in the photograph.

Shells on upper edge of rose window: Pipe a row of shells along the joining of the large rose window and the pediment (triangular piece above it).

Large stars and rosette for roof points above side rose windows and roof point above main rose window: Select the best large stars and 1 rosette and attach the stars to the roof points above the side rose windows and the large open flower rosette at the roof point above the main rose window.

Structural imperfections: If any of the substructural support shows through, use the tinted Royal Icing to mask it.

Gilding

It is helpful to refer to the photograph for extra guidance.

In a small glass dish, mix about 1/2 teaspoon of gold petal dust and 3 to 4 drops of vodka to a paint consistency. Make more as needed, but a little goes a long way and the vodka evaporates quickly.

With the numbers 1 and 3 pointed brushes, carefully paint the following:

• stones around the Gothic windows; stems in the center of the panes
• stones around the edges of the 5 upper rear windows
• stone arches around the front door
• stars (all except for those piped onto the lower roof edge)

- rosette on the front
- dots around the quartrefoil shapes
- the dough portion (filigree lines) of the 3 rose windows
- tip of the steeple

Light Attachment and Storage

A fluorescent light is the safest light to use to illuminate the interior of the cathedral because it generates very little heat. However, the quatrefoil openings on the steeple are left open to serve as vents for any heat buildup that does occur.

Set the fluorescent light fixture into the slot that was created for it in the base of the cathedral board. Tape it in place with a piece of electrical tape. It is best to have someone help you hold up the board while you place the light.

If your cathedral is stored in a cool place in low humidity, it will last through to the following Christmas. Small mesh bags of silica gel help to absorb any moisture. To keep it safe from dust and pets, construct a simple rigid box from Fome-Cor.

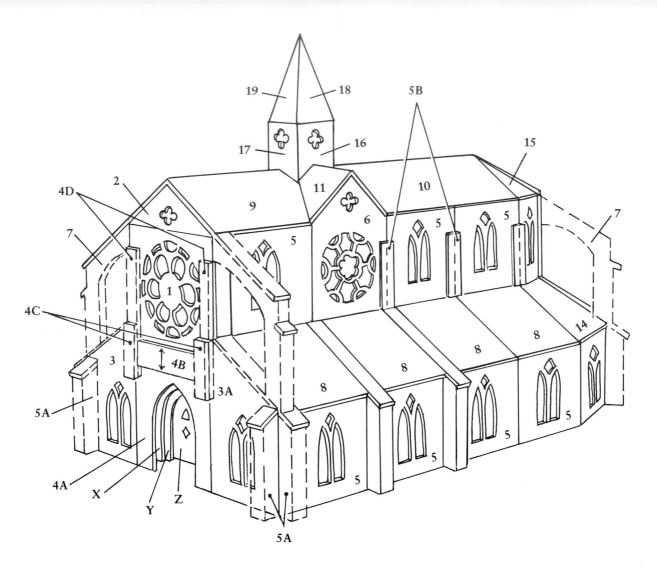

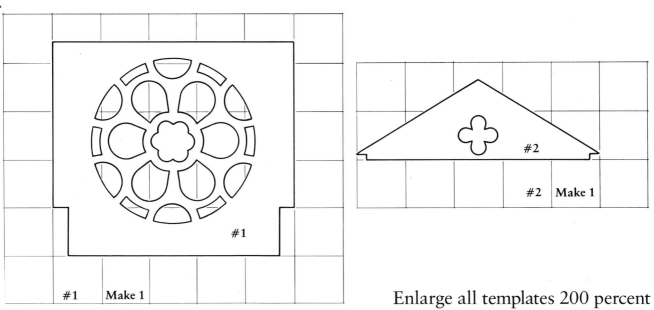

#1 Make 1

#2 Make 1

Enlarge all templates 200 percent

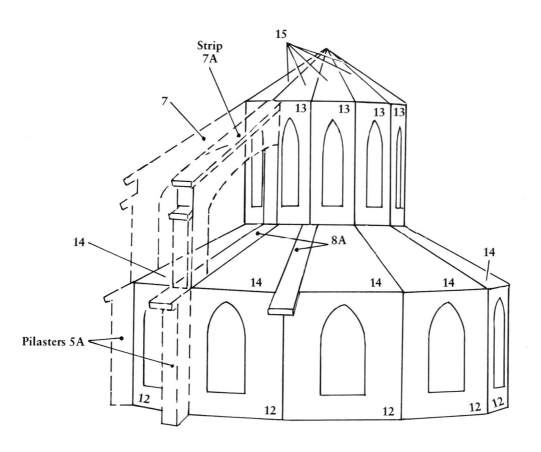

Strip 7A

7

15

13   13   13   13

14

8A

14   14   14   14

Pilasters 5A

12   12   12   12   12

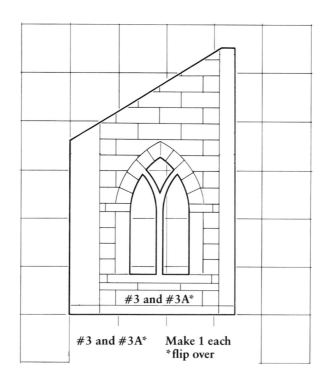

#3 and #3A*

#3 and #3A*   Make 1 each
                *flip over

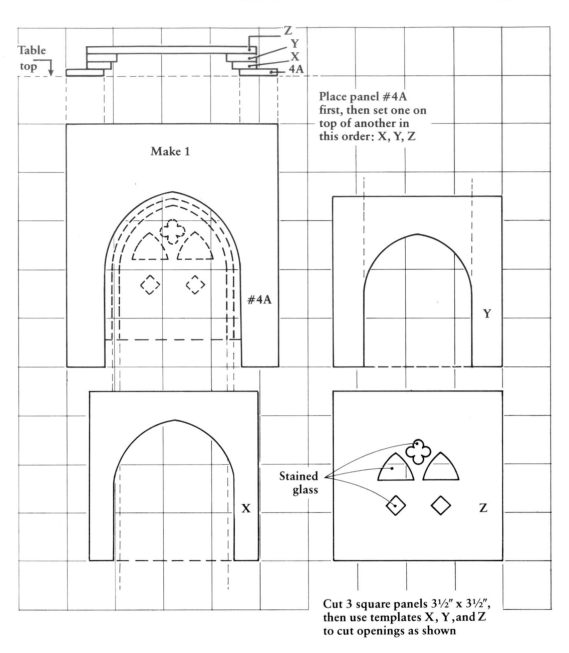

Table top ↓

Z
Y
X
4A

Make 1

Place panel #4A first, then set one on top of another in this order: X, Y, Z

#4A

Y

X

Stained glass

Z

Cut 3 square panels 3½″ x 3½″, then use templates X, Y, and Z to cut openings as shown

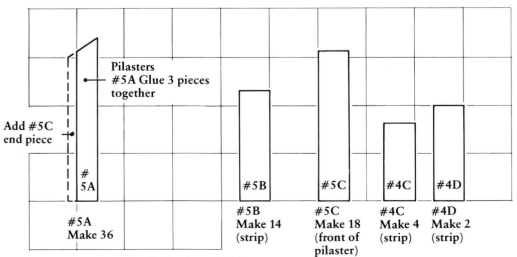

Pilasters #5A Glue 3 pieces together

Add #5C end piece

#5A

#5A Make 36

#5B

#5B Make 14 (strip)

#5C

#5C Make 18 (front of pilaster)

#4C

#4C Make 4 (strip)

#4D

#4D Make 2 (strip)

Notre Dame Gingerbread Cathedral   200

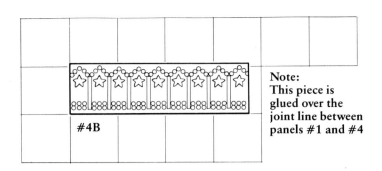

#4B

Note:
This piece is
glued over the
joint line between
panels #1 and #4

Note: Square = 1″

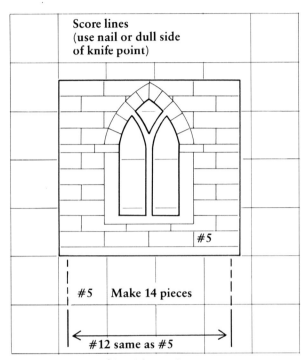

Score lines
(use nail or dull side
of knife point)

#5

#5   Make 14 pieces

#12 same as #5

except this wide. Make 5 pieces

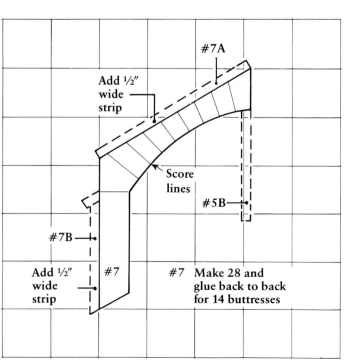

#6

#6   Make 2

Add ½″
wide
strip

#7A

Score
lines

#5B

#7B

Add ½″
wide
strip

#7

#7   Make 28 and
glue back to back
for 14 buttresses

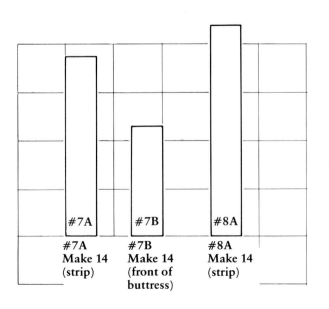

#7A   #7B   #8A

#7A
Make 14
(strip)

#7B
Make 14
(front of
buttress)

#8A
Make 14
(strip)

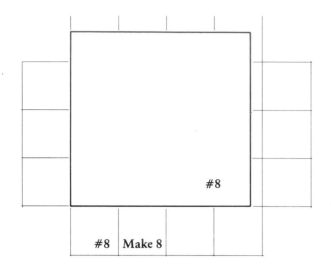

#8   Make 8

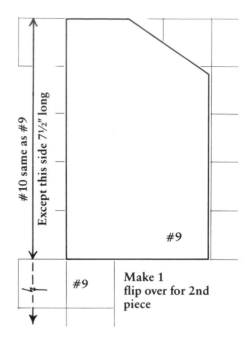

#10 same as #9
Except this side 7½" long

#9   Make 1
flip over for 2nd
piece

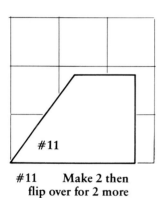

#11   Make 2 then
flip over for 2 more

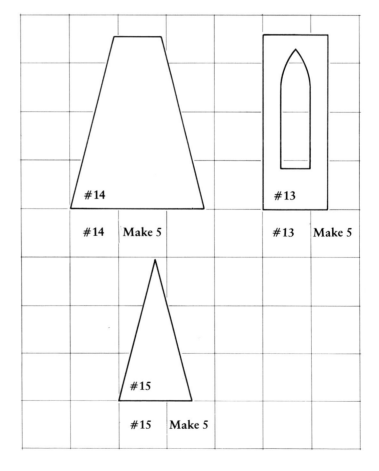

#14   Make 5

#13   Make 5

#15   Make 5

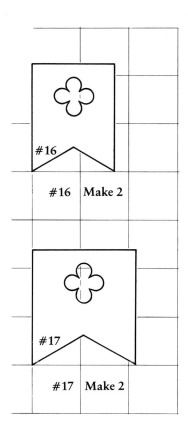

#16   Make 2

#17   Make 2

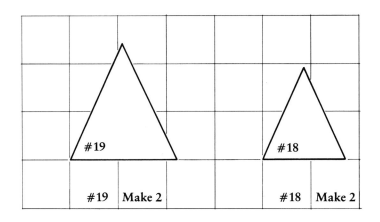

#19   Make 2   #18   Make 2

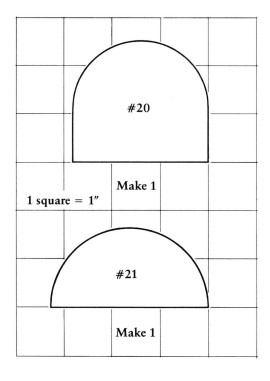

#20

Make 1

1 square = 1″

#21

Make 1

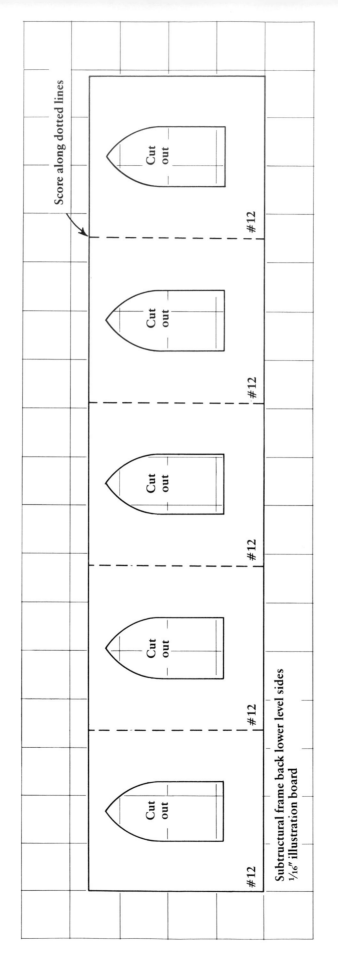

Score along dotted lines

Cut out

#12

Subtructural frame back lower level sides
1/16″ illustration board

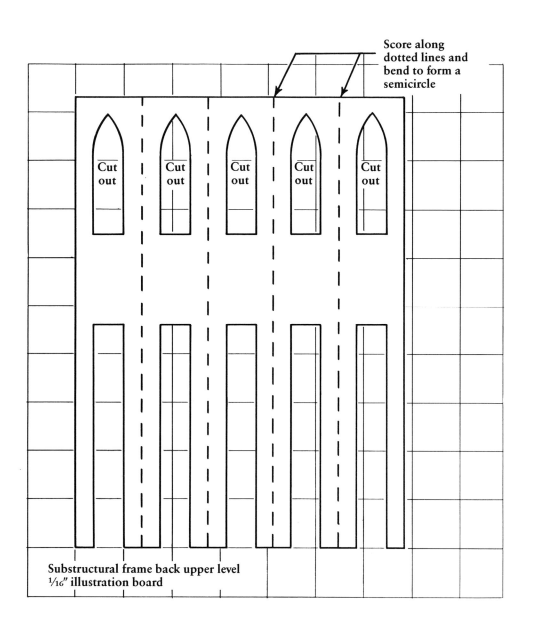

Score along dotted lines and bend to form a semicircle

Cut out

Cut out

Cut out

Cut out

Cut out

Substructural frame back upper level
¹⁄₁₆″ illustration board

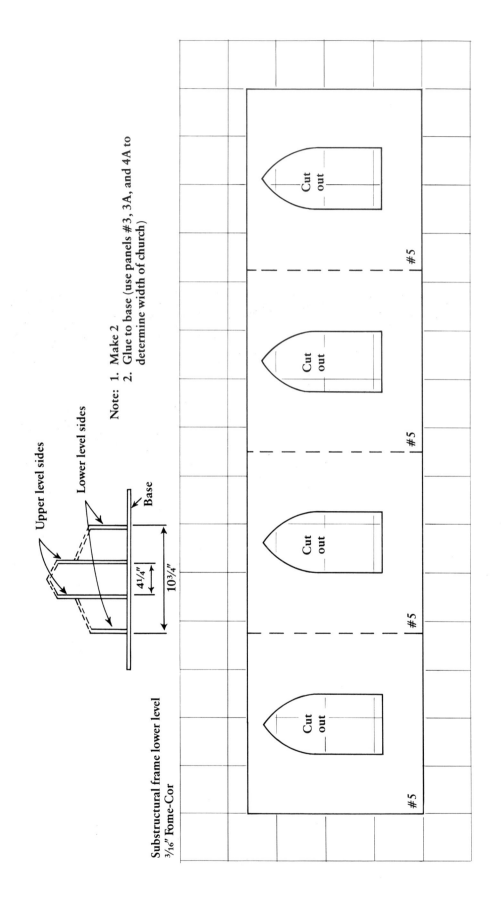

Note: 1. Make 2
2. Glue to base (use panels #3, 3A, and 4A to determine width of church)

Upper level sides

Lower level sides

Base

4¼"

10¾"

Substructural frame lower level
³⁄₁₆" Fome-Cor

Cut out

Cut out

Cut out

Cut out

#5

#5

#5

#5

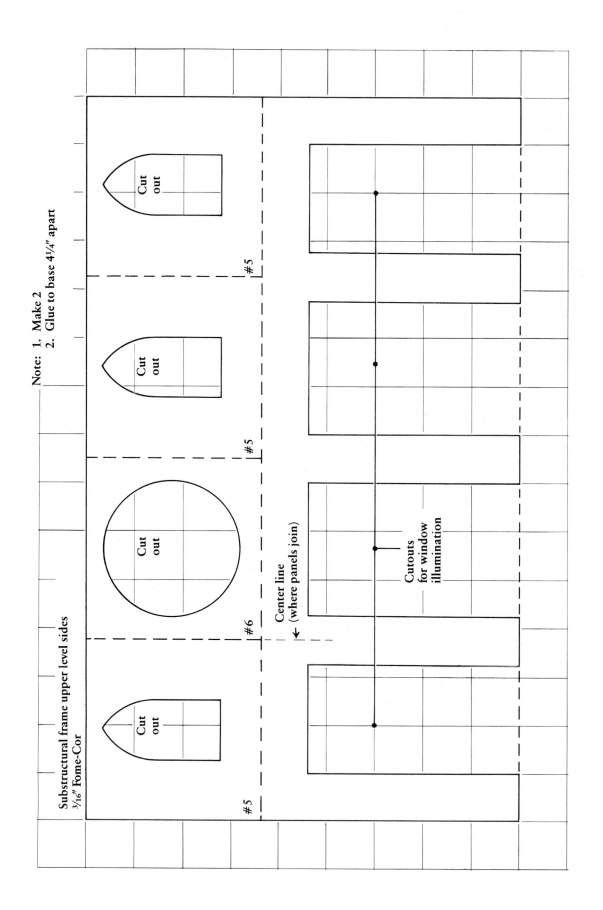

Note: 1. Make 2
2. Glue to base 4¼" apart

Cut out

Cut out

Cut out

Cut out

#5

#5

#6

#5

Center line
(where panels join)

Cutouts
for window
illumination

Substructural frame upper level sides
³/₁₆" Fome-Cor

The weight of all ingredients for recipes in this book is given in both the metric and avoirdupois systems. I have rounded off the ounces to the nearest quarter ounce, the grams to the nearest whole number, without decimal points (except for leavening, which needs to be more precise). Therefore, *do not expect the mathematics of the avoirdupois system to correlate exactly with the metric system.*

There is no doubt about it: Weighing is faster, easier, and more accurate than measuring. Most bakers, including myself, prefer the metric system for its precision in small quantities. There really isn't any adjustment necessary, providing you have a metric scale and the recipe gives metric amounts. If you don't have a scale with a digital readout, simply round off the grams to the nearest convenient number. The amount still will be quite accurate: After all, 1 gram is only about 1/28 of an ounce.

I have presented the volume measures in the way I would measure them when baking. For example, instead of 6 tablespoons of sugar, I indicate 1/4 cup + 2 tablespoons because that is the more convenient approach. Also, the fewer measures used, the less room for error.

On pages 210–213, you will find a chart of weights for your use in converting amounts in recipes from other sources. I arrived at these weights by innumerable trials over a three-year period at seven stories above sea level, using a Mettler scale (page 245), which is used in scientific laboratories. I spent my first pay check earned as a chocolate consultant on this scale, with no regrets. People ask me what is the point in having such accurate equipment when most people will not. My feeling is that if I am to set a standard, I want it to be as close to the absolute as possible. That way, the recipes will still work, despite deviations, because there is always a range of acceptable error.

For those who will measure instead of weigh, the *dip and sweep method* of measuring refers to dipping the measuring cup into a bin containing the ingredient and sweeping off the excess with a long, flat spatula or knife.

Lightly spooned into the cup refers to spooning the ingredient into the cup and then sweeping off the excess with a long, flat spatula or knife. This method yields less of the ingredient than the dip and sweep method.

Sifted means that the ingredient is sifted into a cup that is sitting on a counter. The cup is never touched or (perish the thought) shaken. Only the handle is held when the excess is swept off with a long, flat spatula or knife.

Dry ingredients should be measured in a cup designed for solids. I prefer the Foley stainless-steel set of measuring cups and spoons and Tupperware. The Foley 2-tablespoon cup, however, measures less than

Weights and Measures

How to Measure Flour and Other Dry Ingredients

it should. Other makes of measuring cups may vary in size and are generally less reliable.

How to Measure Liquid Ingredients

Liquid ingredients, including honey and other syrups, should be measured in a liquid measure with a spout. There is a difference in volume between liquid and solid measuring cups. The most accurate liquid measure at the present time is made by Oven Basics, available in some supermarkets throughout the country; 1 cup of water weighs exactly 8.337 ounces/236.35 grams, which is the dictionary definition of an 8-ounce cup of water. The same is not true of many other brands. Some are off by quite a bit, and the markings are not level.

FOOD SUBSTANCE	METHOD OF MEASURE	WEIGHT OF 1 CUP	
		ounces	grams
Fats			
butter		8	227
vegetable shortening		6.75	191
safflower oil		7.5	215
Sugars			
granulated sugar	dip and sweep	7	200
superfine sugar	dip and sweep	7	200
coarse crystal	spooned	7	200
powdered sugar	lightly spooned	4	115
light brown sugar	firmly packed	7.66	217
dark brown sugar	firmly packed	8.4	239
Flours and Other Dry Ingredients			
cake flour	sifted	3.5	100
	lightly spooned	4	114
	dip and sweep	4.5	130
all-purpose flour, bleached	sifted	4	114
	lightly spooned	4.25	121
	dip and sweep	5	145
all-purpose flour, unbleached	lightly spooned	4.55	130
	dip and sweep	5.25	148

FOOD SUBSTANCE	METHOD OF MEASURE	WEIGHT OF 1 CUP	
		ounces	*grams*
cornstarch	lightly spooned or sifted	4.2	120
Dutch-processed cocoa	sifted	2.6	75
	lightly spooned	3.25	92
	dip and sweep	3.33	95
nonalkalized cocoa, such as Hershey's	sifted	2.6	74
	lightly spooned	2.9	82
	dip and sweep	3.33	95
old-fashioned oats	lightly spooned	2.5	74
quick oats	lightly spooned	3	83
Nuts			
almonds	whole	6.75	191
	slivered	4.2	120
	sliced or coarsely chopped	3	85
	finely ground	3.75	107
	powder fine	3.12	89
walnuts, pecans	halves	3.5	100
	coarsely chopped	4	114
hazelnuts	whole	5	142
	coarsely chopped	4	114
	finely ground	3.75	107
cashew	whole	5	142
	coarsely chopped	4.3	124
pistachios	whole	5.32	152
macadamia	whole	5	142
hazelnut praline paste		10.88	308
smooth peanut butter		9.25	266
Liquids			
Dairy			
sweetened condensed milk		11.14	316
heavy cream		8.12	232

FOOD SUBSTANCE	METHOD OF MEASURE	WEIGHT OF 1 CUP ounces	grams
milk		8.5	242
sour cream		8.5	242
Syrups			
molasses		11.25	322
refiner's syrup		12	340
corn syrup		11.5	328
honey		11.75	336
Other Liquids			
lemon juice, strained		8.75	250
orange juice, strained		8.5	242
water		8.337	236.35
Kahlúa		9.6	267
Grand Marnier		8.6	245
Cognac		7.9	225
light rum		7.8	224
Eggs			
1 large egg	in the shell	2	56.7
1 large egg	without the shell (3 tablespoons + $\frac{1}{2}$ teaspoon)	1.75	50
1 large egg white	2 tablespoons	1.05	30
1 large egg yolk	$3\frac{1}{2}$ teaspoons	0.65	18.6
Miscellaneous			
raisins	whole	5	144
cranberries	whole	3.5	100
coconut	grated	2.8	79
chocolate chips or morsels		6	170
Cordon Rose raspberry jam		10.15	290
commercial raspberry jam		10.92	312

FOOD SUBSTANCE	METHOD OF MEASURE	WEIGHT ounces	grams
salt	1 cup	10.25	295
	1 teaspoon		6.7
poppy seeds	1/4 cup	1.25	36
cinnamon	1 tablespoon	•	6.5
baking powder	1 teaspoon	•	4.9
baking soda	1 teaspoon	•	5
gum arabic	1 teaspoon	•	3.25
cream of tartar	1 teaspoon	•	3.1
glycerine	1 teaspoon	•	6
vanilla extract or almond extract	1 teaspoon	•	4
zest (citrus)	1 teaspoon	•	2

The word *approximate* is a key one because converting one ingredient into another is never entirely successful, but in emergencies, it's nice to know how to come close to the original. For example, most substitution charts tell you how to make sour milk with vinegar to replace buttermilk. While the acidity level seems the same, the substitution doesn't begin to re-create the lush, tangy sour taste of buttermilk. Substituting granulated sugar and molasses for brown sugar, however, is another story, because adding molasses to granulated sugar is the way brown sugar is made in the industry as well.

Approximate Equivalencies and Substitutions

FOR	SUBSTITUTE
1 pound unsalted butter	1 pound lightly salted butter but remove 1 teaspoon of salt from the recipe
1 cup milk	1 cup minus 1 tablespoon half and half but remove 1 tablespoon of butter from the recipe and add 2 tablespoons of water
1 cup sifted cake flour	3/4 cup sifted, *bleached* all-purpose flour plus 2 tablespoons of cornstarch (this is 15% cornstarch)
1 cup light brown sugar	1 cup granulated sugar plus 1/4 cup unsulfured light molasses
1 cup dark brown sugar	1 cup granulated sugar plus 1/2 cup unsulfured light molasses
0.25-ounce package (2 1/4 teaspoons) active dry yeast	1 packed tablespoon (0.75 ounce) compressed fresh yeast
1 packed tablespoon (0.75 ounce) compressed fresh yeast	1 packed tablespoon plus 1 packed teaspoon frozen, thawed, compressed fresh yeast

Note: This yeast equivalency is approximate and works well. If you have a scale accurate for small amounts, you may want the more precise conversion:

1 package of active dry yeast = 2 1/4 teaspoons = 0.25 ounce = 7 grams

1 package of compressed fresh yeast = 0.6 ounce = 17 grams

If a recipe calls for dry yeast, × 2.42 is the amount of fresh needed.

If a recipe calls for fresh yeast, × .41 is the amount of dry yeast needed.

Using volume, you need 1.4 times the volume of packed fresh yeast to replace dry.

Chocolate   Substituting one type of semisweet or bittersweet chocolate for another is fine, but it may result in surprisingly different flavors because even if the amounts of cocoa solids, cocoa butter, and sugar are the same, the type of bean and degree of roasting are what cause the most significant variations in taste. Different textures may also result. The surest way to determine which chocolate to use is to taste it.

Ingredients

Almond Extract

Pure almond extract intensifies the flavor of a cookie made with almonds. Be sure to use the pure extract, not imitation flavor, as other types have an artificial and overwhelming quality. Find it at Dean & DeLuca and Cook's Flavoring Company (page 229).

Baker's Joy

This is a combination of oil and flour used to spray on baking molds. It is much faster and neater than greasing and flouring, especially when the molds have fancy indentations. If you can't find it in your local supermarket, get in touch with the manufacturer (Alberto-Culver, page 229) for your nearest distributor. This is a fabulous product.

Baking Powder

Baking powders are mixtures of dry acid or acid salts and baking soda with starch or flour added to standardize and help stabilize the mixtures. Double-acting means that they will react with or liberate carbon dioxide, partially with moisture during the mixing stage and partially when exposed to heat during the baking stage. They make the cookie rise. It is, therefore, important to store baking powder in an airtight container to avoid humidity. There is also a substantial loss of strength in baking powder that is more than 1 year old. Date the bottom of the can when you first buy it, or write the expiration date on the lid with a Magic Marker.

I use Rumford baking powder, which is an all-phosphate product containing calcium acid phosphate. It lacks the bitter aftertaste associated with SAS (sodium aluminum sulfate) baking powders. (The supposed advantage of the SAS powders is that they release a little more carbon dioxide during the baking stage than during the mixing stage, but I find I can still interchange an equal volume and weight of either type of baking powder.) Rumford baking powder is usually available in health food stores (probably because aluminum compounds are considered dangerous by many health-conscious people).

Baking Soda

Baking soda, or sodium bicarbonate, has an almost indefinite shelf life if not exposed to humidity. In Canada I once discovered a wonderful variety called Cow Brand (goodness knows why). It contained a tiny amount of a harmless chemical ingredient that prevented it from clumping. Unless you can obtain this type of baking soda, it is best to sift it before measuring. Baking soda is used when the cookie contains acidic ingredients such as sour cream or molasses. It neutralizes some of the acidity and, in the process, makes the cookie rise.

Chocolate

Chocolate is a very important ingredient in many cookies. Working with it over the past ten years, I have found there is an enormous difference in both texture and flavor among different brands and have developed my own personal preferences. I highly recommend that you do a blind tasting to determine your own.

My preference is for European chocolate, particularly the Swiss. Brands of chocolate differ partly because of special formulas unique to each company, which determine the blend of the beans, the type and amount of flavorings, and the proportion of chocolate liquor and cocoa butter.

Bittersweet and *semisweet* chocolate consist mainly of pure chocolate liquor (cocoa solids and cocoa butter), sugar, extra cocoa butter, and vanilla. They can be used interchangeably in recipes, although their sweetness levels vary according to their individual manufacturer. *Extra bittersweet,* which is occasionally available, contains the least amount of sugar of all and is ideal for adding to particularly sweet cookies, such as those containing caramel.

Milk chocolate also contains milk solids and butter. Because it contains less cocoa solids than the other types of chocolate, it is considerably sweeter.

Cocoa

Cocoa is the pure chocolate liquor of the cocoa beans with about three quarters of the cocoa butter removed. What remains is then pulverized to a powder. *Dutch-processed* means that the cocoa has been treated with a mild alkaline to mellow its flavor and make it more soluble. My favorite unsweetened, Dutch-processed cocoa is Lindt's, from Switzerland, and has recently become available in this country. In Switzerland it comes in dark and light (I prefer the dark) and now is carried here by Maid of Scandinavia (page 229). Pernigotti, an Italian cocoa carried by Williams-Sonoma (page 229), is another favorite. Smelling the cocoa will tell you a lot about its flavor potential but the best test is baking with it.

Storing chocolate and cocoa

The best way to store chocolate or cocoa is to keep it well wrapped in an airtight container (chocolate is quick to absorb other odors and must not be exposed to dampness) and at a temperature of 60-75 degrees with less than 50 percent relative humidity. Under these conditions, dark chocolate should keep well for at least two years. I have used chocolate stored at ideal conditions for several years and it seems to age like a fine wine, becoming more mellow and subtle. (Milk chocolate keeps, even at optimum conditions, for a little over a year and white chocolate, about one year.)

Used primarily in fruitcake and for decorating desserts, these are available through Maid of Scandinavia, Dean & DeLuca, and other specialty food stores (page 229). Stored airtight at room temperature, they last for years. Do not refrigerate them as they become rock hard.

Citron, Angelique,
Glacé Cherries, and
Mixed Candied Fruits

Potassium acid tartrate is a by-product of the wine industry. Its shelf life is virtually indefinite. I have found that by adding 1 teaspoon of cream of tartar per cup of egg whites (1/8 teaspoon per egg white), it stabilizes them so that it becomes practically impossible to dry them out by over-beating.

Cream of Tartar

These little balls of silver or gold consist mainly of sugar. The USDA considers them nontoxic and acceptable for decorative use. Of course, they are not intended to be consumed by the handful. Dragées are carried by cake-decorating supply houses such as Maid of Scandinavia (page 229). When asking for them, it is safer to refer to them as silver or gold balls as no two people seem to pronounce this item the same way!

Dragées
(drahZJAYS)

Eggs contribute both fat (tenderness) from the yolks and protein and water (binding and airiness) from the whites. Cookies made with whole eggs or egg whites are puffier because the water turns to steam while baking.

Eggs

All my recipes use USDA grade large eggs. As a rule of thumb, 5 extra-large eggs equal about 6 large eggs. Values for recipes in this book are given for weight and volume so it's fine to use any size eggs as long as you weigh or measure them. The egg white contains: 87.6 percent water and 10.9 percent protein. The egg yolk contains: 51.1 percent water, 16 percent protein, and 30.6 percent fat.

For smooth meringue cookies, older egg whites are preferable to fresh ones. Commercial eggs are sprayed with a substance that seals the shell, extending freshness so the egg white does not age much in the shell. To age an egg white quickly, whisk it lightly to break it up and allow it to sit covered, overnight, at room temperature, or freeze it for several hours, defrost it, and allow it to warm to room temperature, covered.

Beating egg whites

For the most volume, always beat egg whites at room temperature. Any fat substance, including a drop of egg yolk, is a foam inhibitor and will keep the egg whites from becoming stiff. If a drop of yolk does spill into the whites, use a piece of the broken egg shell to remove it. Adding 1/8 teaspoon of cream of tartar per egg white ensures that during the beating process the egg whites will not start to break down due to inadvertent overbeating. Once all the sugar is added for a meringue, there is no longer any danger of this because the sugar-to-egg white ratio is so high.

Because sugar is hygroscopic (readily absorbs water), it is best to make meringue cookies on dry days or they may be soft and sticky and not set well.

Storage Egg whites, stored in an airtight container, freeze perfectly for at least a year. They can be refrozen once defrosted. It is also possible to freeze yolks. Stir in at least 1/2 teaspoon of sugar per yolk to keep them from becoming sticky after they are defrosted. (Remember to subtract this amount of sugar from the recipe.)

Fat The function of fat in a cookie is to bind it together, to tenderize it, to control its shape, and to give it flavor. Some fats, such as butter, change from solid to liquid quickly within a short range of temperatures, while vegetable shortening and lard remain the same consistency over a relatively long range of temperatures. For example, when a butter cookie bakes, the butter melts and spreads, while a vegetable shortening cookie holds its shape more. The butter cookie will, therefore, be flatter and crisper, the vegetable shortening one will be higher, lighter, and softer.

Also, different fats have different moisture contents. Butter contains about 15.5 percent water. Margarine may contain as much as as 40 percent water and low-fat spreads may contain as much as 58 percent water. Cookies made with low-fat spreads are not going to melt very much so they will hold their shape and puff up a great deal from the steam produced by the high water content.

Almost without exception, butter is my preferred fat for cookies. Not only is it one of my favorite flavors, but because of its low melting point (close to body temperature) it also conveys tastes more quickly than does other fats. (The faster a fat melts, the more quickly the other ingredients give up their flavors to the palate.)

Salted butter does not have the glorious flavor of fresh, unsalted butter. If only salted butter is available, per pound of butter remove 1 teaspoon of the salt called for in a recipe to achieve the same salt level as unsalted butter would offer. Since cookie recipes do not have much salt to begin with, removing 1 teaspoon of salt per pound of butter is not feasible so the resulting cookies will be saltier.

When buying commercial butter, grade A or AA contains about 81 percent fat, 15.5 percent water, and 6 percent protein. Lower grades contain more water. If the butter you buy remains fairly soft after being refrigerated and releases droplets of water when cut, it contains a high water content. Excess water can be removed by kneading the butter in ice water for several minutes and then drying it thoroughly using paper towels.

When using an electric mixer, butter should be softened until it is malleable or it tends to jump out of the bowl. It can be softened in the microwave oven on low power for about 1 minute (check after 30 seconds) or high power if you check it and turn it every 3 seconds without fail. If you inadvertently melt the butter, use it for another purpose as melting changes the structure and makes it unsuitable for most cookies. If you are using a food processor, the butter can be used cold straight from the refrigerator. For ideal blending, cut it into a few pieces and drop it in with the motor running.

To store butter, wrap it airtight as it absorbs other odors very readily. Avoid wrapping it directly in foil as butter may absorb a metallic odor. Butter freezes well for several months.

Flour

Flour contributes a major part of the structure of a cookie. I recommend *bleached all-purpose flour* in most of my recipes because it possesses just the right protein content needed to create the ideal texture and flavor. *Unbleached all-purpose flour* and *bread flour* contain higher amounts of protein. They tend to produce cookies that are browner, flatter, and tougher. More protein absorbs more liquid, forming gluten, which is tough, and leaving less available liquid in the cookie dough to turn to steam and aerate the cookies.

Cake flour contains less protein, so because less water is tied up by the flour, it turns to steam and makes the cookies rise more. Less gluten forms as well, so the cookies tend to be fragile. The cookies brown less because the protein is also responsible for browning.

The protein content of flour is listed on the bag and refers to the number of grams of protein per 4 ounces/113 grams of flour.

> *Swan's Down or Softasilk Cake Flour:* 8 grams of protein per 4 ounces/113 grams flour
>
> *all-purpose flour:* between 8 grams and 14 grams of protein per 4 ounces/113 grams flour

To calculate the percentage of protein in flour, multiply the number of grams of protein per 113 grams of flour by 100 and divide the resulting number by 11.3. For example, for cake flour: 8 × 100 divided by 113 = 7 percent.

Self-rising cake flour contains 1 1/2 teaspoon of baking powder and 1/2 teaspoon of salt per 1 cup of flour.

Storage

Flour should be stored away from the heat so that it doesn't dry out. I find that cake flour can be stored for several years, but bread flour, after 2 years, seems to lose some of its strength. Unbromated bread flour, which I purchased from a mill, became rancid after about 8 months. Flour with the bran removed, such as cake flour and supermarket bread flour, does not become rancid or attract bugs readily.

Weighing or measuring

How much flour you use in a cookie recipe will make all the difference in the quality of your finished cookie. To measure flour accurately, refer to page 209.

Food Coloring   Liquid food coloring, available in grocery stores, mixes well with egg yolks to create a paint you can apply to cookies before baking or shortly before the end of baking. It produces vivid colors. Powdered food coloring (available in candy-making supply stores) achieves very deep colors in Royal Icing without altering its texture. The colors will intensify as the icing sits, so it is best to mix the colors with the icing a few hours before you use them. Then, if a color is too dark, more uncolored icing can be added.

Gold Powder   Called petal dust, this is not actually gold but looks very much like it. It is available in candy-making supply houses such as Maid of Scandinavia and the Chocolate Gallery (page 229).

Gum Arabic   A fine white, tasteless, edible powder made from the gum of the acacia tree, gum arabic was used in paints in Egypt more than four thousand years ago. Today it is used in chewing gum and jellies. When boiled with water and brushed on a cookie, gum arabic produces the most impeccably shiny and transparent glaze. It is available through Maid of Scandinavia and the Chocolate Gallery (page 229).

Nuts   Salted nuts impart far too much salt to a cookie. If the unsalted variety is unavailable, place the salted nuts in a strainer and rinse them in hot tap water. Spread them out on a cookie sheet and recrisp them in a 350°F. oven for about 10 minutes. Cool completely before chopping them.

In general, freshly shelled nuts release the best flavor but the shelled, canned variety are also excellent and a lot more convenient.

The dark brown color and strong flavor of the peel on *hazelnuts* is too bitter for some of the subtler cookies and can be difficult to remove. In most recipes, I recommend boiling hazelnuts in water with baking soda for about 3 minutes. The water turns black but the peel slips off easily. Once the nuts have been recrisped in the oven and allowed to stand for a few hours, or are baked into the cookie, there is no taste from the baking soda. Alternatively, the nuts can be baked in the oven, wrapped for a few minutes in a clean towel, and then rubbed. Some of the peel falls off this way, but there is always more that will not come loose without scraping.

Pistachio nuts may lose some flavor if boiled. Their peel is not bitter, but if it is added to mixtures, they will not have a lovely, pale-green color. To remove this peel, simply toast the pistachios in a 350°F. oven for about 10 minutes and use your fingers or fingernails to remove the peel. If your supermarket or health food store does not carry unsalted pistachio nuts, they can be ordered, shelled and unsalted, from Keenan Farms (page 229).

Lightly toasting all nuts greatly enhances their flavor. Occasionally it is desirable to leave the nuts untoasted so that they blend better and don't overpower other ingredients.

Nuts, particularly almonds, come in many forms. *Unblanched* means that the brown skins are still on the nuts.

Size and form of nuts

unblanched whole

blanched whole

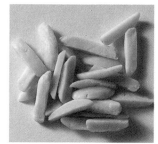
blanched slivered

unblanched sliced

blanched sliced

unblanched chopped
very coarsely

unblanched chopped
coarsely

unblanched chopped
medium coarsely

unblanched chopped finely

blanched chopped
very finely

blanched ground
powder fine

A nut grinder produces nuts that are ground finely. Shaking them in a strainer will separate the portion that is ground powder fine. A chef's knife will do the same things but it will take much longer. I prefer to use a sharp heavy chef's knife when I want nuts chopped very coarsely to coarsely and a food processor fitted with a metal blade for fine to powder fine. Care must be taken with the processor that the nuts are not ground

How to chop and grind nuts

to a paste, especially almonds, which are the softest of all nuts. One way to avoid this is to start with almonds that are already sliced. (If a recipe calls for ground almonds, for every cup of ground almonds needed, start with 1¼ cups of sliced almonds). If only the whole nuts are available, first use the shredder disc and then the metal blade to pulse them until the desired consistency is achieved.

Never process the nuts while frozen or hot as they will become pasty. Nuts should always be at room temperature before grinding in order to prevent them from exuding too much oil. Whenever possible, process the nuts with either some of the sugar or some of the flour in the recipe. This helps to absorb oils and keep the nuts from clumping together.

No matter what grinding method you choose, a certain amount of nut powder will always result. If you wish to eliminate it, simply place the nuts in a strainer and shake them over a sheet of wax paper to catch the powder. It can be collected and frozen for a recipe that calls for nuts that are ground powder fine.

If you should need blanched whole almonds and only unblanched are available, soak the nuts in boiling water for 1 or 2 minutes. Test one by running it under cold water and squeezing it between your thumb and fingers. The nut should pop out of the skin. Drain the remaining nuts and remove the skins. Recrisp the nuts in a 350°F. oven for 5 minutes or for 10 to 15 minutes to brown them lightly.

Storage Nuts will keep well over 1 year if stored airtight in the freezer. I use either freezer bags, expelling all the excess air, or glass canning jars, filling the empty head space with wadded-up plastic wrap.

Praline Paste

Praline paste consists of hazelnuts, or a combination of almonds and hazelnuts, and about 50 percent sugar. (Lesser qualities of paste have a higher percentage of sugar.) I prefer the 100 percent hazelnut and caramelized sugar variety, which can be purchased in small, expensive quantities through Maison Glass (page 229). G. B. Ratto's International Grocers (page 229) on the West Coast also carries praline paste. A small amount goes a long way, and it is well worth every penny. I have experimented endlessly, only to find that homemade praline paste always has a slightly gritty consistency, so I prefer to purchase it.

Praline paste keeps about 1 year, refrigerated, and just about indefinitely frozen. On storage, some of the oil separates and floats to the top. This can be stirred back into the praline paste before using it.

Pam

I prefer Pam to other nonstick vegetable cooking spray products that don't contain flour because is has virtually no odor. It is composed of lecithin, a natural emulsifying agent derived from soybeans, and a tiny amount of soybean oil. It can be used whenever a recipe calls for greasing or buttering a pan or counter.

A cookie is supposed to be sweet, but how sweet is sweet? To my taste, the ideal ratio of sugar to flour is 6 tablespoons of sugar to 1 cup of flour (2.6 ounces/75 grams sugar to 5 ounces/142 grams flour) or 7.5 tablespoons of sugar to 1 cup of flour (3.25 ounces/94 grams sugar to 5 ounces/142 grams flour) if there is cinnamon or spice in the dough to balance the additional sweetness. This results in a sweet cookie, but one that is a little less sweet than you may find in many other recipes. Meringue cookies, by their very definition, have a much higher amount of sugar and contain no flour.

Sugar raises the setting point of the dough while it bakes, so the more sugar a cookie contains, the more the cookie can spread before it sets. This results in a thinner, more crunchy cookie.

The finer the granulation of the sugar, the less the cracking in the surface of the dough. Fine granulation results in a finer crumb and lighter texture because, with the smaller crystals, more surface area is available to trap air. In the creaming process, the sharp or angular surfaces of the sugar crystals catch air. If the surface of the grains of sugar were smooth, such as in powdered sugar, the grains would clump together and not allow air in between. The more crystals there are, the more air will be incorporated. Finer sugar also dissolves more easily and makes lighter, more delicate meringues. Powdered sugar, however, does result in an incredibly fragile, dissolving cookie such as the Mexican Wedding Cakes (page 51). Meringues made with half powdered sugar and half superfine sugar (by weight) combine both airiness and tenderness and therefore seem the lightest of all!

How sugar is made

Sucrose, ordinary *granulated sugar,* is a sugar obtained from sugar beets or sugar cane. There is absolutely no difference between these two sources in the final product if the sugar is refined to 99.9 percent sucrose. A molecule of sucrose is composed of one fructose and one glucose molecule, joined together to form what is a simple carbohydrate, easy to digest and full of energy. Other plants are capable of making sugar, but both cane and beet make it in quantities large enough to support refining. Sugar from the plants is dissolved in water and the resulting syrup is boiled in large steam evaporators. The substance that remains is crystallized in heated vacuum pans and the liquid, now called *molasses,* is separated from the crystals by spinning it in a centrifuge. At this stage, the sugar is known as *raw sugar,* containing about 3 percent impurities or extraneous matter. The raw sugar crystals that have been separated in the centrifuge are washed with steam and are called *turbinado sugar,* which is 99 percent pure sucrose. Although it closely resembles refined white sugar in sweetening ability and composition, it cannot always be substituted in recipes. Its moisture content varies considerably, which, coupled with its molasses flavor and coarse granulation, can affect a recipe without careful adjustment.

Refined white sugar is processed from turbinado sugar. The turbinado sugar is heated again to a liquid state, centrifuged, clarified with lime or phosphoric acid, and then percolated through a column of beef-bone char or mixed in a solution of activated carbon. This last process whitens the sugar and removes all calcium and magnesium salts. Finally, the sugar is pumped back into vacuum pans where it is heated until it crystallizes. The resulting sugar is 99.9 percent sucrose. Sugar that is less refined may be somewhat gray in color, and the protein impurities may cause foaming when the sugar is added to the liquid in a given recipe.

Brown sugar Most brown sugar is ordinary refined sucrose with some of the molasses returned to it (3.5 percent for light brown sugar, 6.5 percent for dark brown). In recipes calling for dark brown sugar, I like to use dark Muscovado sugar from Malawi, a country in southeastern Africa (available at Dean & DeLuca, page 229). Muscovado natural raw sugar doesn't have its natural molasses removed from it, so its flavor seems more pure and subtle.

Equal volumes of either type of brown sugar compared to white sugar have the same sweetening power, but the brown sugar must be measured by packing it into the cup. Dark brown sugar weighs the most; light brown is next, because of the added molasses. Molasses also adds moisture to the sugar. Brown sugar contains 2.1 percent water while plain sucrose contains only 0.5 percent. If you run out of brown sugar and have white sugar and molasses on hand, it's easy to make your own (page 215).

Granulations and forms of sugar All 99.9 percent refined sucrose has equal sweetening power, despite its degree of granulation. Powdered sugar has 3 percent cornstarch added to prevent lumping, but aside from this small percentage, 1 pound of sugar equals 1 pound of sugar.

Regular granulated or fine granulated is the all-purpose sugar found in most sugar bowls and available in all supermarkets. This granulation is suitable for making syrups, but for most other baking, a finer granulation is preferable. Using a food processor, it is possible to make a more finely granulated sugar. Don't confuse the term *fine granulated* with *superfine*, which is much finer.

Baker's special is available commercially and is almost as fine as superfine (bar sugar), available in some supermarkets. This is the perfect granulation for all cookies. I buy it in 100-pound sacks and use it for all my baking. A close approximation can easily be made in the food processor using a coarser granulation and processing for a few minutes.

Castor sugar is a term that appears in British cookbooks. The sugar, commonplace in England, is slightly finer than baker's special. When converting a British recipe, substitute baker's special or the more widely available superfine sugar.

Bar sugar, superfine, or ultrafine sugar is the finest granulation of sugar and comes only in 1-pound boxes in the supermarket. It is sometimes called bar sugar because it is used in bars to make drinks that require fast-dissolving sugar. For the same reason, it is ideal for making meringues and cookies.

Crystal and colored sugars are coarsely granulated sugars. Crystal sugar comes in coarse and medium granulations. Colored sugars also come in fine granulations. These sugars are used for decorating. They are available from Maid of Scandinavia and candy-making supply stores (page 229).

Powdered, confectioner's, or icing sugar can only be made commercially. At one time powdered sugar was stone ground, but now it is ground in a steel magnesium rotary that turns against varying degrees of fine screens, each one determining a different fineness of the grind. The coarser the granulation of the initial sugar, the more even will be the final grind. As might be expected, the finer the granulation, the greater the tendency of the sugar to lump, which explains why 3 percent cornstarch is added to powdered sugar during its manufacture to help prevent lumping. It absorbs any moisture from the air before the sugar has the opportunity to do so. The cornstarch adds what is perceived as a raw taste and makes powdered sugar less suitable than granulated sugar for use with ingredients that are not to be cooked. Powdered sugar comes in three degrees of fineness: 10X, which is the finest (available in supermarkets), 6X, and 4X, which are available commercially.

Syrups
Molasses

Contains 24 percent water. Unsulfured molasses such as Grandma's has the best flavor because it is refined from the concentrated juice of sugar cane. The sulfured variety is usually a by-product of sugar making and tastes of the residues of sulphur dioxide introduced during the sugar-making process.

Refiner's syrup

Contains 15 to 18 percent water. It is a delicious by-product of sugar refining. When syrup, after many boilings, ceases to yield crystals, it is filtered and concentrated into this golden-colored syrup. Lyle's, a British company, packages it under the name Lyle's Golden Syrup. It can be used interchangeably with light corn syrup. Refiner's syrup is carried by specialty stores such as Dean & DeLuca (page 229).

Corn syrup

Contains about 24 percent water. Corn syrup consists of glucose (from corn sugar) with fructose added to prevent crystallization. It is susceptible to fermentation if contaminated, so care should be taken not to return any unused portion to the bottle. Fermented corn syrup has a sour taste and should be discarded.

Vanilla

My favorite pure vanilla extract is produced by Méro and comes from Grasse, the perfume region of France. It is available from La Cuisine (page 229). I like to transfer it to a plastic squeeze-bottle dispenser with pointed tip and add a Tahitian vanilla bean. (This is a great use for used vanilla beans that still have lots of flavor, even after the seeds have been removed. Be sure to rinse the bean in water if it has been used to flavor another liquid and dry it first in a low oven or with the heat of the oven's pilot light.)

The recipes in this book that call for pure vanilla extract refer to the supermarket variety for purposes of standardization. When I use the Méro vanilla extract, I use a little less than half the amount specified in these recipes.

Another wonderful vanilla is Nielsen-Massey vanilla, which is carried by many specialty stores such as Dean & DeLuca (page 229). Recently, Nielsen-Massey introduced an excellent Tahitian vanilla extract. Another fabulous vanilla I have discovered recently is Cook's Pure Cookie Vanilla, which contains the perfect blend of both Madagascar and Tahitian vanillas and is available from Cook's Flavoring Company or G. B. Ratto's (page 229). Imitation vanilla *flavor* does not have the wonderful qualities of the pure extract and often has an off flavor that is undesirable.

Yeast

I prefer using fresh yeast to dry, just on general principle. I like its lively reaction and forthright, earthy smell. But if the yeast isn't absolutely fresh, the final baked product will have a slightly sour taste. The best way to determine freshness is by smell, as the color may not have changed even when slightly past its prime. Fresh yeast freezes almost indefinitely, but certain precautions must be taken in defrosting. Yeast is a live organism and must be "awakened" gradually from the frozen state. To defrost the yeast, place it in a refrigerator for a minimum of 48 hours. Since a few yeast cells will have been destroyed in the process, use one quarter more than the amount specified in the recipe.

It's fine to use dry yeast (page 215), but the quick- or rapid-rise yeasts need a different procedure. For one thing, they cannot be proofed. In the 10 minutes of proofing time, they will have thoroughly exhausted all their energy and leavening power.

Zest

Zest refers to the colored portion of the citrus peel. The white portion, or pith, should be avoided; it is quite bitter. Citrus fruit is a lot easier to zest before squeezing. A zester is the ideal piece of equipment to remove only the outer peel (page 248). The fine strips should then be chopped with a knife or food processor. I like to add some of the sugar from the recipe and process it together with the zest. This keeps the zest from clumping together and allows it to disperse more evenly when added to the larger mixture. A vegetable peeler will also work to remove wider strips that can then be cut or finely chopped.

Note: If citrus fruit is heated (about 10 seconds in a microwave oven on high power) and rolled around while pressing lightly, it will release a significantly greater quantity of juice.

Alberto-Culver Company (Baker's Joy): 2525 Armitage Avenue, Melrose Park, Illinois 60160. (312) 450-3000

Chocolate Gallery: 34 West 22 Street, New York, New York 10010. (212) 675-2253

Cook's Flavoring Company (pure cookie vanilla, pure almond extract): P.O. Box 890, Tacoma, Washington 98401. (206) 627-5499

Dean & DeLuca: 560 Broadway, New York, New York 10012. (212) 431-1691; outside New York: (800) 227-7714, Monday-Friday, 9 A.M.-5 P.M.

Hazy Grove Nuts (hazelnuts): P.O. Box 25753, Portland, Oregon 97225. (503) 244-0593

Keenan Farms, Inc. (unsalted pistachio nuts): P.O. Box 248, Avenal, California 93204. (209) 386-9516

La Cuisine: 323 Cameron Street, Alexandria, Virginia 22314. (800) 521-1176

Maid of Scandinavia: 32-44 Raleigh Avenue, Minneapolis, Minnesota 55416. (800) 328-6722

Maison Glass (praline paste): 52 East 58 Street, New York, New York 10022. (212) 755-3316

Nielsen-Massey Vanillas: 28392 North Ballard Drive, Lake Forest, Illinois 60045. (708) 362-2207

Paprikas Weiss Importer: 1546 Second Avenue, New York, New York 10028. (212) 288-6003

Parrish Decorating Supplies, Inc.: 314 West 58 Street, Los Angeles, California 90037. (213) 750-7650; outside California: (800) 736-8443

G. B. Ratto's International Grocers (Lindt chocolate, pure almond extract, praline paste): 821 Washington Street, Oakland, California 94607. (415) 832-6503

Williams-Sonoma (Pernigotti cocoa): Mail Order Department, P.O. Box 7456, San Francisco, California 94120-7456. (415) 421-4242

Equipment

No two people's cookies are exactly alike. One's personality shines through in the size and shape of cutters chosen or how the dough itself is shaped. The skill and even the temperature of the hands are also factors. But probably the most significant factor of all is the equipment and how it is used.

How you weigh or measure, how your oven bakes, and what kind of equipment you choose will be directly reflected in your finished cookies. This section is intended to suggest possibilities for good-quality equipment and technique (how to use it) that will give you the best results. Your own creativity and individuality will provide the rest.

Bench Scrapers

Metal bench scrapers are excellent for cleaning counters without scratching the surfaces.

Cookie Cutters

If you don't have a cookie cutter collection, start one immediately. Not only are they fun to use to cut decorative cookies, they also make great kitchen decorations when hung on the wall. The most beautiful and unusual cutters in my collection are handmade by Bob and Bill Cukla and Julie Flaherty of Hammer Song (page 249).

For cutters with intricate designs, they recommend rolling a small piece of the cookie dough around the edges of the cutter to create a greasy film and then dipping the edges of the cutter into flour. This helps to keep the cookie dough from sticking to the cutter. While cutting out the cookies, repeat this process as necessary to prevent sticking. To cut the cookies, press the cutter firmly into the dough until it reaches the counter. To release the dough from the cutter, use a north-south movement and then a west-east movement. Lift up the cutter and lightly rap it with a pastry brush, if needed, to further release the dough. With the pastry brush, gently brush off the excess flour from the cutouts of dough.

I also prize my round scalloped nested cutters from Matfer of France, available at The Bridge Company, La Cuisine, and Charles Lamalle (page 249). Cookie cutters also come on metal or plastic rollers that create different shapes when rolled across the dough. Yields for rolled, cut cookies always vary in accordance with the size of cutters used. A $1/8$-inch difference in a $13/4$-inch cutter can make a 40 percent difference in quantity produced.

Cookie Presses

Cookie presses (also called guns) are metal cylinders with templates. The cylindrical container is filled with soft cookie dough that is then pressed through the opening in the template to form different shapes. A pastry

1 Cuisinart food processor
2 KitchenAid mixer
3 pastry frame and cloth
4 Cuisinart scale
5 Krups hand-held electric mixer
6 large mixing bowl
7 French wire cooling rack

8 8-inch aluminum cake pan
9 baking parchment
10 rolling pin (Teflon)
11 nonstick mini-muffin pan
12 madeleine pan
13 Parrish 2-piece 8-inch by 8-inch by 2-inch baking pan
14 springerle mold

15 rolling pin sleeve
16 Parrish 10-inch by 15-inch cookie sheet
17 Parrish 10-inch by 15-inch by 1-inch jelly roll pan
18 Parrish 2-piece 9-inch by 13-inch baking pan
19 Matfer Tefal 11-inch by 15-inch cookie sheet

1 Hammer Song cookie cutter
2 triangular icing comb
3 pastry brush
4 feather
5 wooden spoon
6 flexible pancake turner
7 small metal spatula
8 small angled metal spatula
9 large Rubbermaid spatula
10 Foley stainless-steel measuring spoons
11 large wire whisk
12 small wire whisk

13 nested scalloped cutters
14 number 30 (2-inch) scoop
15 number 100 (1¼-inch) scoop
16 porcelain spoon
17 Tupperware measuring cups
18 2-cup heatproof liquid measure
19 1-cup heatproof measure
20 shortbread press
21 quart-size reclosable freezer bag with coupler and decorating tube
22 polyester decorating bag with pastry tube

23 cookie press
24 cookie press templates and nozzles
25 Krups timer
26 1¾-inch tiny tartlet pans
27 1-inch foil bonbon cups
28 Williams-Sonoma vegetable peeler
29 citrus zester
30 Cordon Rose candy/deep-fat thermometer
31 Albert Uster 14-inch wavy-edge slicer
32 4-cup heatproof liquid measure

bag (or a reclosable freezer bag) with a large star pastry tube is even easier to use to pipe rosettes or star shapes (page 239).

Cookie Sheets

The ideal cookie sheet for evenly baked cookies is one of heavy-gauge aluminum with a shiny (not a dark) finish and flat or very low rolled edges. Darkened pans absorb the heat, causing the cookies to bake too quickly, and result in a crumbly texture and an overbrowned flavor. Pans with edges do not allow the heat to flow over the cookies and prevent cookies from crisping. It is possible to bake the cookies on a jelly roll pan if you bake on its underside (so that its raised sides are facing down and are below the cookie).

A cookie sheet that is thin will burn the bottoms of the cookies. If your cookie sheets are thin, use one on top of the other for insulation. (The Cushionaire cookie sheet works on this principle. It is excellent for baking soft cookies, but don't use it for crisp ones.)

A cookie sheet must be small enough to allow at least 2 inches of clearance on all sides between it and the oven walls for adequate air flow. An 11-inch by 17-inch cookie sheet is a good size, but some ovens will not accommodate this large a sheet with adequate clearance. Sheets 10 or 11 inches by 15 inches are also standard sizes that will fit in almost all ovens. My favorite nonstick cookie sheet is an 11-inch by 15-inch heavy aluminum one coated with Tefal, a nonstick coating. It is made by Matfer in France and is carried by The Bridge Company (page 249). It bakes very evenly and never needs greasing.

Some cookies need to be baked on an ungreased surface, so uncoated cookie sheets are also desirable. (Such cookies will spread too much on a nonstick coating or you won't be able to stamp them with a design; they will come off the sheet too easily and stay attached to the stamp.)

My favorite cookie sheets (without nonstick linings) are made by Parrish and are of heavy-gauge shiny aluminum. They are available in the 10-inch by 15-inch size and the 11-inch by 17-inch size at Parrish, The Broadway Panhandler, and Dean & DeLuca (page 249).

To grease or butter a cookie sheet, use a light spray of nonstick vegetable shortening or use a piece of wadded plastic wrap to spread on a thin film of solid vegetable shortening or unsalted butter. Do not grease the sheet too heavily as the cookies will spread out too thinly and burn around the edges.

Always distribute the cookies at even intervals on the sheet or the heat will be drawn to the empty areas and the cookies near these areas will bake faster. For cookies cut from soft dough, use a small, angled metal spatula or pancake turner to transfer them to the cookie sheet.

If you do not have enough cookie sheets for a whole batch of cookies, you can bake them in stages, being sure to cool the cookie sheet under cold running water and dry it for each batch. (Cookies placed on a hot cookie sheet will start to spread prematurely.) Alternatively, you can lay pieces of aluminum foil the size of your cookie sheet on the counter and place the cookies on the foil. When the first batch is baked, remove them from the cookie sheet and simply slip the cookie sheet under the foil of the next batch. There is no need to cool the sheet first if you immediately place it with the cookies on it in the oven.

For cookies that are rolled into balls and then flattened on the cookie sheets, you can use a lightly greased, buttered, or water-moistened tumbler or a decorative object to both press the cookie flat and to emboss a distinctive design on the surface of the cookie. Cookie stamps (great collectors' items) are available in ceramic, wood, and plastic, but you can also create your own design with a meat-tenderizing mallet, a potato masher, or even a large decorative button. Wooden or metal springerle molds are also fun to collect and look beautiful on the wall when not in use.

Cookie Stamps

The food processor method of mixing cookie dough is listed first because making cookie dough in a food processor is so quick and easy (you don't even have to soften the butter) that I wouldn't consider using my mixer most of the time. The only minimal difference is with cookies that contain liquids (such as the Cashew Puffies, which contain sour cream) or a large amount of egg. They are slightly puffier when made with a mixer.

Another benefit to using the processor for cookie dough is that the sugar can be processed to superfine, which results in a better texture. And often it is not necessary to chop the nuts separately for the cookie dough. (They get chopped when mixing the sugar or flour). If you are grating and chopping nuts in a food processor, it spoils you for life for any other method. For chopping whole nuts I like to use the shredding disc first and then the metal blade. This keeps the chopped nuts drier and more uniform in size.

In my experience, the strongest, most effective and well-designed food processor has always been the Cuisinart. The model I find to be the most convenient size for general use is one that has a work bowl measuring 7 inches by 5 inches. But the standard-size model, which is slightly smaller, will also work for the recipes in this book. For most of these recipes, use a model that can handle a minimum of two pounds of cookie dough. (This information is listed in the instruction booklet.)

Food Processors

The vast majority of cookies contain nuts in one form or other, so if you don't have a food processor, some sort of nut grater or nut chopper is indispensable. (Chopping nuts powder fine with a chef's knife can be done, but it will take forever.) The Mouli hand grater comes with three drums, but only the finest one works to grate nuts evenly, and will produce nuts that are finely ground.

Graters (Nut)

Icing Combs   This is a metal or plastic triangle with different size teeth on each edge. It is used to create an attractive wavy pattern in a chocolate glaze after it is spread on top of a cookie but before it fully sets.

Knives   A small sharp paring knife is useful for many purposes, such as shaping the cookie dough. For cutting bar cookies, I like to use a serrated knife with a long blade. The serration is especially effective for cutting through pieces of nuts without dislodging them from the cookie. This is a difficult knife to find, but fortunately Albert Uster Imports (page 249) carries an excellent 14-inch blade version called "wavy edge slicer 14-inch round tip."

Liners
Parchment   Parchment paper is available at cake-decorating supply houses, specialty stores, and some supermarkets in rolls to line cookie sheets and in triangles to make piping bags (page 242). When you are lining a cookie sheet, it is helpful to grease the sheet lightly with solid vegetable shortening or butter. This helps the parchment to stay in place.

Reusable nonstick pan liner   This is a great optional product because absolutely nothing sticks to it, which makes it especially ideal for meringue cookies. It has been around for many years, but it is usually difficult to find. One excellent brand called sanStick™ is available from European Home Products (page 249).

Foil (Aluminum)   I became a great fan of aluminum foil many years ago while working for Reynolds Metals Company. (The first lesson we were taught was never to say "tinfoil.") Part of my job was to find new and unusual ways to use aluminum foil. We used it for just about everything. Aluminum foil, shiny side out, is excellent for lining cookie sheets and pans for bar cookies. Be sure to use heavy-duty foil to line pans for bar cookies as the foil can then be used to lift out the cookie in one piece, enabling it to be cut on a cutting surface instead of in the pan (which ruins the knife and the pan).

To line a baking pan with foil, turn the pan upside down and drape a piece of foil (a little larger than the pan) over it, shiny side against the pan. Fold the corners against the pan, smoothing the foil to conform to the shape of the pan. Lift away the foil, turn the pan right-side up, and place the pan-shaped foil in it. Because the foil was shaped on the outside of the pan, it will be a little too large, so smooth and press it into the pan.

The most accurate and well-marked heatproof measuring cups I have found are made by Oven Basics, available in some supermarkets. When shopping for measuring cups, look for ones with level markings. A cup of water, read below the meniscus (the curved upper surface) should be close to 8 ounces to be acceptable. In addition to measuring liquids, these cups are ideal for pouring hot sugar syrups and caramel. The handles remain cool to the touch and the spouts control the way the liquid pours. I use my 1-cup measures the most, but 2-cup and 4-cup ones are often useful as well.

Foley stainless-steel cups are the most attractive and among the most accurate. Tupperware's cups are also excellent and include practical 2/3-cup and 3/4-cup sizes. Solid measures must have unbroken, smooth rims, making it possible to level off excess ingredients.

Foley stainless-steel measuring spoons (not the oval ones, page 233) and Tupperware heavy-duty plastic are my favorites. I especially like the Tupperware spoons because they include unusual extra sizes such as 1/8 teaspoon, 4 teaspoons, and 1/2 tablespoon. I have found other brands of measuring spoons to be somewhat smaller than these two types.

An electric hand-held mixer can be used for most cookies except those with stiff doughs, such as Grandmother Schorr's Moravian Spice Crisps (page 135), which will need to be finished by hand with a wooden spoon. Most hand-held electric mixers are also not powerful enough to handle Royal Icing. Both Krups and KitchenAid produce excellent hand-held electric mixers.

People who do a lot of baking sooner or later end up with a heavy-duty mixer on a stand. The two best mixers of this sort are the KitchenAid K5 series and the Kenwood Major from England. They are both excellent. The Kenwood has a larger capacity (7 quarts compared to 5 quarts), but it works as well with small amounts. It also has a stronger motor with a device that protects the motor from burning out if overheated. The conical shape of the bowl and the ability to adjust the beaters to come as close as possible to the bottom makes for thorough and even mixing.

Heavy-duty mixers offer the choice of a flat "spade" beater and a whisk beater. The flat beater is intended for general mixing, and the whisk beater for whenever the aim is to beat as much air as possible into the mixture, such as egg whites for meringue-type cookies. The advantage of the mixer over the food processor when making cookies is mainly cleanup. The dough can be mixed and stored in the same bowl (not of particular significance to me because I always need the bowl for another use, but worth mentioning). Also, cookies containing liquids or a large amount of egg will be slightly more airy when prepared in a mixer.

Ovens

The golden rule for most cookies is that underbaking is usually preferable to overbaking. One way to ensure that cookies bake evenly is to shape them all the same size and thickness. Another way to ensure even baking is the placement of the oven racks. Baking the cookies too close to the top of the oven will overbrown their tops. Baking too close to the bottom will overbrown the bottoms. The ideal placement for most cookies is as close to the center of the oven as possible.

If your oven is not large enough to allow for at least 2 inches between all sides of the cookie sheets and the sides of the oven and you want to bake 2 sheets at a time, the oven racks should be placed so that they divide the oven in thirds. Partway through baking, rotate the cookie sheets from top to bottom and front to back.

Cookies will continue to "bake" and harden after removal from the oven, so most types of cookies need to be removed while they are still a little soft in the center. They must also be removed from the cookie sheets to wire racks as soon as they are rigid enough to transfer with the help of an angled spatula or pancake turner.

Oven temperature is important to the cookies' texture. Most oven thermometers are quite inaccurate, so I usually use my Cordon Rose sugar syrup thermometer, wiring it to the rack to hold it in position. (The thermostat in most ovens fluctuates at least 10°F. above and below the ideal temperature.) A simple and effective test for finding out your oven's temperature is to make a batch of cookies. If, for example, it takes longer than the recommended time, you will know that your oven is too cool at the setting used, so next time you can turn it up a bit.

Always preheat your oven for at least 15 minutes before baking the cookies. The heat sets the cookies so that they don't spread too thinly and burn around the edges.

Pans

My favorite pans for bar cookies are heavy-gauge shiny aluminum ones made by Parrish. They have corners that are at perfect right angles, not rounded, so all the bars can be uniform in size after cutting. (I have asked Parrish to produce a 9-inch by 13-inch by 2-inch pan and an 8-inch by 8-inch by 2-inch pan of this type with removable bottoms, making it possible to remove the cookie in one piece from the pan without having to line it with aluminum foil or invert it, which sometimes mars the top surface. To unmold the cookie, you simply place the pan on a sturdy cannister slightly smaller than the opening on the bottom of the pan and press down on the rim. The sides of the pan slip down and away from the cookie and onto the counter.) Parrish also makes an excellent 10-inch by 15-inch by 1-inch jelly roll pan.

If you use glass pans, be sure to lower the oven temperature by 25°F.

Mini-muffin pans, measuring 1¾ inches in diameter across the top, are used for several cake-type cookies and are readily available from all sources that carry baking pans. I prefer mini-muffin pans that are lined with a nonstick surface, although I still spray them with Baker's Joy or grease and flour them. The nonstick lining, together with this treatment, results in the best release.

Tiny tartlet pans, measuring 1³/₄ inches across the top, are available in candy-making supply stores such as Maid of Scandinavia and the Chocolate Gallery. The more heavy-gauge ones, shaped like miniature brioche pans, are from France and available at Charles Lamalle. Madeleine molds, also made in France, are available from Dean & DeLuca, Charles Lamalle, and La Cuisine (page 249).

Pastry Cloths

A canvas pastry cloth and knitted cotton rolling pin sleeve are very helpful for rolling out soft, sticky doughs. About ¹/₄ cup of flour is rubbed into the cloth and about 1 tablespoon into the sleeve. The dough picks up just what is needed, preventing overflouring. Foley makes my favorite pastry cloth. It comes with a frame that keeps it from slipping and moving on the counter. It is available at many better hardware stores and Maid of Scandinavia (page 249).

Pastry Bags, Parchment Cones, and Reclosable Freezer Bags

Pastry bags are useful not only for piping and decorating cookies but also for filling small molds and tart tins with batter and filling. I like to use reclosable quart-size and gallon-size freezer bags because they are readily available and disposable. Simply cut off a small piece from one corner of the bag and insert a tube (if you are using a large pastry tube) or a coupler first (if you are using a small decorating tube that would otherwise work its way back into the bag). Invert the bag over a blender container or large glass, fill the bag with the mixture, and close it securely.

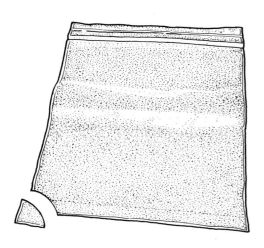

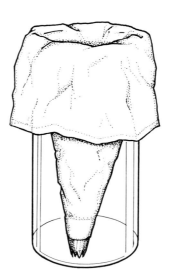

Preparing a polyester decorating bag

One of the major advantages of the polyester bag, aside from being reusable and comfortable to hold, is that it can be used with a coupler so you can change tubes without emptying or changing bags.

To cut a bag to accommodate the coupler, separate the coupler and drop the base, narrow end down, into the bag. Force down the coupler as far as it will go. With a pen or pencil, mark the spot on the outside of the bag where the bottom thread is outlined against the material (fig. 1).

Push the base of the coupler back up into the bag and cut across where the mark was made, cutting in a slight curve rather than sharply across it. The beginning and end of the cut should be slightly higher than the middle so that when the end is open, it will be round (fig. 2).

Push the coupler base back through the bag opening. Two threads should be showing (fig. 3). To secure a tube in place, slip it onto the coupler base and twist the ring over it, threading it onto the base (fig. 4).

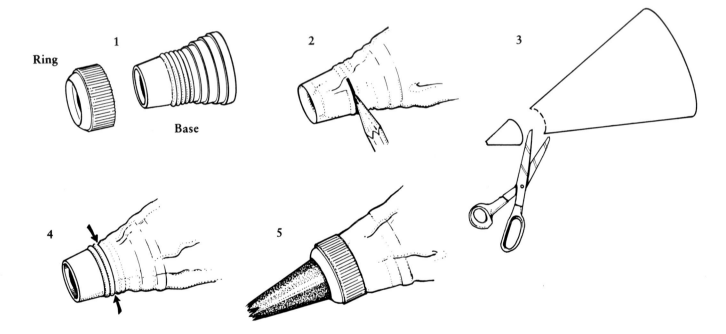

Ring   1

Base

2

3

4

5

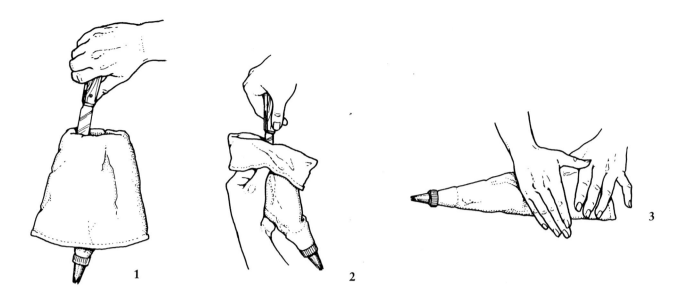

To fill bag: Fold down the top to form a generous cuff and hold it beneath the cuff. Use a long spatula to fill the bag half full. Filling it more risks melting and softening the icing from the heat of your hand (fig. 1).

To remove the icing from the spatula, hold the bag on the outside between your thumb and fingers and pull the spatula out of the bag, pinching the icing (fig. 2). Unfold the cuff and, using the side of your hand, force icing toward the tip (fig. 3). Twist the bag closed. To be sure that no air is trapped in the bag, squeeze a small amount of icing into a bowl. It is a good idea to do this when refilling the bag or the little explosion of air when old icing meets new can disrupt the piped decoration.

To hold bag: Place the twisted part of the bag in the V between your thumb and forefinger. Lock your thumb over your forefinger to keep the icing in the lower part of the bag (fig. 4). Press your remaining fingers against the side of the bag so that when you squeeze out the icing, you squeeze from the side while your thumb presses from the top (fig. 5).

Steady the front end of the bag with the fingers of the other hand to support the weight of the bag and to establish the direction of the tip (fig. 6).

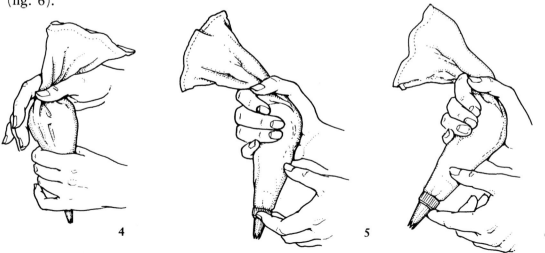

There are two major advantages to a parchment cone: It is disposable, and its stiffness keeps the heat of your hand farther from the icing.

In an emergency I have used a triangle of wax paper. It works well but does not hold up quite as long.

In these illustrations, the points of the triangle have been labeled A, B, and C.

Place the triangle on a flat surface with A pointing toward you (fig. 1). Curl C up and under, bringing it toward you until points A and C meet. The curled edge from C should lie on top of the edge between A and B. The parchment will curve more easily if you extend your right elbow while doing this (fig. 2). Hold points C and A together with your left hand while picking up B with your right (fig. 3). Wrap B around to meet points A and C in the back, forming a cone (fig. 4). Hold the bag with both hands, thumbs inside, and slide B and C in opposite directions to make a W formation (fig. 5). Tugging point B slightly upward will help to form a sharp, closed point (fig. 6).

Turn down the top and secure with a staple (fig. 7). Tape the outside seam of the bag. Use a small strip of tape near the pointed end. This will keep the cone from unfolding and the icing from coming out the side (fig. 8).

If piping chocolate, cut off the tiniest amount possible from the tip. If piping icing, make an opening for the tube by clipping off 3/4-inch from the tip (fig. 9). Too large a hole will allow the tube to fall through, too small and the parchment will cut off part of the frosting's design. Make the cut slightly curved, as for the polyester bag, so the opening will be round and icing will not creep out around the edges.

Drop the tube into the cone, narrow end first, and push forward to make sure the tip is exposed. The weight of the icing will hold it securely in place.

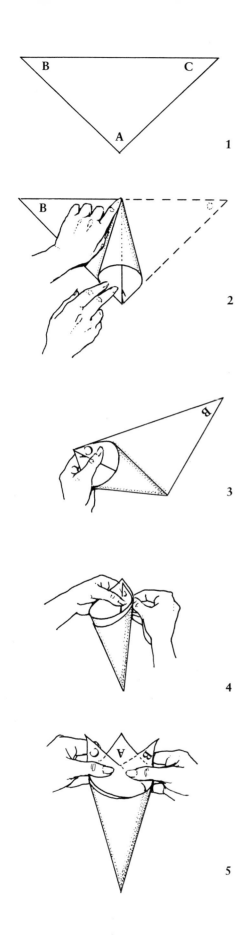

1

2

3

4

5

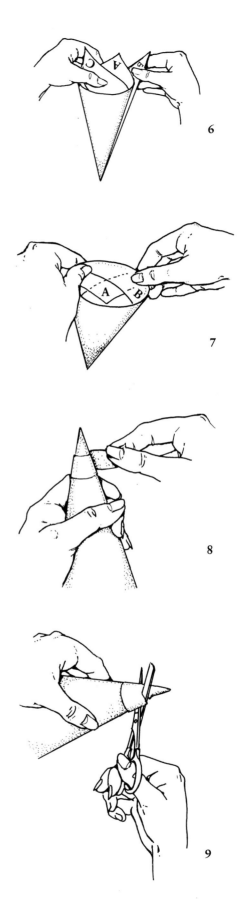

6

7

8

9

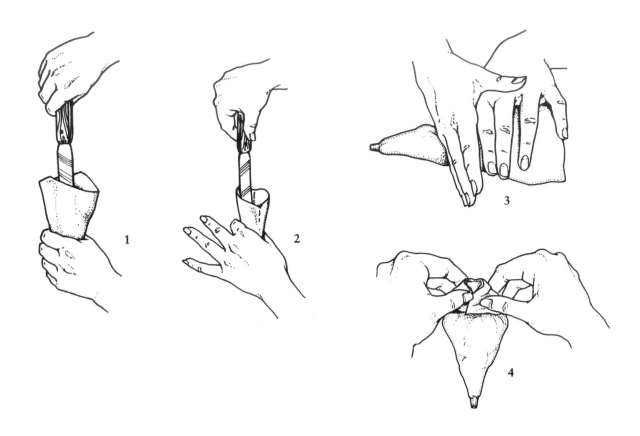

To fill cone: Hold near the bottom and use a long spatula to fill with icing, forcing it down (fig. 1). Fill half full, removing the icing from the spatula by pinching it between thumb and fingers from outside of bag, while withdrawing spatula (fig. 2).

Closing the cone: Parchment cones must be closed tightly to keep icing from escaping through the top. First, smooth the top flat, using the side of your hand to force the icing toward the tip (fig. 3). Then fold in each side and roll down the top until it is close to the icing (fig. 4). Lock your thumb over the top with your remaining fingers curled around the side.

Pastry Brushes or Feathers

Natural or nylon bristles, or feathers, work well both for brushing off excess flour from rolled cookies and for glazing them.

Porcelain Spoons

These spoons, made of French porcelain, are designed to be tasting spoons because they don't conduct heat and they don't absorb odors. These qualities also make them perfect for stirring hot liquids. They can also be used in the microwave oven. I especially like to use porcelain spoons for making caramel. It's easier to see the true color of the caramel against the white of the porcelain. They are available at Charles Lamalle (page 249).

Bar cookies are cooled in the pan set on a wire rack to allow the air to circulate for quick cooling. Individual cookies are removed to wire racks as soon as they are rigid enough to hold their shape. The best wire racks I have found are from France because the wire is closer together, offering more support for the cookies. They are available at Charles Lamalle (page 249).

Racks (Wire)

I collect rolling pins. I have ones in marble, antique glass, wood, solid stainless steel, and my most recent prize pin from France, in solid white Teflon, 1 3/4 inches in diameter and close to 20 inches long. They are fun to collect and fun to use to roll out cookie dough. But in a pinch, cookie dough can be rolled with a round glass bottle.

Rolling Pins

A medium-size heavyweight saucepan such as Wearever with a nonstick lining is ideal for sugar syrups and reducing liquids because very little of the liquid sticks to the pan. It is available at housewares stores and The Broadway Panhandler (page 249).

Saucepans (Nonstick)

An accurate scale makes baking much faster and more reliable. My favorite scale for traveling is produced by Cuisinarts. It weighs only up to 10 ounces/300 grams but is designed on the pendulum principle rather than spring, and is thus accurate to plus or minus 2 grams. At home I use the Mettler PM 16 electronic scale, which is a top-quality, very expensive laboratory scale from Switzerland, accurate to within 0.2 gram. (It weighs up to 35 pounds/16,000 grams, which makes it convenient for large-scale cake baking such as wedding cakes.) Both scales can be used to weigh in avoirdupois or metric systems.

Scales

Stainless-steel ice cream scoops from Italy come in many sizes and make quick work of dropped cookies, ensuring uniformity of size and evenness of baking. The ones I use most are a tiny number 100 (1 1/4-inch diameter) scoop, which equals 2 level teaspoons and produces cookies about 1 3/4 inches in size, and a number 30 (2-inch diameter) scoop, which equals 2 tablespoons plus 2 teaspoons and produces cookies about 3 inches in size. They are available through Dean & DeLuca (page 249).

Scoops

There is no reason to sift flour for cookies except, in some rare instances, when it serves as an accurate way to measure the flour if you are not weighing it. Baking soda, which tends to clump, needs to be sifted with some of the dry ingredients to keep it separate. But both these siftings can be accomplished with a strainer. Simply tap the side of the strainer with a spoon or use the spoon to press the dry ingredients through the strainer.

Sifters or Strainers

Sifting dry ingredients does not evenly mix them together. This is best accomplished by whisking them together briefly.

A strainer can also be used to dust cookies with powdered sugar.

Spatulas

A small metal spatula with a narrow 4-inch blade and wooden handle is an ideal implement with many uses ranging from dislodging bar cookies from the sides of the pan to spreading frosting on sandwich cookies.

Small and large angled or offset spatulas are also handy for spreading mixtures evenly in pans or even for lifting small cookies.

A small cake turner and a broad, flexible pancake turner are also useful for lifting cookies from the counter onto cookie sheets and from cookie sheets onto wire cooling racks.

Large commercial and regular Rubbermaid spatulas are very efficient for scraping bowls and folding together certain ingredients, but they retain odors, so it is best to reserve a separate set for baking. Spatulas are available at candy-making supply and cake-decorating supply stores such as The Bridge Company, The Broadway Panhandler, Maid of Scandinavia, Parrish, and the Chocolate Gallery (page 249).

Thermometers

A candy thermometer is not necessary for 99 percent of the recipes here, but an accurate candy thermometer is useful for toffee and caramel. I have found the thermometers on the market to be so inaccurate that I produce my own. The Cordon Rose candy/deep fat thermometer has a range of 20°F. to 500°F. in two-degree increments. It can be found at Dean & DeLuca, The Broadway Panhandler, La Cuisine, and Maid of Scandinavia (page 249).

How to read a thermometer

Since many people hold a thermometer with their left hand while stirring with the right, I designed the Cordon Rose thermometer with two opposing scales so that it can be read either left- or right-handed. The thermometer should be read at eye level, slanted slightly to one side. The immersion level, indicated by an etched ring toward the base, is the point at which a thermometer is calibrated to read most accurately. The thermometer should be immersed up to this level when read. If you are working with a small amount of liquid, tilt the pan slightly to increase the depth of the liquid when reading the thermometer.

How to care for the thermometer

It is best to hang a thermometer out of harm's way, as rattling around in a drawer may cause the mercury to separate. This can also occur if the thermometer was handled roughly during shipping. To reunite mercury, it will be necessary to send it back to the store where it was purchased.

To prevent breakage, avoid extremes in temperature. When removing the thermometer from a hot liquid, for example, do not place it on a cold drain board. Also, do not allow the thermometer to rest on the pan's bottom, because when it lies on its side, the uneven heat distribution could cause it to crack. Clips to attach thermometers to the side of a pan are prone to slipping because they do not conform to a universal pan size or shape. I prefer to hold the thermometer, which is possible because the glass does not conduct the heat.

Tubes

Small tubes, referred to as decorating tubes, are used for just that. Larger tubes, referred to as pastry tubes, can be used to shape (pipe) the actual cookies themselves. If you prefer, you can always spoon the cookies onto the cookie sheet instead of piping them. Piping them, however, gives them a more uniform and decorative shape.

In these recipes, I have listed the numbers of the tubes and their diameters. The numbers apply to both Wilton and Ateco tubes, but tube numbers from other countries do not correspond to these, so it is best to check the diameters. Wilton tubes are available from Wilton; Ateco from Maid of Scandinavia and other cake-decorating supply houses (page 249).

Wilton and Ateco produce pastry tubes that are nickel coated, with welded, almost invisible, seams, and that are sturdy enough to resist crushing (except underfoot). (Ateco also has a less expensive line in which the seams are visible, resulting in less precise piping.) When tubes flatten and become deformed through much use, an inexpensive plastic tube corrector is all that is needed to put them back into shape. Plastic couplers make it possible to change tubes without emptying the pastry bag.

I keep a separate set of tubes for working with Royal Icing because even a trace of grease will break it down. Only hot water is needed to wash tubes encrusted with Royal Icing. Alternatively, tubes can be well washed and soaked in a little vinegar to remove grease.

Whisks

I use a small wire whisk in cookie making only to combine the dry ingredients. With just a little more effort, a fork will do about as well. A larger wire whisk, however, is ideal for folding powdered sugar into beaten egg whites for meringue-type cookies. It results in the most effortless incorporation with the least amount of breakdown in the volume of the whites.

Wooden Spoons

Most cookie doughs can be mixed by hand, using a large bowl (at least 4-quart capacity) and a wooden spoon (which has not been used for spicy or savory ingredients). In making the recipes, follow the same basic instructions as for the electric mixer with the following modifications: Instead of beating the butter and sugar together, start by beating the butter until it is creamy. Then add the sugar and beat the two together for a few minutes or until the mixture becomes very light in color. If eggs are used, beat them lightly before adding them.

Wraps   Plastic wrap is handy both for rolling out certain cookie doughs and for wrapping the dough airtight during refrigerating. My favorite plastic wrap is Saran Wrap because it is very smooth and absolutely airtight. If it is unavailable at any given time, I prefer to use wax paper for rolling out the dough as other wraps do not lie as flat and tend to get caught up in the dough.

Wax paper is ideal for layering between sticky cookies or crisp cookies when storing. It will keep the cookies crisp longer because it absorbs very small amounts of moisture.

Zesters and Strippers   A zester has a small metal head with tiny rough holes in it. When scraped across a citrus fruit, it penetrates just deeply enough to remove the peel without removing the bitter pith beneath. The stripper, on the other hand, removes wider strips of the same peel. A vegetable peeler also works to remove the zest, but care must be taken so that it does not remove the pith as well. For finely grated zest, if you are not using a food processor, first use the zester and then a chef's knife to chop it very fine.

Albert Uster Imports Inc.: 9211 Gaither Road, Gaithersburg, Maryland. (800) 231–8154

The Bridge Company: 214 East 52 Street, New York, New York 10022. (212) 688–4220

The Broadway Panhandler: 520 Broadway, New York, New York 10012. (212) 966–3434

La Cuisine: 323 Cameron Street, Alexandria, Virginia 22314. (800) 521–1176

Dean & DeLuca: 560 Broadway, New York, New York 10012. (212) 431–1691; outside New York: (800) 227–7714, Monday-Friday, 9 A.M.-5 P.M.

European Home Products: P.O. Box 2524, Waterbury, Connecticut 06723. (203) 866–9683; Outside Connecticut: (800) 225–0760

Fante: 1006 South Ninth Street, Philadelphia, Pennsylvania 19147. (215) 922–5557

Hammer Song: 221 South Potomac, Boonsboro, Maryland 21713. (301) 432–4320

Kitchen Bazaar: 1098 Taft Street, Rockville, Maryland 20850. (301) 424–7474

Charles Lamalle: 36 West 25 Street, New York, New York 10010. (212) 242–0750

Maid of Scandinavia: 32–44 Raleigh Avenue, Minneapolis, Minnesota 55416. (800) 328–6722

Mettler Instrument Corporation: Box 71, Hightstown, New Jersey 08520. (609) 448–3000

Parrish Decorating Supplies, Inc.: 314 West 58 Street, Los Angeles, California 90037. (213) 750–7650; Outside California: (800) 736–8443

Williams-Sonoma: Mail Order Department, P.O. Box 7456, San Francisco, California 94120–7456. (415) 421–4242

Wilton Enterprises: 2240 West 75 Street, Woodridge, Illinois 60517. (312) 963–7100

Index

About the Author

Rose Levy Beranbaum has her B.S. and M.A. cum laude in food science and culinary arts. In addition to continuing her studies at many of the world's leading cooking schools, she has also studied art and design at the Fashion Institute of Technology in New York City. Rose has received accreditation from the International Association of Culinary Professionals as a food writer and a teacher.

A frequent contributor to all the major food magazines and *The New York Times,* she is also a consultant to the baking and chocolate industries. For ten years Rose was owner and director of the Cordon Rose Cooking School in New York City.

Rose translated and adapted the award-winning *A Passion for Chocolate* and is author of the multiaward-winning best cookbook of 1988, *The Cake Bible.*